跨文化交际阅读文本

蔡静　主编

山东大学出版社

图书在版编目(CIP)数据

跨文化交际阅读文本/蔡静主编．—济南：山东大学出版社，2018.9

ISBN 978-7-5607-6197-8

Ⅰ.①跨… Ⅱ.①蔡… Ⅲ.①文化交流—高等学校—教材 Ⅳ.①G115

中国版本图书馆CIP数据核字(2018)第230019号

责任编辑：王 翎
封面设计：张 荔

出版发行：山东大学出版社
社 址 山东省济南市山大南路20号
邮 编 250100
电 话 市场部(0531)88363008
经 销：新华书店
印 刷：济南新科印务有限公司
规 格：720毫米×1000毫米 1/16
16.5印张 303千字
版 次：2018年9月第1版
印 次：2018年9月第1次印刷
定 价：32.00元

《跨文化交际阅读文本》编委会

主　　编　蔡　静

副 主 编　马应心　袁　颖　宋　辉　张锦辉

参编人员　盖颖颖　孟丽莉　黄　倩　李　龙

　　　　　冯海英　钟云霞　朱纪燕　葛云峰

项目来源：

1.山东省本科高校教学改革研究项目“基于成果导向教育的大学英语教学改革体系构建研究”(Z2016Z029)

2.山东省本科高校教学改革研究项目“基于学科专业与课程体系建设CBI理念的大学英语教学新模式与综合评价体系建设研究”

3. 山东省“十二五”教育科学规划课题“微课视阈下大学英语教师学习共同体的建构研究”(CBW15015)

4. 德州学院2018年校级教学改革项目“大学英语教学中的文化自觉建构研究”(2018018)

5. 第九批中国外语教育基金项目“一带一路背景下的国际化英语人才培养研究”(ZGWYJYJJ2018B77)

序言

构建人类命运共同体是当今世界的重要命题，也是外语教育者的时代责任。人类命运共同体的构建需要培养具备“中国情怀”“国际视野”和“跨文化沟通能力”的国际化人才。因此，跨文化能力培养成为外语教学领域的重要课题之一。

本教材基于多年教学实践经验，以长篇阅读为媒介，以拓展学生的思辨能力为手段，从中西对比角度讲授跨文化交际知识，旨在提升新时代大学生的跨文化交际意识与能力。

本书共分 8 个单元，每单元包含 3 个阅读版块。第 1～2 单元介绍跨文化交际的相关理论和概念；第 3～6 单元从中西对比角度展示价值观、语言交际、非语言交际、商务跨文化交际等内容；第 7～8 单元阐述中国传统文化的核心内容和现代形象的传播。内容的编排既能改善学生缺乏跨文化交际理论基础的现状，又能帮助学生切实实现跨文化交际的双向交流。

每单元的 3 个阅读版块由精读、泛读和学术阅读构成。阅读练习题涵盖阐述、分析、评价、推理等一系列思辨技能训练，使学生通过全方位的阅读训练构建跨文化交际知识与能力。

本教材以语篇阅读为视角，突破了以往教材篇幅较小，注重语言点而忽略语篇理解的局限。阅读材料多为以跨文化交际为主题的经典文章和高水平学术论文，部分文章篇幅较长，但是难度适中，符合本科学生的英语水平。使学生了解跨文化基本理论、掌握跨文化交际知识的同时，能够提高语篇理解能力和学术文章的写作能力。

内容设计具体有以下特色：

1. 语篇阅读类型丰富，能够多方位地训练学生的能力

精读版块侧重跨文化知识的传播；泛读版块注重中西文化对比；学术阅读版块主要使学生熟悉跨文化交际学术文章的写作和观点的表达方式。除了本

教材提供的语篇，每单元最后还列出了“推荐阅读书目”，旨在扩大学生的阅读视野。

2. 阅读长度和难度适当增加

以往跨文化交际教材多注重文化内容和语言等知识点的讲解，学生缺乏在长篇阅读中获取跨文化交际要点的能力。因此，本教材在阅读长度方面适当增加，在阅读难度方面增设了学术阅读板块。文章多选自于跨文化领域的经典文章，使学生通过原汁原味的阅读获得确切的跨文化知识。

3. 注重跨文化交际理论

改善以往教材重实践、轻理论的现状，引用经典文章，深入浅出地展示跨文化交际相关理论和概念。

4. 增加中国文化部分

响应“中国文化走出去”“讲好中国故事”的号召，内容不仅包含文化表层，更突出中国文化内核。通过学习，使学生能够用英语输出中国传统价值观，实现跨文化交际的平等交流。

5. 阅读习题注重思辨能力的训练

题型包括语言知识检测、概念辨析、观点分析与对比等，重在提高学生的思辨能力和跨文化交际能力。

本书适合英语专业和非英语专业的本科、专科学生使用。

本书是山东省本科高校教学改革研究项目“基于学科专业与课程体系建设CBI理念的大学英语教学新模式与综合评价体系建设研究”和“基于成果导向教育的大学英语教学改革体系构建研究”(Z2016Z029)、山东省“十二五”教育科学规划课题“微课视阈下大学英语教师学习共同体的建构研究”(CBW15015)、德州学院2018年校级教学改革项目“大学英语教学中的文化自觉建构研究”(2018018)，以及第九批中国外语教育基金项目“一带一路背景下的国际化英语人才培养研究”(ZGWYJYJJ2018B77)的研究成果。为培养具备文化自觉和国际视野的新时代国际化人才提供资源和指导。

本书在编写过程中，承蒙德州学院马应心教授、袁颖老师等学者的指导，在此深表感谢。书中引述了一些学者的观点，在此一并致谢！

由于时间仓促，以及本人能力和水平有限，书中难免出现错误和不妥之处，希望广大师生和学者批评指正。

蔡　静

2018. 9. 10

目录

Unit 1 Culture and Communication

To know another's language and not his culture is a very way to make a fluent fool of one's self.

—Winston Brembeck

Objectives:

To increase intercultural awareness and sensitivity;

To get familiar with the basic concepts on intercultural communication;

To understand the relationship between culture and communication.

Warm-up Activity

Different Attitudes Toward a Fly in a Beer

In the dining hall, if a fly was seen in a glass of beer...

—An Englishman would say, "May I have another, please?"

—A Frenchman would pour the beer out.

—A Spanish man would put the money on the table and leave without a word.

—A Japanese would summon the manager and criticize, "Do you do all your business like this?"

—An Arab would give the beer to the waiter and say, "I'll buy you a drink."

—An American would say to the waiter, "Please serve the fly and beer separately. If the customer likes the fly, he could put it into his beer himself. "

Question for discussion

From this case, can you figure out the orientation of different nations' mainstream culture through people's different reactions?

Part One

Intensive Reading

Intercultural Awareness and Communication

We live in a time when the need for understanding and mutual respect across cultural boundaries is imperative. Implicit in the achievement of understanding and respect is the successful interchange between two human beings that we call communication. Language is, of course, a key component of communication, and although the accurate use of linguistic forms is necessary for effective communication, in most communicative situations, the communicators do more than simply talk to each other in grammatically well-constructed sentences; there has to be familiarity with the culture of the language being used by the communicators.

Even between two fluent speakers of the same language there has to be some awareness of cultural differences. I still remember the parting words from a Nigerian student of mine who assured me "I will remember you until tomorrow". I understood his sentiment because I was aware that the English word "tomorrow" in a Nigerian context was a much less definite time expression than the day that follows today—or at least I hope so. The point is that language and culture, as we all know, are linked together and that communication, even between two people speaking the same language can be difficult if there is a cultural difference between the two speakers.

For the average person, a complete assimilation of a second culture may be even more impossible than speaking with flawless grammar and accurate pronunciation. What may be more realistic and valuable than striving for total assimilation of the target culture is the development of an awareness of culture and the intercultural skills that one develops on the way to cultural awareness.

Cultural awareness can be seen as the recognition that culture affects perception and that culture influences values, attitudes and behavior. The development of this awareness can be described as having four sequential stages leading ideally toward toleration and appreciation of cultural diversity.

Intercultural adjustment skills are a range of skills that are implicit in the concept of cultural awareness. These skills must be developed if we are to adjust to living in a new culture or even travel comfortably through a new culture.

In fact, one could make the case that the skills must be developed before an awareness will develop. Using the four stages of cultural awareness as a basis, we can describe four general skills that must be developed at each stage in the process.

Stage One: Recognition

At this stage we recognize the existence and pervasive influence of culture. For most of us, this begins with the growing consciousness of our own cultural group, and except for those individuals in extremely isolated cultural groups, we also begin to recognize the existence of other cultures. A pronouncement such as "I am an American" is the starting point, and implicit in this statement is the recognition that Americans do things in a particular way. Simultaneously, the concept of foreigner also begins to have meaning, and at this stage there is the recognition that foreigners do things differently. As we develop, so does our recognition that cultural differences are not only obvious and concrete (food, shelter, clothing), but subtle and abstract (values, attitudes, mores) as well. It is probably safe to say that as our recognition of foreign cultures increases, so does our conscious recognition of our own cultural heritage.

At the recognition stage, the key skill is "non-judgmental observation". This is the ability to see and describe culture with minimal judgment that what is seen is good or bad or right or wrong. In other words, we should avoid quick and easy labeling of cultural behavior as "funny" or "dumb" or "backward" or "progressive". Ideally, the intercultural traveler takes on the attitude of a scientist who simply reports what he or she sees. The first step toward understanding is seen clearly.

Stage Two: Acceptance or Rejection

Almost simultaneously with our recognition of culture and cultural differences there is a reaction that is most often either positive or negative. The techniques in this article attempt to encourage a neutral, non-judgmental attitude of acceptance, but in fact what often occurs is rebellion against our own culture or rejection of the foreign culture.

The set of skills we hope to develop during this acceptance or rejection stage can be labeled "coping with ambiguity". When we become aware of the fact that there is more than one way to behave or more than one way to organize society, it becomes necessary to live with a certain amount of ambiguity until we see enough of the total picture to see how the various pieces of the cultural puzzle fit together.

Stage Three: Intergration or Ethnocentrism

At this stage we reach either a somewhat more sophisticated point of view where we begin to act and think biculturally or, at the other extreme, we solidify our monocultural point of view into rigid ethnocentrism. For the ethnocentric individual, the road toward cultural awareness has come to an end.

At this third stage, where we have started to come to terms with the culture in an intercultural situation, we are beginning to develop into a bicultural being who is not only becoming more fluent in the language but is also beginning to take on a second identity. To achieve biculturalism, we must develop a set of skills that can be called "the ability to empathize". This involves not only projecting ourselves into the role of a person in the target culture, but it also requires a willingness to let go of our close identity with our native culture. In the face of an impending identity crisis, when questions such as "Who am I, after all?" begin to emerge, our self image as "a 100% American", for example, must be sacrificed in order to embrace a new identity.

Stage Four: Transcendence

When we reach the final stage of cultural awareness, we are able to value and appreciate our own cultural roots, whether they are native or acquired, and also to value and appreciate all other cultures as well. at this level of understanding, however, we are also able to transcend particular cultures and see their individual weaknesses and strengths, to become, in effect, a citizen of the world, searching for universals but also valuing the vitality and variety of earth's cultures.

Finally, after we have reached the point where we can transcend culture and see ourselves as a product of culture, but no longer a prisoner of culture, and when we can see the strengths and weaknesses of the cultures we embrace, we need a set of skills that can be labeled "the ability to respect". This is what understanding is all about. It is important to note that the ability to respect still allows for disagreement and criticism. We can, after all, adopt an attitude of "live and let live" while both showing respect for another way of doing things and questioning whether it is the only or best way.

More importantly, however, we should remind ourselves on a daily basis that theories and frameworks such as the four stages of cultural awareness apply only to an idealized individual, and that individuals not only look different from each other, but also think, feel and grow in ways that never quite match the idealized "we" of the preceding paragraphs. Ultimately, the journey toward cultural awareness is made by individuals who, like the six blind men in Saxe's poem, may never know the whole truth or the best answer, but whose handicap should not prevent them from the search.

(GASTON J. Cultural awareness teaching techniques[M]. Brattleboro: Pro Lingua Associates, 1984.)

Vocabulary

mutual *adj.*	having or based on the same relationship one towards the other
imperative *adj.*	very urgent or important; needing immediate attention; implied, but not expressed directly
sentiment *n.*	tender, romantic, or nostalgic feeling or emotion
assimilation *n.*	people of different backgrounds come to see themselves as part of a larger national family
sequential *adj.*	in regular succession without gaps
pervasive *adj.*	spreading or spread throughout
simultaneously *adv.*	at the same instant
concrete *adj.*	not abstract or imaginary
recognition *n.*	the state or quality of being recognized or acknowledged

neutral *adj.* without strong feelings or opinions on either side of a question or argument

ambiguity *n.* unclearness by virtue of having more than one meaning

sophisticate *vi.* change the meaning of or be vague about in order to mislead or deceive

solidify *vi.* make solid or more solid

ethnocentric *adj.* centered on a specific ethnic group, usually one's own transcendence

Exercises

A. Words in Use

Fill in the blanks with the words given below. Change the form when necessary. Each word can be used only once.

imperative	sentiment	pervasive	concrete	ambiguity
neutral	sophisticate	mutual	implicit	recognition

1. Switzerland remained ________ during World War Ⅱ.
2. Should ________ be controlled by reason?
3. If you are wrong, admit it rather than ________.
4. It is ________ that we make a quick decision.
5. Gaps in health outcomes have multiple causes, but poverty is the most ________ factor.
6. Democracy is based on good will and ________ understanding.
7. Her attitude was ________ in the answer she gave us.
8. We should make a analysis of each specific ________ question.
9. The scientist deserves ________ for his talent.
10. She can hear when the ________ creeps in between the words, and that tells her that she needs to find something out.

B. Questions for Discussion

1. Each culture has its own way of saying and doing things and therefore each person tends to make a judgment based on his or her own culture. What would happen if each person sticks to his or her own judgment?
2. Since cultural differences are unavoidable in intercultural communication, what role can intercultural awareness play then?

3. How would you understand the statement "... also to value and appreciate all other cultures as well" ?

C. Translation

1. The point is that language and culture, as we all know, are linked together and that communication, even between two people speaking the same language can be difficult if there is a cultural difference between the two speakers.
2. Cultural awareness can be seen as the recognition that culture affects perception and that culture influences values, attitudes and behaviors.
3. When we reach the final stage of cultural awareness, we are able to value and appreciate our own cultural roots, whether they are native or acquired, and also to value and appreciate all other cultures as well.
4. Ultimately, the journey toward cultural awareness is made by individuals who, like the six blind men in Saxe's poem, may never know the whole truth or the best answer, but whose handicap should not prevent them from the search.

D. Case Study

Case 1

In Hong Kong, a Chinese policeman (A) goes to his British superior (B) and asks for leave to take his mother to the hospital.

A: Sir?

B: Yes, what is it?

A: My mother is not very well, sir.

B: So?

A: She has to go to hospital, sir.

B: Well, get on with it. What do you want?

A: On Thursday, sir.

B: Bloody hell, man. What do you want?

A: Nothing, sir.

Questions

1. Why does B turn out to be angry at A in the conversation?
2. What caused the conflict between the two speakers?

Case 2

Henk van der Meijden is one of the most successful impresarios and circus directors in Europe. He has had a very good relationship with Chinese culture for over twenty-five years. He brought the Xi'an Ballet and Peking Opera groups to Europe several times. However, definite cultural difference was also encountered in their cooperation. For example, at the finale of the show, though the public gave standing ovations for a few minutes, the artists still looked straight ahead as if they were not enjoying this success themselves. It confused Henk van der Meijden at the very beginning. After exchanging their opinions, the situation changed a lot.

Question

Do Chinese artists dislike enjoying success themselves?

Part Two

Extensive Reading

An Introduction to Intercultural Communication

Human beings have a great desire to be with people who are similar to themselves. This is because they share the same ways of doing things, the same values and operate by similar rules. When we are with people who are similar to ourselves, the ways we have of doing things just seem like common sense. However, sometimes work or study or a sense of adventure take us out of our comfort zone. When this happens we realize that the things we took for granted about human interaction are not necessarily the same for everyone. This can be a very difficult, even shocking experience. This helpsheet explains what happens when people step out of their comfort zone by experiencing other cultures, either by travelling to another country or by being in contact with people from other cultures who are in your home country. It explains how we react, why we react the way we do and how to make the interaction with people from other cultures a positive experience.

What Is Culture?

Culture can be defined as human creation. It is the human part of the environment. In other words, culture is the non-biological aspects of life. It is the process of generating and sharing meaning within a social system. This social system is comprised of values, norms and ways of behaving and so culture comprises the ways we interact, behave, and communicate with one another. Culture is something that is learned from parents, schools, the media and the broader community. Singer (1998) defined culture as:

> a pattern of learned, group-related perception—including both verbal and non-verbal language, attitudes, values, belief systems, disbelief systems and behaviours that is accepted and expected by an identity group.

Yet cultures are not fixed. They are changing and interconnected although change may be slow or irregular. Cultures are dynamic as they are created and recreated through shared interactions. However, these changes may be slow or irregular.

The important thing to remember about culture is that while it may be fundamental, it is not innate. Yet it's often not discussed, analysed or critiqued but is seen as being "common sense". Culture is made up of the shared values and assumptions of a particular group of people. Because these values and assumptions are shared, it is easy to take them for granted and believe that they are "normal". In this way it is possible for people to believe that the ways in which they behave and the things they value are right and true for everyone.

However, in order to facilitate communication between cultures it is necessary to understand human reality as socially constructed. If we can understand that then we can begin to understand that different groups may have different values, different ways of communicating, different customs, conventions and assumptions. While these may conflict with our own understandings and assumptions it does not necessarily mean that they are inferior, "wrong" or "rude".

The essential features of culture are:

(1) Culture is the human made part of the environment.

(2) Culture reflects widely shared assumptions about life.

(3) Culture is so fundamental that most people do not and cannot discuss or analyse it.

(4) Culture becomes evident when someone encounters someone from another country who deviates from his/her own cultural norms.

(5) Culture is transmitted from generation to generation.

(6) Even in new situations, people can make a judgment about what is

expected in their own culture.

(7) Cultural values endure and change takes place over a number of generations.

(8) Violations of cultural norms have an emotional impact.

(9) It is relatively easy (although not necessarily helpful) to make generalisations about cultural differences.

These key features are useful when we consider communication between cultures.

What Is Intercultural Communication?

Today the world we live in is "a global village" where no nation, group or culture can remain anonymous. What happens in one part of the world affects all parts of the world. As the world is becoming smaller, we are increasingly interacting with people from many different cultures. While modern technology has made it easier for us to communicate with people anywhere in the world, such interactions can be difficult if we do not know how to deal with people and cultures different from our own. Here are examples of some of the obvious mistakes politicians and businesses have made when it comes to dealing with other languages cultures:

(1) In China, KFC's "finger-licking good" was translated as "eat your fingers off".

(2) Chevrolet attempted unsuccessfully to market its Nova compact car in Latin American countries. In Spanish, "no va" means "does not go" or "it doesn't run".

(3) In Australia, President Bush flashed a backhanded peace sign in motorcades. Many in Australia interpret that gesture as obscene.

These language and cultural mistakes can clearly be avoided if we increase our knowledge and understanding of other people and their cultures. The study of intercultural communication addresses this need by examining the communication and interactions between people of different cultures or subcultures. Fundamental to intercultural communications is the belief that it is through culture that people learn to communicate. A Chinese, an Egyptian, or an Australian, for example, learns to communicate like other Chinese, Egyptians, or Australians. Their behavior conveys meaning because it is learned and shared. In other words, it is cultural. Thus the ways in which people communicate, their language patterns, style, and nonverbal behaviors are all culturally determined.

Samovar and Porter point out that as cultures differ from one another, the communication practices and behaviours of people will inevitably vary as a result of their different perceptions of the world. Intercultural communication, more precisely then, is defined as the study of communication between people whose "cultural perceptions and symbol systems are distinct enough" to alter their communication. In their model of intercultural communication. Samovar and Porter illustrate the process of how the meaning of a message changes when it is encoded by a person in one culture and decoded by a person in another culture in the context of his or her own cultural background (see Figure 1-1). In some cases, the message may be interpreted to carry a different meaning that was not intended.

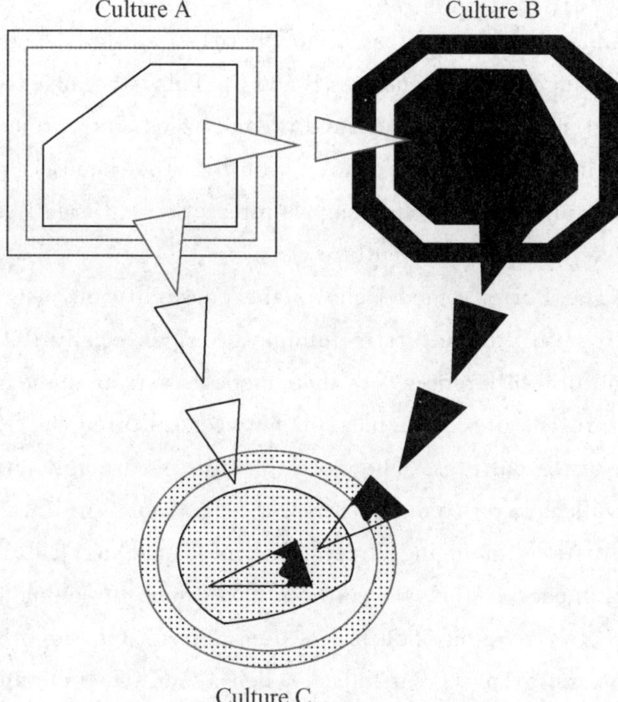

Figure 1-1 Intercultural Communication Model

(Source: Samovar and Porter, 1997)

In Figure 1-1, A, B and C represents three different cultures. Cultures A and B are similar to one another while culture C is quite different. Within each culture is another form similar to the shape of the influencing parent culture.

This represents the person who has been molded by his/her culture. However, the shape of the person is somewhat different from that of the parent culture since we are all shaped by our culture, but are also influenced by other factors as well (e. g. age, gender, class, race, etc.). Also, within any culture there is internal variation.

The series of arrows connecting the figures represents the production, transmission, and interpretation of messages across cultures. When a message leaves culture A, for example, it carries the content of the message as it is intended. When it reaches culture B, the message changes because the new culture influences how the message is interpreted and hence its meaning. Also, the greater the differences between the cultures are, the more likely the message is changed.

For example, the change that occurs between cultures A and B is much less than the change between cultures B and C. This is because there is greater similarity between cultures A and B and the message is interpreted more nearly like it was originally intended. Culture C, on the other hand, is quite different from cultures A and B and the message is interrupted differently there and becomes more like the pattern of culture C.

Samovar and Porter's model shows the possibility of misunderstandings that always exist in intercultural communication, especially if there is great variation in cultural differences. As their model illustrates, the amount of influence a culture has on communication between cultures clearly depends on the similarity of the cultures. The more the cultures are alike, the less influence culture will have on communication. For example. in intercultural communication situations involving Americans and Canadians, culture would not have a strong impact as the two cultures have much in common (e. g. language, geography, religion, political system, etc.). On the other hand, we can expect culture to have great impact when a German communicates with a Chinese as the two cultures differ greatly (e. g. physical appearance, language, religion, concept of self, etc.).

When communicating with someone from a different culture, we can therefore expect cultural differences to have an influence. Cultural differences stem from our differing perceptions, which in turn determines how we communicate with people of other cultures. By understanding how people perceive the world, their values and beliefs, we can better understand what they say and can anticipate potential cross-cultural misunderstandings. Let's now look more closely at what we mean by perceptions, beliefs and values in the intercultural context.

Perceptions

Perceptions are defined as "the internal process by which we select, organise and interpret information" from the outside world. In other words, our perceptions of the world are what we tend to notice, reflect upon and respond to in our environment that is meaningful and significant to us. As a result, no two of us perceive our surroundings in exactly the same way. This is especially the case if we interact with people who come from cultures very different from our own. The way in which each one of us perceives the world is learned and is part of our cultural experience. Whether it is the judgment we make of a certain kind of food or the responses to the fact we have to going to see the doctor, we all react to these different events in the way that our culture has taught. Our perceptions are culturally determined and in return influence the way we communicate with others.

Beliefs

Beliefs are the judgments we make about what is true or probable. They are usually linked to objects or events that possess certain characteristics that we believe to be true with or without proof. For example, we have beliefs about religion (there is a God), events (the meeting was successful), other people (she is friendly) or even about ourselves (I am hard-working). According to Price, most of our beliefs are ideas about how things work, why things are the way they are, and where things come from. Many of our beliefs are also concerned with providing an explanation for things which would otherwise be unpredictable or inexplicable, such as the weather, death and romance. Like our perception, our beliefs are determined by our cultural backgrounds and experiences. We are taught very early on what to believe based on what our culture considers worthy and true. Subsequently, our belief systems form the basis of our values, which determine in large measure how we behave and relate to others.

Values

Values are defined as "an enduring set of beliefs that serve to guide or direct our behaviours". They represent the norms of a culture and specify, for instance, what is good or bad, right or wrong, rude or polite, appropriate or inappropriate. In other words, they provide us with a set of rules for behaving, making choices and reducing uncertainty. Like our perceptions and beliefs, values are learned and hence subject to interpretation. When we interpret behaviour, an object, or an event. we are applying value judgments, which reflect our particular culture.

For instance, an English person who values personal space very highly may consider it rude when a Mexican stands too close. A Japanese who values conformity may find it inappropriate when an American express too much of his or her own opinions. The relative importance of values within each culture can also be revealed through sayings, such as "Time is money"(American), "A zebra does not despise its stripes"(African) or "No need to know the person, only the family"(Chinese). Such sayings impart values that are important in each culture and can provide us with a better understanding of others' cultural beliefs.

One of the criticisms of discussions of intercultural communication is that it can be said to generalise about cultures. However, our aim is not to oversimplify, or to claim that "Asian students are like this" and "Australian students and like that". The idea that there is such a thing as an "Asian student" is clearly an over generalisation as Asia is a vast area, comprising many nations. Even the idea of a "Chinese'student" is a difficult one. Do we mean only mainland China? Clearly not. Do we mean Chinese speaking? Not necessarily. The notion of an "Australian" is also a difficult one as this is a new country comprised of the original inhabitants, the Aborigines, the white colonists and more recent migrants from a wide range of backgrounds.

When thinking about communication between cultures, rather than thinking of them as entirely separate and static, it is more useful to consider them as dynamic and interconnected. However, it is also important to consider that for particular characteristics (for example individualist/collectivist), while individuals in each culture will be found across the spectrum, in any one culture people will be clustered around a certain point. Although people are clustered around a certain point, there is also an area of overlap where they may share some similarities.

(GUDYKUNST W B. Intercultural communication theory: current pespectives[M]. Beverly Hills, CA: Sage Publications, 1983.)

Language focus

helpsheet *n.* 文本
irregular *adj.* 不合法的;不合规矩的
innate *adj.* 天生的;固有的
assumption *n.* 假定;设想;假装
inferior *adj.* 次等的;下级的
deviate *vi.* 偏离;脱离
backhanded *adj.* 反手的;反向的
inevitably *adv.* 不可避免地
impart *vt.* 传授;赋予;告知
spectrum *n.* 系列;幅度;范围
disbelief *n.* 不相信;怀疑
dynamic *adj.* 动态的;有活力的
critique *n.* 批评;评论
facilitate *vt.* 促进;帮助
encounter *vt.* 遭遇;偶然碰到
norm *n.* 规范;标准
anonymous *adj.* 匿名的;没特色的
despise *vt.* 轻视
overlap *n.* 重叠部分;覆盖物
cluster *vt.* & *vi.* 群集;丛生;使成群

Exercises

A. Text Reading

Decide whether the following statements are true (T) or false (F).

1. ______ Culture is taken for granted and right and true for everyone.
2. ______ Culture is changeable, although the change is sometimes slow and abnormal.
3. ______ Culture could be transmitted from generation to generation.
4. ______ Culture is a part of the environment.
5. ______ Different groups have different perceptions, values and beliefs.
6. ______ Intercultural communication refers to the change of communication between people sharing different cultural systems.
7. ______ People perceive their surroundings and perceptions in the same ways.
8. ______ The amount of cultural influence on communication depends on the similarity of the cultures.
9. ______ The base of people's value comes from the belief systems.
10. ______ There are still similarities on culture even though people are clustered around a certain point.

B. Terms Understanding

Find the definitions of the following terms in the text. If you cannot find the exact definition, try to use your own words to interpret it.

1. comfort zone
2. culture
3. encode
4. decode
5. perception
6. belief
7. value

C. Classroom Activities

1. Could you name as many cultural groups as you can?
2. Please discuss together to develop a list of characteristics that make each of the culture groups different from the others.
3. Work in pairs and exchange views on the meanings of the following proverbs, and discuss the values transmitted. Then try to find out their Chinese equivalents if there is any.

   Proverb 1: East is East, and West is West, and never the twain shall meet.

   Proverb 2: The early bird catches the worm.

Part Three

Academic Reading

A Review on Intercultural Communication

Introduction

Intercultural or cross-cultural communication is an interdisciplinary field of research that studies how people understand each other across group boundaries of various sorts: national, geographical, ethnic, occupational, class or gender. In the United States it has traditionally been related to the behavioral sciences, psychology and professional business training; In Europe it is mostly associated with anthropology and the language sciences. Researchers generally view intercultural communication as a problem created by differences in behavior and world views among people who speak different languages and who belong to different cultures. However, these problems may not be very different from those encountered in communication among people who share the same national language and culture.

Background

Teaching English to Speakers of Other Languages (TESOL) has always had as its goal the facilitation of communication among people who do not share the same language and national culture. But before the Second World War, the term "culture" meant knowledge about great works of literature, social institutions and historical events, acquired through the translation of written texts. The rise of linguistics and of the social sciences after the Second World War, and the demands of market economies, gave prominence to spoken language and to communication across cultures in situations of everyday life.

While the term "intercultural communication" became prominent in TESOL only in the 1980s, as the necessary supplement to communicative language teaching first developed in Europe in the early 1970s, the field itself can be traced to the work in the 1950s of Georgetown University linguist Robert Lado and of anthropologist and U. S. Foreign Service Institute (FSI) officer Edward T. Hall. Lado's *Linguistics Across Cultures* (1957) was the first attempt to link language and culture in an educationally relevant way; Lado had an enormous influence on the teaching of English around the world. In *The Silent Language* (1959), Hall showed the complex ways in which "culture is communication and communication is culture" (1959: 191). The principles of intercultural communication developed by Hall and his colleagues in the Foreign Service Institute were used by the Peace Corps., founded in the early 1960s. They gave rise to simulation games, studies of "critical incidents" where miscommunication occurred, and comparative studies of Asian and American cultures, especially Japanese culture. In the 1970s these studies were employed by the international business community and applied to the training of salespeople and corporate executives. In the 1980s, following the Civil Rights Movement and demands for cultural recognition by ethnic groups and minorities, intercultural communication became relevant also to ethnically diverse groups within one and the same country and was used by social workers and educators.

By contrast, the field of intercultural communication in Europe was a direct outcome of social and political upheavals created by the large scale immigrations into the industrialized countries. It has therefore been much more closely linked to fields such as anthropology, sociolinguistics, pragmatics and discourse analysis even though behavioral training is also part of the field in Europe.

Some of the major facets of human interaction that intercultural communication has helped to define are:

(1) the situation of communication itself, e. g. the socially conventionalized roles adopted by participants, their expected norms of interaction and interpretation, the way they construct a shared sense of reality;

(2) the stereotypes they entertain of each other, as individuals and as members of a social group;

(3) their non-verbal and preverbal behavior;

(4) the way they save their own and each other's face;

(5) the way they structure their discourse to meet their communicative goals;

(6) the attitudes, values and beliefs (also "discourses") they share with the social group they belong to;

(7) the way their language reflects these deeper discourses;

(8) the way members of different groups realize various speech acts (like making compliments, requests or apologies).

Research

One of the major concerns in the beginning of the field was how to help FSI officers interact with people in the foreign countries to which they were dispatched. Thus, in *The Silent Language* (1959), Hall studied particularly the "out-of-awareness" aspects of communication—the paralanguage of pitch, rhythm and intonation, the "silent language" of gestures and movements (kinesics), and the use of time (chronemics). In his next book, *The Hidden Dimension* (1966), he studied the use of space (proxemics) and found that Anglo-Americans establish a greater distance between face-to-face interlocutors than, say, Japanese or Arabs. In *Beyond Culture* (Hall, 1981), he discussed the concepts of "high-context communication", where most of the information is implicit because it is located in the physical context or part of a shared world view, and "low-context communication", where the bulk of the information is to be found in the words uttered. The latter, he claimed, is more typical of Northern European style communication, whereas high-context communication is particularly characteristic of Chinese speakers.

Many intercultural researchers were influenced by work in cross-cultural psychology: Segall (1979) identified human universals in visual perception and cognitive processing of which each culture showed specific variations. Triandis (1995) —drawing on Hofstede (1983) —propagated the concepts of individualistic vs. collectivist cultures (e. g. American or Germany vs. Brazil or Japan). Today, many studies in cross-cultural psychology seem simplistic because they ignore the cultural diversity within a given nation, state and the increasing potential for change within a global economy.

Besides these psychological studies, linguistics entered the field with Kaplan's (1966) contrastive study of the various rhetorical patterns found in the writing of English as a Second Language (ESL) learners. This study illustrated the different ways various cultures have of expressing themselves. "Westerners" were claimed to prefer a direct mode of expression: "Semitics" and "Latin-Americans" to use a more hoop-like way of argumentation, and "Orientals" were said to favor digression and "beating around the bush". Today, such characterizations sound dangerously ethnocentric. They show the difficulty of expressing one culture in terms of another without sounding critical or condescending.

Since the 1980s, the field has been broadened to include sociolinguistics and linguistic anthropology. The most prominent work here is that of Ron and Suzanne Scollon. In their first book *Narrative, Literacy, and Face in Interethnic Communication* (1981) they documented the different nature and value attributed to literacy and orality practices among Anglo-Americans and Athabaskans. In the way they told stories, their own three-year-old daughter, Rachel, and her ten-year-old Athabaskan friend, Big Sister, were differentially literate. Even before she could read and write. Rachel told stories she made up according to a tripartite pattern (orientation—complication—resolution) familiar to her from the English bedtime stories she was read by her parents. By contrast, Big Sister's spoken and written stories conformed to a four-part, repetitive pattern favored by members of her culture.

In their second book *Intercultural Communication* (1995), the Scollons focus on the professional discourse between Americans and East Asians, especially Chinese. Scollons pass in review the parameters of intercultural speech situations, the strategies of politeness and power, the conversational inferences, topics and face systems that regulate cross-cultural communication, and the realization of speech acts across cultures. They also extend the usual boundaries of intercultural communication by discussing the discourse systems (or discourses, ideologies and stereotype) that underlie the way people talk and interact with one another; examples of such systems are corporate discourses, professional discourses, generational discourses and gender discourses.

As intercultural communication moves into a critical examination of systems of thought, the works of linguists like Gee and Pennycook have yielded important insights into intercultural communication in recent years. Cultural differences are often of political importance and are linked to issues of power and control. For example, Gee (1990) shows how our autonomous concept of literacy is a Western construct, favoring the academic-essay type of literacy and the individual literate performance over more creative and community-based uses of the written language. Gee's work has far-reaching implication for the teaching of English reading and writing to members of cultures that have a view of literacy different from Western ones.

(CARTER R, NUNAN D. The cambridge guide to teaching English to speakers of other languages [M]. Cambridge: Cambridge University Press, 2001.)

Comprehension Check

A. Questions for Discussion

1. What do you think of the "culture"?
2. What is the definition of "high-context communication"? Can you illustrate it with an example?
3. Try to use your own words to interpret the term "chronemics" and "proxemics".

B. Detail Understanding

Find out the following people's works or contributions.

Name	The book(s) or the Contribution(s)
Robert Lado	A.
Hall and his colleagues	B.
Segall	C.
Ron and Suzanne Scollon	D.
Triandis	E.
Kaplan	F.
Gee	G.

Suggestions for Further Reading

HALL E. The silent language[M]. New York: Doubleday, 1959.
胡文仲. 跨文化交际学概论[M]. 北京:外语教学与研究出版社, 1999.
王宏印. 现代跨文化传通——如何与外国人交往[M]. 天津:南开大学出版社, 2012.

Unit 2 Intercultural Adaptation

The greatest distance between people is not space but culture.

—Jamake Highwater

Objectives:

To know what culture shock is and how it occurs;

To understand the barriers of intercultural communication;

To learn how to adapt to a new cultural environment.

Warm-up Activity

Imagine you are attending your first invitation to dinner at the home of a foreign friend. How would you respond in the following situations?

Situation 1

You are eating some food which you have never tried before. What would you say?

A. What's this?

B. Is this sweet or salty?

C. What are the materials?

Situation 2

You are offered some food you don't really like. What would you say?

A. No thanks, I don't like it.

B. No thanks, I don't want any.

Part One

Intensive Reading

Studying Abroad and Culture Shock

Are you planning to study in the U. K. ? Are you looking forward to an exciting time, with high expectations of life in Britain?

If you have been to the U. K. already, then you will roughly know what to expect. If it is your first time in the country—and perhaps your first time abroad—you may find that settling in is not an automatic process. It requires a bit of effort. You may be surprised, and at some stage you will probably use the term "culture shock" to explain your reactions. But what exactly is culture shock? What does it feel like? Can you prevent it? Probably not, but you can minimise its effect. Read on and find out how. You may settle in more easily if you know in advance how you are likely to feel after your arrival.

Research into Culture Shock

For over thirty years, culture shock has been a bona fide field of research for European and American anthropologists and psychologists. They have studied the reactions and experiences during the first few months in a new country of travellers and diplomats, businesspeople and international students.

Some researchers describe five stages; others believe it is a six or even seven stage process. Not everyone experiences the exact stages, but most travellers will go through the highs and lows, the positive as well as the negative aspects of living in a new culture. The different stages roughly are as follows:

At first you are excited by the new environment and a few frustrations do not spoil your enthusiasm. When experiencing some difficulties with simple things like making telephone calls or using public transport, you tend to down-play negative emotions.

Then follows a period in which cultural differences in behaviour and values become more obvious. What previously seemed exciting, new and challenging is now merely frustrating. You may feel isolated and become withdrawn from life around you. You seek security in the familiar. Food from home, possibly even the one that you never particularly enjoyed, becomes a focus, maybe an obsession.

In the next stage you may reject what is around you, perhaps becoming opinionated and negative. You may feel that everyone is against you and that nobody understands you. Limpet-like you cling to other students from your home country, hoping to have your negative stereotypes of the British and life in Britain reinforced. However, you are beginning to re-assert yourself.

Based on your successes in negotiating a variety of social situations and, maybe, increased language skills, your self-esteem grows. You can accept the negative differences and tolerate them. Knowing that you cannot change your surroundings, you now enjoy certain aspects of British culture and feel relieved and strengthened from having overcome the difficulties. You may even feel a sense of belonging.

The Symptoms

Just as everyone's experience of culture shock is unique, the symptoms associated with it vary, too. They can range from the physical-headaches, lethargy, sleep problems, loss of appetite, and digestive irregularities to the psychological irritability and anger over minor frustrations, confusion about morals and values. Suffering from culture shock often leaves people feeling moody, isolated and insecure.

Researchers believe that the beginning of the negative phases happen most often within two to six months of living in a new culture, but many travellers experience the full gambit of emotions associated with culture shock in a much narrower time span.

Not Everyone Experiences Culture Shock

Research has shown that the more well-travelled and practised at absorbing, accepting and adapting you are, the more early you overcome culture shock.

If you are confident of speaking the language and possess a thorough knowledge of your new home, you can feel settled after a relatively short period.

If you have adjusted well to your new environment, you would perform competently the roles that each social context requires and thus avoid the frustrations resulting from inappropriate behaviour.

Preparing for Culture Shock

What strategies can you use to minimise, and cope with, culture shock? Research has shown that our expectations affect how we react to a new country. Therefore, thorough pre-departure preparations are necessary:

(1) Read the very useful booklet *How to live in Britain* (from the British Council).

(2) Perhaps you know someone who has lived in the U. K. , or—better still—studied at the university or college you are going to. Talk to them but beware, they may indulge in some nostalgia when looking back on their student days. Ask them what problems and disappointments they have experienced. Contact former students and find out whether the institution you are going to supports an alumni group in your country.

Do not rely on TV or cinema films to provide you with cultural pointers. British soap opera and films only give you a stereotypical and often idolised view.

How to Overcome Culture Shock

After arriving at your new university or college, the following suggestions may assist you in reducing the strain of culture shock:

(1) Be aware of the signs, including the physical symptoms.

(2) Soon after arriving, explore your immediate environment. Having taken advice on personal safety, walk around and get to know your neighbourhood. Creat a mental map of your surroundings.

(3) Be courageous and introduce yourself to your neighbours. If you live in university accommodation, there are likely to be other students who feel just the way you do.

(4) Locate useful places such as the post office, the doctor's surgery and the university welfare office so that you know where they are when you need them.

(5) Read a local newspaper and find out what the topical issues are. If you are well informed, you can hold conversations with British people without always feeling as an outsider.

(6) If you are unsure of your English, boost your confidence by remembering that most British people do not speak a foreign language. Make an effort

at improving your language skills by watching TV and listening to the radio. Your institution may run free courses for international students.

(7) Take a break from studying and take part in social activities. Enquire about things like etiquette and dress code if you are at all unsure.

(8) Ask questions about social customs from people with whom you feel comfortable. You will always find someone who will assist you in finding out about life in Britain. This can be a two-way exchange, with you telling people about life in your home country.

(9) Keep in touch with your own culture. The university's International Welfare Officer should know, for instance, where the nearest temples and mosques are and where you can buy the cookery ingredients that you are used to from home.

(10) Avoid mixing only with compatriots or other international students. Contact with British people allows you to adapt more quickly. By asking questions you have a point of contact when trying to make friends.

(11) A good way of meeting British people is to take part in a hosting scheme where British families invite international students into their homes for a meal, or a weekend stay. Ask the International Welfare Officer about this.

(12) Ask yourself which situations irritate or confuse you the most. Are you sure that you have always understood people's reactions to you, or could it be that you misinterpret their behaviour?

(13) Avoid comparing them with us, good with bad. Establishing why people behave the way they do and then placing their behaviour in a social or economic context are more helpful.

(14) Help to reduce stress on your body by keeping fit physically.

(15) If you are feeling very low, talk to someone about it. This could be your fellow students, your landlord, or university staff such as the International Welfare Officer or Student Counsellor.

(16) Write down things you like and do not like. Can you change them? If not, perhaps you can find a way of living with them.

(17) And finally, remember that other students probably go through the same experiences as you do. Even British students have to adjust to living away from home.

Adapting to a different climate, different social conventions and different cultural values can be a complex and sometimes painful process, but coming out at the other end is rewarding and definitely worth the effort!

(StudyModeResearch. Culture shock when studying abroad[EB/OL]. (2011-11-24)[2018-09-04]. http://www. studymode. com/essays/Culture-Shock-When-Studying-Abroad-851452. html.)

Vocabulary

bona fide *adj.* undertaken in good faith

withdrawn *adj.* seeking solitude; tending to reserve or introspection

obsession *n.* an unhealthy and compulsive preoccupation with something or someone

opinionate *adj.* obstinate in one's opinions

stereotype *n.* a conventional or formulaic conception or image

reinforce *vt.* strengthen and support with rewards

assert *vt.* to declare or affirm solemnly and formally as true; insist on having one's opinions and rights recognized

self-esteem *n.* a feeling of pride in yourself

lethargy *n.* inactivity; showing an unusual lack of energy

digestive *n.* relating to or having the power to cause or promote digestion

irregularity *n.* behavior that breaches the rule or etiquette or custom or morality

gambit *n.* an opening remark intended to secure an advantage for the speaker; a maneuver in a game or conversation

indulge *vt.* enjoy to excess

nostalgia *n.* longing for something past

idolised *adj.* regarded with deep or rapturous love (especially as if for a god)

strain *n.* difficulty that causes worry or emotional tension

boost *vi. & vt.* increase; contribute to the progress or growth of

compatriot *n.* a person from your own country

irritate *vt.* cause annoyance in; disturb, especially by minor irritations

Exercises

A. Words in Use

Fill in the blanks with the words given below. Change the form when necessary. Each word can be used only once.

obsession	assert	strain	irritate	reinforce
indulge	digestive	opinionate	boost	lethargy

1. Although he is thin, he has good ________ power.
2. Reporters, however, are often reluctant to create their own analogies as they may seem to be too ________.
3. I was suffering from ________ that my career would be ended.
4. She ________ that he was innocent.
5. I shall forget about dieting today. I'm just going to ________.
6. A warm-up is important before a run so as not to ________ any muscles.
7. Several hours after the surgery, she was still in her ________.
8. The publication of this book ________ my confidence.
9. Any good speaker should be able to ________ his argument with facts.
10. His letter ________ me a little.

B. Questions for Discussion

1. According to this article, what should students do in order to reduce culture shock?
2. What is your attitude toward culture shock?
3. What suggestions would you make to those who plan to study abroad? Why?

C. Translation

1. Not everyone experiences the exact stages but most travellers will go through the highs and lows, the positive as well as the negative aspects of living in a new culture.
2. They can range from the physical-headaches, lethargy, sleep problems, loss of appetite, and digestive irregularities to the psychological irritability and anger over minor frustrations, confusion about morals and values.
3. If you are unsure of your English, boost your confidence by remembering that most British people do not speak a foreign language.
4. Avoid mixing only with compatriots or other international students. Con-

tact with British people allows you to adapt more quickly. By asking questions you have a point of contact when trying to make friends.

D. Case Study

Case 1

W: (Showing C the sofa) Sit down, please.

C: No, no. I'll sit here. (Moving towards a chair)

W: Oh, do sit over here on the sofa.

C: No, no. This chair is perfectly all right.

(W=Waiter, C=Customer)

Questions

Can you interpret the response of C?

Case 2

This is a story told by a Chinese student in Britain about her first invitation to have dinner in an English family.

"After I had settled down at Warwick University for my M. A. course. I was invited to give a talk to a professional women's organisation about my first impressions of Britain. After the talk, quite a few participants gave me their addresses and invited me to visit their families. They were really very friendly and helpful. The first visit left a lasting memory because it was my first time to have dinner in an English home. My hostess picked me up at the university and showed me around the city till sunset. I was very excited about the visit, but at the same time I was wondering who would cook the meal. Her husband? In China, if I am going to have some visitors to dinner, it usually takes me at least three hours to prepare the eight courses. As soon as we arrived at the house, the lady asked me to sit at the table and said everything was in the oven and ready to serve. She told me she had put food in the oven before she went to the university and after two hours of touring the city, dinner was ready. Can you imagine how many dishes I had? Only one—a stew with meat and vegetables. The meat was overdone and too hard to eat; green vegetables were no longer green. Compared with Chinese food, they were tasteless. I was very much disappointed at their hospitality. However, after I had stayed in Britain for a year and visited many different families, I became more used to the British way of showing hospitality. In Britain, hospitality is not measured by how many dishes are provided as in China. It is shown by giving you freedom to choose whatever you really want. They never press you. They never put food on your plate but just ask you to help yourself. If you, as a guest, are shy or modest, waiting for the food to be put on your plate, you will remain half-starved. Maybe that is why I lost nearly 20 pounds after a year in Britain!"

Questions

1. Why was the Chinese student so disappointed?
2. What is stew?
3. Do you think British people are inhospitable?

Part Two

Extensive Reading

Culture Shock: Adjustment to New Cultural Environments

Culture shock is precipitated by the anxiety that results from losing all our familiar signs and symbols of social intercourse. These signs or cues include the thousand and one ways in which we orient ourselves to the situations of daily life: when to shake hands and what to say when we meet people, when and how to give tips, how to give orders to servants, how to make purchases, when to accept and when to refuse invitations, when to take statements seriously and when not. Now these cues which may be words, gestures, facial expressions, customs, or norms are acquired by all of us in the course of growing up and are as much a part of our culture as the language we speak or the beliefs we accept. All of us depend for our peace of mind and our efficiency on hundreds of these cues, most of which we do not carry on the level of conscious awareness.

Now when an individual enters a strange culture, all or most of these familiar cues are removed. He or she is like a fish out of water. No matter how broadminded or full of good will you may be, a series of drops have been knocked from under you, followed by a feeling of frustration and anxiety. People react to the frustration in much the same way. First they reject the environment which causes the discomfort: "the ways of the host country are bad because they make us feel bad." When Americans or other foreigners in a strange land get together to grouse about the host country and its people, you can be sure they are suffering from culture shock. Another phase of culture shock is regression. The home environment suddenly assumes a tremendous importance. To an American everything becomes irrationally glorified. All the difficulties and problems are forgotten and only the good things back home are remembered. It usually takes a trip home to bring one back to reality.

Individuals differ greatly in the degree in which culture shock affects them. Although not common, there are individuals who cannot live in foreign countries. Those who have seen people go through culture shock and on to a satisfactory adjustment can discern steps in the process. During the first few weeks most individuals are fascinated by the new. They stay in hotels and associate with nationals who speak their language and are polite and gracious to foreigners. This honeymoon stage may last from a few days or weeks to six months depending on circumstances.

But this Cook's tour type of mentality does not normally last if the foreign visitor remains abroad and has seriously to cope with real conditions of life. It is then that the second stage begins, characterized by a hostile and aggressive attitude towards the host country. This hostility evidently grows out of the genuine difficulty which the visitor experiences in the process of adjustment. There is maid trouble, school trouble, language trouble, house trouble, transportation trouble, shopping trouble, and the fact that people in the host country are largely indifferent to all these troubles. They help but they just don't understand your great concern over these difficulties. Therefore, they must be insensible and unsympathetic to you and your worries. The result, "I just don't like them." You become aggressive, band together with your fellow countrymen and criticize the host country, its ways, and its people. But this criticism is not an objective appraisal but a derogatory one. Instead of trying to account for conditions as they are through as honest analysis of the actual conditions and the historical circumstances which have created them, you talk as if the difficulties you experienced are more or less created by the people of the host country for your special discomfort. You take refuge in the colony of your countrymen and its cocktail circuit which often becomes the fountain-head of emotionally charged labels known as stereotypes. This is a peculiar kind of invidious shorthand which caricatures the host country and its people in a negative manner. The "dollar-grasping American" and the "indolent Latin American" are samples of mild forms of stereotypes. The use of stereotypes may salve the ego of someone with a severe case of culture shock but it certainly does not lead to any genuine understanding of the host country and its people. This second stage of culture shock is in a sense a crisis in the disease. If you overcome it, you stay; if not, you leave before you reach the stage of a nervous breakdown.

If the visitor succeeds in getting some knowledge of the language and begins to get around by himself, he is beginning to open the way into the new cultural environment. The visitor still has difficulties but he takes a "this is my cross and I have to bear it" attitude. Usually in this stage the visitor takes a superior attitude to people of the host country. His sense of humor begins to exert itself. Instead of criticizing he jokes about the people and even cracks jokes about his or her own difficulties. He or she is flow on the way to recovery. And there is also the poor devil who is worse off than yourself whom you can help, which in turn gives you confidence in your ability to speak and get around.

In the fourth stage your adjustment is about as complete as it can be. The visitor now accepts the customs of the country as just another way of living. You operate within the new milieu without a feeling of anxiety although there are moments of strain. Only with a complete grasp of all the cues of social intercourse will this strain disappear. For a long time the individual will understand what the national is saying but he is not always sure what the national means. With a complete adjustment you not only accept the foods, drinks, habits, and customs, but actually begin to enjoy them. When you go on home leave you may even take things back with you and if you leave for good you generally miss the country and the people to whom you have become accustomed.

Now before going on to consider the nature of culture shock, it might be well to point out that the difficulties which the newcomer experiences are real. If individuals come to a tropical area from a temperate one they quite often suffer from intestinal disturbances. Strange food sometimes upsets people. In Rio, for instance, water and power shortages are very real. When these physical difficulties are added to those arising from not knowing how to communicate and the uncertainties presented by strange customs the consequent frustrations and anxieties are understandable. In the course of time, however, an individual makes his adjustment. You do what is essential about water, food, and the other minutiae of daily life. You adapt yourself to water and power shortages and to traffic problems. In short the environment does not change. What has changed is your attitude towards it. Somehow it no longer troubles you, you no longer project your discomforts onto the people of the host country and their ways. In short, you get along under a new set of living conditions.

Another important point worth considering is the attitude of others to a person suffering from culture shock. If you are frustrated and have an aggressive attitude to the people of the host country, they will sense this hostility and in many cases respond in a hostile manner or try to avoid you. In other words, their response moves from a preliminary phase of ingratiation to aggressive ridicule and on to avoidance. To your own countrymen who are well adjusted you become somewhat of a problem. As you feel weak in the face of the host country people you tend to wish to increase your dependence on your fellow countrymen much more than normal. Some will try to help you; others will try to avoid you. The better your fellow countryman understands your condition the better he is able to help you. But the difficulty is that culture shock has not been studied carefully enough for people to help you in an organized manner and you continue to be considered a bit queer—until you adjust yourself to the new situation. In general, we might say that until an individual has achieved a satisfactory adjustment he is not able to fully play his part on the job or as a member of the community. In a sense he is a sick person with a mild or severe case of culture shock as the case may be. Although I am not certain, I think culture shock affects wives more than husbands. The husband has his professional duties to occupy him and his activities may not differ too much from what he has been accustomed to. The wife, on the other hand, has to operate in an environment which differs much more from the milieu in which she grew up, and consequently the strain on her is greater.

The question now arises: What can you do to get over culture shock as quickly as possible? The answer is to get to know the people of the host country. But this you cannot do with any success without knowing the language, for language is the principal symbol system of communication. Now we all know that learning a new language is difficult, particularly to adults.

This task alone is quite enough to cause frustration and anxiety, no matter how skillful language teachers are in making it easy for you. But once you begin to be able to carry on a friendly conversation with your maid, your neighbor, or go on shopping trips alone, you not only gain confidence and a feeling of power but a whole new world of cultural meanings opens up for you.

You begin to find out not only what and how people do things but also what their interests are. These interests, people usually express by what they habitually talk about and how they allocate their time and money. Once you know this value or interest pattern it will be quite easy to get people to talk and to be interested in you. When we say people have no interest, we usually admit the fact that we have not bothered to find out.

At times it is helpful to be a participant observer by joining the activities of the people, to try to share in their responses. These activities could be a carnival, a religious rite, or some economic conferences.

Yet the visitor should never forget that he or she is an outsider and will be treated as such. He or she should view this participation as a role playing. Understanding the ways of people is essential but this does not mean that you have to give up your own. What happens is that you have developed two patterns of behavior.

Finally a word on what your fellow countrymen can do to help you get over culture shock. It is well to recognize that persons suffering from culture shock feel weak in the face of conditions which appear insuperable. It is natural for them to try to lean heavily on their compatriots. They may be irritating to the long-term resident but he should be patient, sympathetic, and understanding. Although talking does not remove pain, I think a great deal is gained by having the source of pain explained, some of the steps towards a cure indicated. And the assurance given that time, the great healer, will soon set things right.

(OBERG K. Culture shock: adjustment to new cultural environments [J]. Practical Anthropology, 1960, 7: 177-182.)

Language focus

precipitate *vt.* 使沉淀；使陷入；促成
orient *adj.* 东方的；新生的
regression *n.* 回归；退化
appraisal *n.* 评价；估价；估计
indolent *adj.* 懒惰的；无痛的
milieu *n.* 环境；周围；出身背景
hostile *adj.* 敌对的；怀敌意的
queer *adj.* 奇怪的；不舒服的
grouse *vi.* 埋怨
cue *n.* 提示；暗示；线索
maid *n.* 女仆；少女
derogatory *adj.* 贬损的
crack *n.* 裂缝
disturbance *n.* 干扰；骚乱
ingratiation *n.* 逢迎；讨好
carnival *n.* 狂欢节，嘉年华会

Exercises

A. Text Reading

Decide whether the following statements are true (T) or false (F).

1. ______ Anxiety resulting from experiencing a different culture will lead to culture shock.
2. ______ People react to the frustration in much different ways.
3. ______ Individuals differ greatly in the degree in which culture shock affects them.
4. ______ When people go through culture shock, the second stage begins with a hostile and aggressive attitude towards the host country.
5. ______ Getting to know the language will help people to recover from culture shock.
6. ______ In the fourth stage, You still suffer from a feeling of anxiety when there are moments of strain.
7. ______ The physical difficulties will add to the anxiety arising from intercultural communication.
8. ______ It is useless to observe the activities of the people in host country.
9. ______ Understanding the ways of people does not mean that you have to give up your own.
10. ______ Getting to talk to the fellow countrymen ia a good way to get over culture shock.

B. Terms Understanding

Find the definitions of the following terms in the text. If you cannot find the exact definition, try to use your own words to interpret it.

1. culture shock
2. honeymoon
3. negotiation
4. adjustment
5. adaptation
6. ego

C. Classroom Activities

1. Have you suffered from culture shock in your university life?
2. Should intercultural training be required of those who intend to study abroad? What do you expect to learn from it?
3. Work in pairs and exchange views on the meanings of the following proverbs; then try to find out their Chinese equivalents if there is any.
   Proverb 1: There's more than one way to bake a cake.
   Proverb 2: All work and no play makes Jack a dull boy.

Part Three

Academic Reading

Becoming More Intercultural

This chapter provides guidelines for the individual who wishes to become more interculturally competent in a communication sense. How does one become more capable in intercultural communication? Does intimate contact with another culture lead to better intercultural communication? How can one overcome the obstacles that prevent effective intercultural communication?

Intercultural Competence

Intercultural competence is the degree to which an individual is able to exchange information effectively and appropriately with individuals who are culturally dissimilar. Individuals vary widely in their ability to communicate with culturally unalike others. There is much evidence that intercultural communication is a difficult process.

The stated or implied purpose of most research, training, and teaching in the field of intercultural communication is to improve the intercultural competence of individuals. This objective has been apparent since the beginnings of the field of intercultural communication at the Foreign Service Institute in the 1950s. One of the most important skills for cultural competence is the ability to suspend our assumptions about what is "right". The greater the range of alternatives to which we are exposed, the more choices we have for deciding what makes sense for us. Knowing another culture gives you a place to stand while you take a good look at the one you were born into. Anthropologists are taught to be nonjudgmental about cultural differences. Even though they may study a culture that has sexual practices considered bizarre by European and North American standards, anthropologists seek to understand the functions fulfilled by these sexual practices from the point of view of the culture in which they occur.

We live in a world that is increasingly diverse in a cultural sense. Large U.S. cities, for example, have populations that are extremely diverse. Improved communication technologies and transportation make intercultural contact increasingly common. This trend will continue in the future, the "global village" becomes more real every day. If individuals could attain a higher degree of intercultural competence, they would presumably become better citizens, students, teachers, business people, and so forth. Society would be more peaceful, more productive, and become a generally more attractive place in which to live. Individuals would be better able to understand others who are unlike themselves. Through such improved understanding, a great deal of conflict could be avoided, the world would be a better place. Most North Americans want to become more interculturally experienced. College students, for example, want to learn about individuals unlike themselves. They often attend religious services of religions other than the one in which they were raised. They make friends with individuals from nations other than their own. They may date someone from another ethnic group, attracted to someone who does not think exactly as they do. Many students take vacations in other nations, go on student exchanges, or study at foreign universities. Heterophilous contacts with culturally different people provide an opportunity to become more interculturally competent, but they do not guarantee it. Our ability to learn from other individuals depends on our ability to overcome the barriers of culture.

Willingness to expand one's skills to include intercultural communication is an essential first step in overcoming barriers to intercultural communication. However, despite good intentions, we should be mindful of possible negative outcomes. Intercultural contact in many cases lends an individual to become more ethnocentric, prejudiced, and discriminatory. Even when we are aware of the barriers that make intercultural communication particularly difficult, we may mistakenly attribute problems to other people rather than examining our own skills or lack of them. Misunderstandings are as likely to result from intercultural contact as are understandings. How do we develop sufficient intercultural communication competence to ensure more successes than failures? The following sections revisit major barriers to intercultural communication and suggest ways to improve one's skills.

Overcoming Ethnocentrism

One of the most important barriers to intercultural competence is ethnocentrism, the degree to which other cultures are judged as inferior to one's own culture. Ethnocentrism can lead to racism and sexism. Racism categorizes individuals on the basis of their external physical traits, such as skin color, hair, facial structure, and eye shape, leading to prejudice and discrimination. Sexism is the assignment of characteristics to individuals on the basis of their sex, so that the genders are treated unequally. In many cultures, the female gender is treated as inferior and subjected to prejudice and discrimination.

How can ethnocentrism, and its attendant racism and sexism, be decreased or eliminated? Decreasing ethnocentrism is usually not just a matter of increased information but rather one of bringing about an emotional change on the part of the individuals involved. Greater contact between unalike individuals may be one means to lessen ethnocentrism. Many individuals study other national cultures or travel to visit them because they think that closer contact will help them toward better understanding of an unalike culture. However, the nature of such intercultural contact is an important determinant of whether such travel decreases or increases ethnocentrism toward the culture that is visited. Many tourists who visit another culture for a brief period, often without knowing the language, become more ethnocentric toward that culture. Touristic sojourning often does little to decrease ethnocentrism toward a national culture. Language competence, contact over a lengthy period of time, and a more intense relationship with members of the foreign culture (such as through close personal friendships) can help decrease ethnocentrism. The key is that only positive contacts produce positive feelings about another culture.

The various elements of a culture are integrated so that each element generally makes sense in light of the other elements. When a stranger encounters only one cultural element, independently of the other elements, it may seem exotic, unusual, or weird. Only when the outside observer experiences and understands all of the cultural elements, does that culture make sense. This level of cultural understanding can be achieved more fully if an individual has fluency in the language that is spoken and has had extended personal contact. Only then can the stranger perceive all of the elements of an unfamiliar culture and understand that the totality is coherent.

The nature of contact also applies to the case of ethnocentrism toward another religion, race, or any outgroup within one's own society. Just as most individuals have only limited, and socially distant, contact with foreigners, so do most North Americans communicate mainly with others who are ethnically much like themselves. The degree of interpersonal contact with heterophilous others is infrequent, but when interpersonal relationships occur, they have a rich potential for behavior change. Direct, personal (one-on-one) contact with an unalike other can decrease ethnocentrism.

More individuals today have the opportunity to meet people from another culture. Frequently the reasons for increased contact are related to studying or working abroad. Sojourning cannot be an effective type of intercultural communication in decreasing ethnocentrism, especially if the stay time is long enough. The special cultural patterns created, shared and learned by individuals who have lived in a culture other than their own have been termed "third culture". Even though the sojourning individuals may have a different first culture (the culture into which they were born and reared) and a different second culture (the culture in which they sojourned), they learn to share a world-encompassing perspective (the third culture). Someone who was born in the United States and then lived in India has a third culture experience in common with another individual who was born in Japan and then sojourned in Mexico.

Most people learn the third culture as adults when they sojourn abroad. Their children may learn the third culture by accompanying their parents on the sojourning experience. Third culture young people have much in common and, in fact, often marry each other. Third culture individuals are unusually tolerant and understanding of cultural differences. They are less likely to think in terms of borders between ingroups and outgroups.

Some individuals have a third culture from birth. Biracial children, for example, can often operate effectively within each of their parents' cultures and can connect the two. Biracial people, who never leave their home nation, have a third culture. In the United States, the number of interracial marriages is increasing, as is the number of multiracial children. Today there are more than two million people of mixed racial ancestry in the United States; this number may be a substantial underestimate.

Experiential Training

Ethnocentric attitudes are firmly entrenched in cultural norms and thus are extremely difficult to change. Change is not, however, impossible. One means of decreasing ethnocentrism is intervention through training. There are courses designed to help individuals understand the nature of their ethnocentric beliefs. One example of an ethnocentrism intervention is a two-week training course in India that is designed to decrease the sexism of male government employees.

This Women's Awareness Training puts the male trainees in the daily role of an Indian woman. The trainees carry water from a distant well, wash their clothes and dishes, cook, and clean their living quarters. The male trainees are not allowed to go outside of their residences without permission of a female trainer. Nor are the trainees permitted to drive a vehicle. Thus, the Indian men are taught to empathize with the subservient role of Indian women. Individuals who have completed this training say that it has a powerful effect on their sexist attitudes and, more generally, in decreasing their ethnocentrism. The training is intended to increase empathy not just with women but with all heterophilous others, including lower-caste individuals and those considered inferior.

Intercultural communication training must be highly experiential in order for it to increase intercultural competence. Thus intercultural communication courses often use simulation games, exercises, videos, and other types of learning in which another culture can be experienced by the learner. In other words, if intercultural communication training is to have an effect on individuals' behavior, the unalike culture must be experienced. One cannot just talk about intercultural communication. One has to do it.

Cultural Relativism

Cultural relativism is the degree to which an individual judges another culture by its context. One can then understand the behavior of another individual in the context of the other's culture. Thus cultural relativism is in a sense the opposite of ethnocentrism. Rather than picking out a specific cultural element as unusual or odd, the individual who is culturally relativistic considers that element in light of the total culture of which it is a part. When judged from the viewpoint of the entire culture, the cultural element usually can be understood for the functions that it serves.

For example, the Hindu value on sacred cows seems bizarre to many visitors to India. In a land where millions of individuals go hungry, cows roam the streets of large cities, causing traffic problems, but cannot be slaughtered for meat. To Westerners who are accustomed to an entirely different culture, one that stresses eating steak and hamburgers, the beliefs about cows seem illogical. But the sacred cows are very functional for Indian society. Their manure is gathered and used for fuel and fertilizer. Sacred cows are milked to provide an important source of protein for the human diet in a largely vegetarian society. Hindu religion, which believes in reincarnation, preaches that the cows may represent a former (or a future) form of human life. So the idea of sacred cows makes sense in light of the total culture of India, including its dominant religion, its vegetarianism, and the need for protein in the diet.

The Navajo approach to housing is another example of a behavior serving a germane function within a culture. Tom Begay lives in a hogan whose door faces east because the Navajo feel a spiritual closeness with the sun. The hogan belongs to Tom's wife, because the Navajo are matrilocal, which means that when they marry the husband goes to live in the wife's mother's hogan. All of these elements of Navajo culture make sense to a culturally relativistic individual who understands this culture and who appreciates its coherence. Cultural relativism means that we understand a culture from the inside and that we look at the behavior of people from their point of view. Furthermore, we respect the differences that contrast with our own culture.

From Ethnocentrism to Ethnorelativism

The variable of ethnocentrism versus ethnorelativism (that is, cultural relativism) is marked by a series of stages through which an individual may pass:

(1) A parochial denial of cultural differences, in which there is little contact with unalike others. For example, when Edward Hall was training diplomats and technicians at the Foreign Service Institute, many of the trainees initially insisted that all people are alike, once you get to know them.

(2) An evaluative defense against understanding cultural differences, because they may be threatening to one's view of the world. An individual may say, "I don't want to understand what those people think. They are so different from U. S."

(3) A minimization of cultural differences, through which cultural similarities are stressed.

Edward Hall found that the mid-career agricultural technicians that he was training at the FSI frequently stated: "I have worked extensively with U. S. farmers in the past, and I expect that Latin American farmers will be about the same."

(4) The acceptance of cultural differences, which are acknowledged and understood. Here a trainee in a cultural diversity workshop might say: "Okay, people in India do not use their left hand for eating, and I understand why."

(5) The adaptation of one's thinking and behavior to cultural difference. A trainee may state: "Now I understand why women in the United States feel they are underpaid for doing the same work as a man."

(6) The integration of cultural differences into one's own worldview, so that one's identity is both a part of, but apart from, the different culture, and a new "third culture" perspective replaces the native culture perspective. A returned Peace Corps volunteer from Nigeria explained that she now felt she viewed North American culture from a different perspective than before her sojourn in Africa.

Training can move an individual through these six stages toward a greater degree of cultural relativism.

Pluralism is the degree to which an individual is open to others' points of view. Such broadmindedness is closely related to cultural relativism but may be even wider in scope. For example, one could be pluralistic regarding another individual's point of view on some issue like abortion. An ethnorelativistic individual would accept a viewpoint if it was coherent with the rest of the culture.

Societies, as well as individuals, can be pluralistic. Often a system that is characterized by diversity (defined as the degree to which a system is composed of a variety of individuals with different cultures) is also pluralistic. Diversity can encourage tolerance for other points of view. Of course, diversity can also lead ethnocentric individuals to think in terms of ingroups and outgroups.

Overcoming Stereotypes

In order for individuals to become more interculturally conscious, they must learn to question stereotypes, the building blocks of prejudice, and to break through the arbitrary borders that have been taught to separate people from one another. The interculturally competent communicator judges each individual on a person-to-person basis, rather than categorizing people into stereotypes.

Derivation of Stereotypes

What is the origin of the word "stereotype"? In the early history of U. S. newspapers, more than 100 years ago, cartoons were extremely popular. Photography was not yet well developed, and newspapers were eager to publish illustrative material. The works of famous cartoonists were syndicated in a number of newspapers. The cartoonist's daily cartoon was distributed by sending a paper-made mirror image of the cartoon through the postal service. A stereotype was made of the cartoon by converting the cartoon to lead type, and the cartoon was published in the local newspaper. The cartoons often featured exaggerated images of Uncle Sam, John Bull, the cunning Asian, bloated politicians, and other social figures. Gradually, these cartoon images came to be called "stereotypes".

A stereotype is a generalization about some group of people that oversimplifies their culture. Many stereotypes are completely incorrect and others greatly distort reality. For example, many North Americans have a stereotype of the college athlete as an individual who is not a serious student. The stereotype was generalized from well-known examples. While there may be some truth in the stereotype (some athletes, like all other students, may not be exceptional scholars), it is greatly exaggerated. A stereotype is often self-fulfilling. If we accept a stereotype as an accurate description, we tend to see only evidence that supports it and to overlook the frequent exceptions to it.

In public opinion, Walter Lippmann spoke of "the pictures in our heads" and the role of the mass media in forming such stereotypes. One of the most shameful episodes in U. S. history resulted from the stereotypes depicting the enemy during World War Ⅱ. Anti-Japanese propaganda convinced many people in the United States that the Japanese were cunning, tricky, and willing to fight to the death to win. The negative stereotype was mainly formed by news accounts carried by the media about warfare in the Pacific theater, by cartoons and posters, and by interpersonal communication influenced by the predominant beliefs of the time. Attitudes help us determine appropriate behavior. Nationalistic sentiments protecting one's country by uniting against an enemy that threatens its national security are essential during a war. However, those stereotypes created an atmosphere in 1942 in which U. S. citizens did nothing while the federal government put 110,000 citizens of Japanese ancestry in internment camps. Japanese Americans were forced to leave their homes, their businesses, and their possessions behind because the stereotype portrayed them as threats to their own country.

Stereotypes as Codes

What is a code? A code is a classification used by individuals to categorize their experience and to communicate it to others. A code is a kind of shorthand that enables an individual to convey a range of phenomena in a single word. For example, ducks, geese, and swans are three variations of waterbirds. Adults are generally familiar with the general category and the three subcategories. A child may learn one of the subcategories and apply it to the other two, calling all birds paddling in a lake "ducks", for example.

A stereotype is a special kind of code. The term stereotype evolved from the printing process of repeatedly casting the same image often exaggerated and usually negative. It is easier to communicate if we don't need to describe every nuance of difference. Rather than exerting the mental effort to evaluate all incoming information carefully and critically, we often resort to categorizing certain information into familiar patterns. Stereotypes are one of these patterns, and they can be positive or negative. For example, many people in the United States think that Asians have a gift for mathematics and science. Another stereotype is that Germans build the finest automobiles; the French have the best chefs; the Italians have the finest opera singers.

We learn stereotypes as one part of our culture. Standardized mental pictures held in common by members of a group make it easier to decide what behavior is appropriate and what behavior to expect. The problem with such an oversimplified approach is that it distorts the reality of what we are perceiving. During initial contact with someone of a certain race or lifestyle, you may have reacted toward the stranger in a way determined by the stereotype that you held. The stereotype may have prevented you from ever getting to know the other individual. On the other hand, if you got to know the individual better, you might first believe that the stereotype did not apply to him or her and, eventually, that the stereotype incorrectly categorized all members of the group. We should recognize that within any stereotyped set of individuals, there is wide variation.

Forming codes and thinking in terms of these categories is a necessary aspect of human communication. Culturally sensitive individuals guard against the dangers of thinking in stereotypes, and they remain flexible in changing these classifications. Culturally competent people use stereotypes as tools with limited functions. Cultural relativism is one means of questioning existing stereotypes. If we learn the codes of other cultures, we can evaluate our own more critically.

Overcoming Prejudice and Discrimination

Certain countries like the United States have a national policy with the objective to lessen discrimination. The Civil War of the 1860s, the Civil Rights Movement of the 1950s and 1960s, and the equal opportunity legislation of recent decades are important landmarks in this historical movement toward lessened discrimination. But making discrimination illegal does not make it disappear. In order to decrease discrimination, individuals and systems must change.

Such a shift in attitudes (prejudice) and in overt behavior (discrimination) ultimately can be encouraged by intercultural communication.

Prejudice

As explained in previous chapters, prejudice is an unfounded attitude toward an outgroup based on a comparison with one's ingroup. Prejudice is usually expressed through communication. For example, an African-American student attending a mainly white people university stated: "In my freshman year, at a university student parade, there was a group of us standing there not knowing that this was an event that not a lot of black people went to. Our dorm was going, and ... we were students too! ... A group of white fraternity boys ... I remember the Southern flag, and one of them pointed and said, 'Look at that bunch of niggers!' I remember thinking, 'Surely he's not talking to us!'... I wanted to cry."

After several such unpleasant experiences, an individual develops an expectation of experiencing prejudice in similar situations. Another African-American student attending a predominantly White university explained: "I still find myself uncomfortable if I walk into a strange environment where there are only Whites and I'm the only Black. And unfortunately, usually someone, at least one person in that environment or in that situation, will say or do something that's negative, if it's no more than just ignore you. So, if you come in defensive... your fear is reinforced."

There are many types of prejudice in the United States, but one of the most obvious is prejudice by European Americans toward African Americans. In the 1940s, Gunnar Myrdal identified racial prejudice as an American Dilemma. In recent decades, White North Americans' negative perceptions of African Americans have softened as a result of the general liberalization of racial attitudes and the decrease of segregation in the United States. However, many prejudiced Whites still cling to negative stereotypes. A national survey of ethnic images found that African Americans are more likely than European Americans, Latinos, Asian Americans, or Southern Whites to be perceived as poor, violent, unintelligent, and welfare-dependent. A 1991 national survey found that 31 percent of White European Americans perceived African Americans as lazy, and 50 percent thought they were aggressive.

This kind of prejudice leads to discrimination. Whites who perceive African Americans as lazy are less supportive of government programs to alleviate poverty. Those who perceive African Americans as unintelligent and violent are less supportive of school integration. Public opinion polls in the United States show that the nation is actually two societies: One Black and one White, separate and unequal. The two groups differ markedly in socioeconomic status and are divided by residential segregation. The public opinion polls show that Blacks and Whites disagree, even on topics that have no explicit racial content. So the "American dilemma" that Gunnar Myrdal wrote about 50 years ago still exists.

Prejudice can take as many forms as the groups who perceive difference as a threat. Earlier we looked at the prejudice against Japanese Americans from 1942 to 1945. Despite the unimaginable discrimination against citizens in a democracy, some 33, 000 Japanese Americans enlisted in the armed forces, some of them serving in the much-decorated 442nd Regiment in Europe. When U. S. President Harry Truman welcomed home this regiment in 1946, he said: "You fought not only the enemy, you fought prejudice and you won."

Prejudice is a kind of cultural blindness. It prevents the U. S. from seeing reality accurately. In order for individuals to become more interculturally competent, they must avoid the prejudiced attitudes that often lead to discrimination and the unequal treatment of others.

(ROGERS E M, STEINFATT T M. Intercultural communication[M]. Mississippi: Waveland Press, 1998.)

Comprehension Check

A. Questions for Discussion

1. How does one become more capable in intercultural communication?
2. Does intimate contact with another culture lead to better intercultural communication?
3. How can one overcome the obstacles that prevent effective intercultural communication?

B. Detail Understanding

Match the terms with their definitions.

Term	Definition
1. Ethnocentrism	A. It is the degree to which an individual is open to others' points of view.

续表

Term	Definition
2. Cultural relativism	B. The degree to which other cultures are judged as inferior to one's own culture. It can lead to racism and sexism.
3. Stereotype	C. It is a classification used by individuals to categorize their experience and to communicate it to others. It is a kind of shorthand that enables an individual to convey a range of phenomena in a single word.
4. Pluralism	D. The degree to which an individual judges another culture by its context.
5. Code	E. It is a generalization about some group of people that oversimplifies their culture.
6. Prejudice	F. It is an unfounded attitude toward an outgroup based on a comparison with one's ingroup. It is usually expressed through communication.

Suggestions for Further Reading

1. SOLER E A, JORDA M P S. Intercultural language use and language learning[M]. Dordrecht: Springer Netherlands, 2008.
2. BENNETT J M, SALONEN R. Intercultural communication and the new American campus[J]. Change, 2007, 39 (2): 46-50.
3. 爱德华·霍尔. 跨越文化[M]. 何道宽，译. 北京：北京大学出版社，2010.

Unit 3 The Basic Value behind Culture

One man's meat is another man's poison.

—English Proverb

Objectives：

To understand the value that gives meaning to words；

To know how to express chinese basic value；

To get familiar with the differences of values between East and West

Warm-up Activity

The following are proverbs from various countries（see Table 3-1）. Different as they are，these proverbs express the same or similar values.

Table 3-1 The values behind proverbs

Proverbs	Chinese Equivalents	Countries
He who speaks first loses.	发言最先，失败最早。	India
The mouth is the cause of calamity.	祸从口出。	Japan
Life is but a candle before the wind.	人生好比风中烛。	Japan
Man does not attain everything he desires; winds do not always blow as the vessels wish.	人无法事事如愿，风也不能时时都顺。	Arabic countries
There is nothing to fear but fear itself.	最大的恐惧是恐惧本身。	U. S.

续表

Proverbs	Chinese Equivalents	Countries
The path is not hard to follow because of the rivers and the mountains, but because, men are reluctant to face the mountains and rivers.	道路的艰难并不是因为有山脉和河流，而是因为人们不愿意直面山脉与河流。	Vietnam

Question for discussion

Identify what these proverbs mean to the people speaking the language and what values these proverbs transmit.

Part One

Intensive Reading

Language Mirrors Values

In addition to reflecting its worldview, a language also reveals a culture's basic value structure. For example, the extent to which a culture values the individual, as compared to the group, is often reflected in its language or linguistic style. The value placed on the individual is deeply rooted in the American psyche. Most citizens of the United States start from the cultural assumption that the individual is supreme and not only can, but should, shape his or her own destiny. That individualism is highly valued in the United States can be seen throughout its culture, from the love of the automobile as the preferred mode of transportation to a judicial system which goes as far as any in the world to protect the individual rights of the accused. Even when dealing with children, Americans try to provide them with a bedroom of their own, respect their individual right to privacy, and attempt to instill in them a sense of self-reliance and independence by encouraging them to solve their own problems.

Owing to the close interrelatedness of language and culture, values (such as individualism in the United States) are reflected in standard American English. One such indicator of how our language reflects individualism is the number of words found in any American English dictionary that are compounded with the word "self". To illustrate, one is likely to find in any standard American English dictionary no fewer than 150 such words, including "self-absorbed", "self-appointed", "self-centered", "self-confident", "self-conscious", "self-educated", "self-image", "self-regard", and "self-supporting". This considerable list of English terms related to the individual is significantly larger than one can find in a culture that places greater emphasis on corporate or group relationships.

In the U. S., individual happiness is the highest good, while in such group-oriented cultures as Japan, people strive for the good of the larger group such as the family, the community, or the whole society. Rather than stressing individual happiness, the Japanese are more concerned with justice (for group members) and righteousness (by group members). In Japan the "we" always comes before the "I"; the group is always more predominant than the individual. As Condon reminds us, "If Descartes had been Japanese, he would have said, 'we think, therefore we are.'"

An important structural distinction found in Japanese society is between *uchi* (the in-group) and *soto* (the out-group), or the difference between "us" and "them". This basic social distinction is reflected in the Japanese language. For example, whether a person is "one of us" or "one of them" will determine which conversational greeting will be used, either *Ohayo gozaimasu*, which is customarily used with close members of one's in-group, or *Konnichiwa*, which is more routinely used to greet those outside one's inner circle. Mizutani has conducted an interesting experiment outside the Imperial Palace in Tokyo which is a favorite place for jogging. Dressed like a jogger, he greeted everyone he passed, both other joggers like himself and non-joggers, and noted their responses. Interestingly, 95 percent of the joggers greeted him with *Ohayo gazaimasu* (the term reserved for in-group members), while only 42 percent of the non-joggers used such a phrase. He concluded that the joggers, to a much greater degree than the non-joggers, considered him to be an in-group member because he was a jogger too.

Group members in Japan don't want to stand out or assert their individuality because according to the Japanese proverb, "The nail that sticks up gets hammered down." In contrast to the United States, the emphasis in Japan is on "fitting in", harmonizing, and avoiding open disagreement within the group. If one must disagree, it is usually done gently and very indirectly by using such passive expressions as "It is said that..." or "Some people think that..." This type of linguistic construction enables one to express an opinion without having to be responsible for it in the event that others in the group might disagree. In a study of speech patterns among Japanese and American students, Shimonishi found that the Japanese students used passive voice significantly more than their American counterparts did.

How language is used in Japan and the United States both reflects and reinforces the value of group consciousness in Japan and individualism in the United States. The goal of communication in Japan is to achieve consensus and promote harmony, while in the United States it is to demonstrate one's eloquence. Whereas language in Japan tends to be cooperative, polite, and conciliatory, language in the United States is often competitive, adversarial, and confrontational, and aimed at making a point. The Japanese go to considerable length to avoid controversial issues that might be disruptive; Americans seem to thrive on controversy, debate, argumentation, and provocation, as is evidenced by the use of the expression "just for the sake of argument". Moreover, the Japanese play down individual eloquence in favor of being good listeners, a vital skill if group consensus is to be achieved. North Americans, by way of contrast, are not particularly effective listeners because they are too busy mentally preparing their personal responses rather than paying close attention to what is being said. Thus, all of these linguistic contrasts between Japan and the United States express their fundamentally different approaches to the cultural values of "groupness" and "individualism".

(FERRARO G P. The cultural dimension of international business[M]. 3rd ed. Upper Saddle River N. J.: Prentice Hall, 1998.)

Vocabulary

psyche *n.* that which is responsible for one's thoughts and feelings; the seat of the faculty of reason

destiny *n.* an event (or a course of events) that will inevitably happen in the future

supreme *adj.* greatest in status or authority or power; highest in excellence or achievement

accuse *v.* blame for, make a claim of wrongdoing or misbehavior against

indicator *n.* a signal for attracting attention

corporate *adj.* done by or characteristic of individuals acting together

righteousness *n.* adhering to moral principles

predominant *adj.* having superior power and influence

counterpart *n.* a person or thing having the same function or characteristics as another

consensus *n.* agreement in the judgment or opinion reached by a group as a whole

eloquence *n.* powerful and effective language

conciliatory *adj.* making or willing to make concessions

confrontational *n.* discord resulting from a clash of ideas or opinions

controversial *adj.* marked by or capable of arousing controversy

provocation *n.* unfriendly behavior that causes anger or resentment

thrive *vi.* make steady progress; be at the high point in one's career or reach a high point in historical significance or importance

Exercises

A. Words in Use

Fill in the blanks with the words given below. Change the form when necessary. Each word can be used only once.

controversial	supreme	predominant	concilliatory	accuse
corporate	consensus	confrontation	eloquence	provocation

1. We resolve not to __________ them to avoid troubles.
2. The __________ feature of his character was pride.
3. We tried to stay away from __________ topics at the dinner party.
4. Even a limited __________ can escalate into a major war.
5. The safety of the people is the __________ law.
6. She sometimes angers with little or no __________.

7. His letter was couched in __________ terms.
8. The two parties have reached a __________.
9. His __________ did not avail against the facts.
10. The owner opened a __________ checking account at the bank.

B. Questions for Discussion

1. How do you interpret the statement "Language is like a mirror which can reflect people's values"? Can you give some examples to account for your arguments?
2. Can you point out the difference between the Americans and the Japanese in terms of their way of speaking?

C. Translation

1. Even when dealing with children, Americans try to provide them with a bedroom of their own, respect their individual right to privacy, and attempt to instill in them a sense of self-reliance and independence by encouraging them to solve their own problems.
2. As Condon reminds us, "If Descartes had been Japanese, he would have said, 'we think, therefore we are.'"
3. Group members in Japan don't want to stand out or assert their individuality because according to the Japanese proverb, "The nail that sticks up gets hammered down."
4. If one must disagree, it is usually done gently and very indirectly by using such passive expressions as "It is said that..." or "Some people think that..."
5. Thus, all of these linguistic contrasts between Japan and the United States express their fundamentally different approaches to the cultural values of "groupness" and "individualism".

D. Case Study

Case 1

A Filipino couple were vacationing in England. While they were strolling along one of the main streets of London with a British acquaintance, they met another Filipino who had been residing there for some time. He was an old friend who they had not seen for several years. They greeted him warmly and effusively and continued their conversation in a loud and animated fashion using their native language. After a while the British became noticeably agitated, and turned his head away and sighed. The Filipinos noticed the reaction, looked at each other, and then resumed their conversation but in a quieter tone.

Questions

Why did the British become agitated?

A. Being a British, he was unwilling to be seen with a group of foreigners.

B. He thought their excitement was not proper in public.

C. He suspected the Filipinos were talking about him.

D. He thought the Filipinos were very rude for not introducing him to their friend.

Case 2

A foreign visitor was looking at the host's potted flowers with obvious admiration. The plants were blooming profusely. The host remarked diffidently, "Growing flowers is my hobby, but I'm not much good at it."

Question

How should the foreigner visitor reply?

Part Two

Extensive Reading

The Fundamental Spirit of Chinese Culture

The Philosophy of Harmony

While "Harmony of Man with Nature" and "Peace Enjoys Priority" are the philosophies and ideals of the Chinese people since ancient times in their pursuit of the harmony between Man and Nature and the harmony among people, building up a harmonious society and achieving harmonious development are the dream and aspirations of the Chinese. To Chinese people, harmony is a powerful word. There is nothing it cannot absorb and nothing it cannot cover. Harmony seeks peace, compromise, concord and unison.

Harmony boasts strong Chinese characteristics, and expresses the traditional Chinese philosophy in pursuit of a balance between man and nature, among people and between man's body and soul. The theory that man is an integral part of nature first originated in the Spring and Autumn and Warring States periods (770BC-221BC). The theory, as a basic notion in Chinese philosophy, insists that the politics and ethics of human beings are a direct reflection of nature.

Harmony is rich in connotation and full of profound philosophy of great wisdom. It advocates, first, diversity and, second, balance and arriving at the same destination by different routes, reaching unanimity after taking many things into consideration: it encourages the virtue of magnanimity, promotes the broad and profound spirit of "great virtue carrying substance with it", featuring tolerance, compatibility, and honesty and moderation. Gathering different things together and making them balanced is called "harmony". Harmony can generate new things. When five-tones are harmonious, the sound is audible; when the five-colors are harmonious, they become a set of well-designed pattern; and when five-flavors are harmonious, they are edible.

When this logics inferred to administration, we must harmonize various kinds of interests, synthesize different opinions and defuse complicated contradictions. If same things are piled up together, they cannot give birth to new things and so they cannot be full of vigor, instead, the phenomenon of "such same things that cannot continue to exist" will emerge.

When harmony is used in interpersonal relations, magnanimity will win over the public; when one treats others liberally, he or she will win others' confidence. For instance, one in a high position should treat others with an attitude of leniency and show his courtesy.

When harmony is used in politics, then there can be logical administration and harmonious people, historical development can be promoted, and prosperous culture can be achieved. "Harmony" can promote the birth of new things and new thoughts and bring about a situation featuring the blossoming of one hundred flowers and a blaze of color. Conversely, there can only be a situation in which ten thousand horses are muted, and neither cow nor sparrow could be heard.

If we use harmony in economy, we can promote the development of production and prosperity of economy. At the beginning of many Chinese dynasties, the rulers pursued a policy of allowing a period of time for recuperation and building up of strength in order to give people an opportunity for the restoration and development of production. This policy of harmony did play a desirable role in restoring and developing production.

Harmony we use in diplomacy can make all nations live together in peace, and by doing so, we have both safeguarded our own national independence, and refrained from practicing external expansion; we do not invade other countries, and absolutely not allow other nations to commit aggression against our country. This is China's fine tradition of loving peace and promoting common development.

When harmony is used in the relations between man and nature, then each of them can live in peace respectively and can accomplish something through respective support. Humanity can develop itself only by making rational use of and maintaining harmony with nature, maintain and develop the civilization itself has created, satisfy intergenerational demand, realize intergenerational fairness and enjoy mutual growth and mutual prosperity with nature and develop together with nature in a harmonious way.

The harmony theory encouraged by traditional Chinese culture is very profound. As a profound philosophy used to regulate social contradiction and to bring a suitable, timely and appropriate state of harmony, harmony has brought stability and auspiciousness to the Chinese nation.

Harmony is both an ancient social ideal as well as our actual choice. Harmony will open up a broader world for future humankind and provide humanity with inexhaustible driving force for its development.

Yin-Yang

This symbol (see Figure 3-1) represents the ancient Chinese understanding of how things work. The outer circle represents "everything", while the black and white shapes within the circle represent the interaction of two energies, called "*Yin*"(black) and "*Yang*"(white), which cause everything to happen. They are not completely black or white, just as things in life are not completely black or white, and they cannot exist without each other.

While *Yin* would be dark, passive, downward, cold, contracting and weak, *Yang* would be bright, active, upward, hot, expanding, and strong. The shape of the *Yin* and *Yang* sections of the symbol, actually gives you a sense of the continual movement of these two energies, *Yin* to *Yang* and *Yang* to *Yin*, causing everything to happen: just as things expand and contract, and temperature changes from hot to cold.

Figure 3-1 *Yin-Yang*

The Five Elements

According to traditional Chinese medicine and philosophy, the Five Elements are the fundamental components of the universe. They are: Wood, Fire, Earth, Metal and Water.

Everything in existence (also known as "matter" or "the ten thousand things") contains some quantity of all these five elements. However, according to the theory, one of the five so particularly predominates or manifests itself in each thing, and may thus be categorized accordingly.

Taoist physicians and sages further determined that each element has special associations with particular organs in the human body as well as to other things such as colors, flavors, the time of day, the seasons of the year, and the way we respond physically and emotionally to external influences and all of the forces of nature.

The Five Elements theory identifies the five different modes (elements) in which *Qi* energy may manifest itself. The five (wood, fire, earth, metal and water) are arranged into a cyclical sequence that represents the flow of energy between these elements as "phases".

Each phase of an element characterizes a stage in a cyclical process. The characteristic of each phase is determined by the "energy dynamic" personified as the never ending round of the seasons in the natural world.

How *Yin-Yang* and the Five Elements Work

The *Yin* and *Yang* accomplish changes in the universe through the five material agents, or *Wu Xing*, which both produce one another and overcome one another. All changes in the universe can be explained by the workings of *Yin and Yang* and the progress of the five material agents as they either produce one another or overcome one another, *Yin-Yang* and the five agents are universal explanatory principles.

All phenomena can be understood with *Yin-Yang* and the five agents: the movements of the stars, the workings of the body, the nature of foods, the qualities of music, the ethical qualities of humans, the progress of time, the operations of government, and even the nature of historical change. All things follow this order so that all things can be related to one another in some way: one can use the stars to determine what kind of policy to pursue in government, for instance.

The *Yin* and *Yang* represent all the opposite principles one finds in the universe. Under *Yang* are the principles of maleness, the sun, creation, heat, light, Heaven, dominance, and so on; and under *Yin* are the principles of femaleness, the moon, completion, cold, darkness, material forms, submission, and so on. Each of these opposites produce the other: Heaven creates the ideas of things under *Yang*, the earth produces their material forms under *Yin*, and vice versa; creation occurs under the principle of *Yang*, the completion of the created thing occurs under *Yin*, and vice versa, and so on.

This production of *Yin* from *Yang* and *Yang* from *Yin* occurs cyclically and constantly, so that one principle does not continually dominate the other or determines the other. All opposites that one experiences—health and sickness, wealth and poverty, power and submission, can be explained in reference to the temporary dominance of one principle over the other. Since one principle does not dominate eternally, all conditions are subject to change into their opposites.

This cyclical nature of *Yin* and *Yang*, the opposing forces of change in the universe, mean several things. First, all phenomena change into their opposites in an eternal cycle of reversal. Second, since the one principle produces the other all phenomena have within them the seeds of their opposite state, that is, sickness has the seeds of health, health contains the seeds of sickness, wealth contains the seeds of poverty, etc. Third, even though an opposite may not be seen to be present, since one principle produces the other, no phenomenon is completely devoid of its opposite state. One is never really healthy since health contains the principle of its opposite, sickness. This is called "presence in absence". Once you have this principle down, the particular Chinese view as expressed in literature, art, and history will become immediately evident.

Chinese Traditional Concept of Health Preserving

Health preserving is a concept in Chinese traditional medicine to enhance physical fitness, prevent diseases, postpone aging and prolong the life by spiritual toning, therapeutic diets and medicated diet, healthy exercises and other methods. Such concept takes the natural point of view in ancient China as the theoretical basis, such as Five Elements Theory, *Yin-Yang* Theory, Pneumatism and Connecting with Macrocosm.

The ancients believe that all things in the world are generated from the five substances: metal, wood, water, fire and earth. This Five Element Theory also can be applied to explain the uniformity of mutual connection between human viscera and tissues as well as between human body and the external environment.

The ancients also believe that, all things in the world can be divided by *Yin* and *Yang*. If applied to medicine, this *Yin-Yang* Theory will define such substances and functions that are driving, warming and exciting the human body as *Yang*, while such substances and functions that are condensing, moisturizing and inhibiting the human body as *Yin*. *Yin* and *Yang* rise and fall by restricting each other to achieve dynamic balance. If this balance is damaged, disease will produce.

The ancients also believe that the *Qi* is the source of changes of *Yin* and *Yang* and the Five Elements; they believe that man and nature communicate and correspond to each other. The theory of Pneuma and Correspondence of Man and Heaven has been also applied to the understanding of human life activities, as well as the explanation for the mutual restraint and effect of man and nature.

The concept of health preserving is the product of such natural views. It is in light of this concept that people established the rich and effective methods of health preserving, such as spiritual toning, guiding and breathing, health care in four seasons, food and medicine diets for health preserving, thus forming a miracle of the traditional Chinese medicine—Health Preserving Theory.

(FAN W W, YU Q H. An introduction to Chinese culture[M]. Beijing: Higher Education Press, 2011: 38-49.)

Language focus

compromise	*n.*	妥协;和解	concord	*n.*	和谐
integral	*adj.*	完整的;整体的	unanimity	*n.*	同意;全体一致
magnanimity	*n.*	慷慨	compatibility	*n.*	兼容
moderation	*n.*	适度;节制	audible	*adj.*	听得见的
edible	*adj.*	可食用的	synthesize	*vt.*	合成;综合
vigor	*n.*	活力;精力	defuse	*vt.*	平息
leniency	*n.*	仁慈;温和	courtesy	*n.*	礼貌;恩惠
mute	*adj.*	沉默的	recuperation	*n.*	恢复
refrain	*vi.*	节制;避免	aggression	*n.*	侵犯;侵害
contradiction	*n.*	矛盾	auspiciousness	*n.*	兴盛;幸运
inexhaustible	*adj.*	用不完的	predominate	*vt.*	支配;主宰
manifest	*vt.*	表明;显示	sage	*n.*	圣人
personify	*vt.*	是……的典型;表现	cyclical	*adj.*	循环的
submission	*n.*	服从	ethical	*adj.*	伦理的;道德的
reversal	*n.*	逆转	therapeutic	*adj.*	治疗的
viscera	*n.*	内脏;内容	tissue	*n.*	组织
moisturize	*vt.*	使湿润	dynamic	*adj.*	动态的
pneuma	*n.*	灵魂;精神;元气			

Exercises

A. Text Reading

Decide whether the following statements are true (T) or false (F).

1. ______ Harmony expresses the traditional Chinese philosophy in pursuit of a balance between man and nature, among people and between man's body and soul.
2. ______ When we use harmony in diplomacy, we should always seeks peace, compromise, concord.
3. ______ Harmony is just an ancient social ideal, but not our rational choice in modern society.
4. ______ This *Yin-Yang* symbol is not completely black or white, which represents the things in life are not completely black or white.

5. ______ Confucian physicians and sages determined that each element has special associations with particular organs in the human body.
6. ______ All phenomena can be understood with *Yin-Yang* and the five agents.
7. ______ According to *Yin* and *Yang* theory, the *Yin* and *Yang* represent all the opposite principles in the universe, and each of these opposites produce the other.
8. ______ *Yin* and *Yang* cannot continually dominates each other.
9. ______ The connotations of *Yin* and *Yang* applied in medicine are exactly the same as they are in the *Yin* and *Yang* Theory.
10. ______ According to the Five Elements Theory, the five elements exist in everything.

B. Terms Understanding

Find the definitions of the following terms in the text. If you cannot find the exact definition, try to use your own words to interpret it.

1. Harmony of Man with Nature
2. Peace Enjoys Priority
3. *Yin-Yang* Theory
4. Five Elements Theory
5. Health Preserving Theory

C. Classroom Activities

1. What aspects of our life have been listed to explain the implication of harmony?
2. Does the philosophy of harmony well fits in the following areas of our daily life? Explain how.
   (1) Keeping a diet
   (2) Agriculture
   (3) Dancing
   (4) Playing computer games
3. Do you know any way of health preserving? What are the theories underlying it/them?

Part Three

Academic Reading

Interpersonal Relationship and Intercultural Communication: East and West

Abstract

This paper makes a comparison of the communication patterns and the interpersonal orientations between the East and West. It also goes beneath the surface and explores the philosophical sources of the differences in these aspects. The assumption in this paper is that communication is essentially a social process and that, as such, it is influenced by the orientations of interpersonal relationship, which in turn is underpinned by value orientations and philosophical foundations.

Interpersonal relationships, the cultural, social, and psychological variable, almost constitute the most important factor that influences communication both in the Chinese context and American context. However, interpersonal relationship in the Chinese contest is underpinned by Confucianism, especially *Ren* (仁) and *Li* (礼), which lie at the very core of Confucianism. It is well-acknowledged that *Ren* and *Li*, which can hardly be appropriately translated into English, virtually determine almost all aspects of the Chinese life. They have become the collective unconsciousness for the Chinese programming their social behavior including speech acts such as apologies, compliments, addressing, etc.; as well as interactional rules, such as conversational principles, politeness principles, face work, etc. In short, *Ren* and *Li* have shaped the way the Chinese behave. And obviously the understanding of *Ren* and *Li* can help explain why the Chinese people behave the way they do.

Ren and _Li_, the Key Concepts of Confucianism

Ren and *Li*, the core concepts of Confucianism, complement each other in nature. If we look at these two concepts in terms of ends and means, we can say that *Ren* serves as the goal of life, while *Li* serves as the norms and means for achieving the acceptable ends of social life. And at the same time, these best two concepts overlap with each other.

Ren, etymologically a combination of the Chinese ideographic characters for "人"(human being, represented by the radical on the left of the Chinese ideograph) and for "二"(two represented by the radical on the right), means, on the one hand, the ideal manhood, defining all the fine qualities that make up an ideal man. On the other hand, the ideal reciprocal relationship that should pertain between people. Men should be warm and benevolent to others or love them and respect themselves. Self or an individual must emerge himself into the group or collective. We can say that *Ren*, the cardinal principle of Confucianism lays great emphasis on relationship. To some extent, the largeness of heart which *Ren* renders knows no boundaries as *Ren* advocates that within the four seas all men are brothers and sisters.

Li, as we have pointed out, serves as a norm or a means for people to achieve ideal manhood or good relationships. It defines almost all the norms or rules for the appropriate conduct and behavior for every social member according to his or her social position. It defines the specifics of obligations and responsibilities for every member in the society. The norm consists of the proscriptions and prescriptions for acceptable behavior concerning almost every aspect of life, such as morality, social and political order, social rituals, customs, social interactions, and so on and so forth.

Ren advocates reciprocity, the reciprocity of love or benevolence, however, is not unlimited. Unlike the Western humanism, the love and reciprocity *Ren* advocates have never been symmetrical in the Chinese context. It is based on the kinship relationships in the patriarchal Chinese society or rather it is a symbol of patriarch. The reciprocity or love *Ren* advocates is best expressed in the obligations and responsibilities ascribed to the people according to their social positions in the society. As for *Li*, it specifies Five Constant Relationships that constitute the warp and woof of social life. The relationships are those between ruler and subject, parent and child, husband and wife, elder sibling and junior sibling, elder friend and junior friend, These relationships are symmetrical. Rulers should be benevolent, subjects loyal; parents loving, children reverential; elder siblings gentle, younger siblings respectful; husbands good, wives obedient. Three of these five relationships pertain within the family while two are the extensions of family relationships, which is indicative of the importance of family institution.

Ren and *Li* in fact is a system of moral codes in the Chinese contest predisposing a society in which relationship is complementary, asymmetrical, and reciprocally obligatory. The relationships are asymmetrical in that behavior that is appropriate to one party in each pair of the five relationship is not identical with what is appropriate for the other party. It is just this asymmetry that predisposes role differentiation and details its specifics.

The Chinese society, traditionally speaking, is hierarchical in nature. In a society as such, *Li* is used as norms and means to maintain this hierarchical social order by differentiating the difference between the emperor and his subjects, father and his sons and daughters, and obligations according to their positions. If the people in lower social positions are obedient to and respect those in higher positions, e. g. the humble respect the venerate, the younger respect the elder, as *Li* advocates, the society will be in order. As a matter of fact, *Li* advocates nothing but vertical or hierarchical relationships and its essential function is to build social order upon this hierarchical relationships. It functions in the society as law does in the Western society.

The Doctrine of the Mean (called "*Zhong Yong*" in Chinese) literally meaning middle and constant, is also central to *Li* canon. The Doctrine of the Mean advocates that men should not go to extremes or should constantly keep themselves in terms of behavior. With nothing in excess as guiding principle, people are expected to constantly be watchful against overdoing and indulgence. The practice of the Mean brings balance and harmony. As a result, men in the society favor compromise and highly value reserve.

Under the influence of *Ren* and *Li*, the core concept of Confucianism, *Lun Li* (伦理) (ethic principle) has ruled over China for several thousands of years. *Lun* (伦) in Chinese means the hierarchical order while *Li*, (理, meaning principle in Chinese) homophonic with *Li* (礼), in fact means exactly what *Li* (礼) means. Therefore *Li* becomes the important principle in China. That is why china becomes a country of *Lun Li*, both in terms of politics and morality. When we say that China lays emphasis on *Li* (for example, 礼仪之邦), we do mean to say that it is a country with *Lun Li*.

In short, the Chinese people, no matter what social positions, can all best be characterized by the spirit of *Li*—people from all walks of life have each his or her own *Li*. People can only do what *Li* allows them to. All the concepts, all the ways of life, modes of thinking, ways of perception, and patterns of behavior are underpinned by the principle of *Li*.

Individualism and Human Rights

Unlike Chinese culture, *Ren* and *Li* find no place in the Western philosophy and religion. What is highly valued in the West is individualism and as a result equal or horizontal relationship is highly valued. Therefore, what is advocated is not the obligations and responsibilities ascribed to each member of the society according to his or her social position, but humanitarianism and human rights and thus the slogan: "everybody is born equal-democracy; liberation of the individual is everybody's wish." In this case, the love and benevolence humanitarianism advocates is entirely different from those advocated by *Ren* in the Chinese context. The love and benevolence advocated by humanitarianism is not selective or asymmetrical but symmetrical in nature. The relationships are symmetrical in that behavior that is appropriate to one person in each pair is identical with what is appropriate to the other person. This symmetry presupposes role equality rather than differentiation as is the case in China.

The Characteristics of Interpersonal Relationship in the East and West

Under the impact of *Ren* and *Li* in the East and individualism in the West, two entirely different interpersonal relationships exist between these two hemispheres of the globe.

1. (Harmonious) Relationship vs. Individualism

As mentioned above, *Ren* the most important principle underlying almost all aspects of the people's life in the Chinese context, deals with relationship. Obviously, relationship must be the predominant value in China. As a matter of fact, every person, ever since he or she was born, was placed into complex and orderly warps and woofs of hierarchical relationships. Though people's social status may be unequal, they are equally essential in making the whole society operate.

Even though people nowadays begin to complain about the overuse of relationship in everyday transactions, according to the investigation conducted among 3, 300 people and the analysis based on 800,000 data, 72. 1% of the people investigated tend to think harmonious relationship is foremost important in the society.

What calls for attention is that harmonious relationship that the Chinese people seek to build up is based on the fulfillment of the obligations and responsibilities ascribed to each member of the society according to his or her social position. In this sight, the reciprocity is asymmetrical in nature.

Today relationship has become so important that it is virtually being taken the most advantage of almost in all kinds of everyday transactions and activities, such as promotions of one's position, opening up a new enterprise, transferring from one place to another, etc. Relationship, in this case, however, including relatives, friends, or even useful persons.

Relationship, while being made the best use of in China, in contrast, is almost something people in the West would expect last as they emphasize the importance of individualism over the important of relationship. "Connected self" or "interdependent construal of self" is almost a negative concept.

In the West, people lay importance on "I" rather than on "we". Given name comes first in the West, only thereafter is family surname added, while in China, where family is the basic unit of the social structure, family surname comes first and only thereafter comes the given name. Individual identity, individual rights and individual needs are emphasized over "we" identity and the interest of the group or in-group, and obligations and commitment. As some scholars have pointed out, there is only one principle in the West that regulates interpersonal relationship and that is individualism. The core building block of individualism is the collective unconscious of "autonomous self ". Unlike the connected self or "we" orientation, individualism tends to dispose each member of the community to sever himself from the mass of his fellows and to draw apart with his family and his friends, so that after he has thus formed a little circle of his own, he willingly leaves society at large to itself (Alexis de Tocqueville). Almost every American believes that "God helps those that help themselves." In this sight, dependence or inter-dependence accompanied by obligations and responsibilities or commitment which are highly valued in China is absolutely devalued or despised as they may be regarded as threats to self-autonomy and freedom of action or individual rights.

2. Power/Authority vs. Solidarity/Equality

Power and solidarity relationships are a universal phenomenon in all societies. However, different societies generally have different attitudes towards these two. That is, comparatively speaking, power may be more important in one culture while solidarity may be more important in another culture. In another word, people in one culture may be sensitive to power while people in a different culture may be sensitive to solidarity.

The Chinese social structure is basically hierarchical or vertical in nature and the principle of *Ren* and *Li* help reinforce the asymmetrical or vertical relationship by advocating the maintenance of differences between the emperor and his subjects, father and his son, elder brother and younger brother, male and female; and obedience of the lower position to those who are in higher position and respect from the humble to those who are superior in the society. Logically, in terms of interpersonal relationship, it has become an unwritten rule that authority and power relationship should be valued in daily transactions. What authority refers to vary with time. Nowadays it may include, for example, father in a family, leaders at different levels, the elder and the aged, and even people who are considered to be useful in the society. In old times, government officials (官) meant control or governance (管, which is homophonic and synonymous to 官), while common people must be obedient to government officials, the phenomenon of which is called *Shun* (顺). In old times, *Shun*(顺) meant *Xun* (循, meaning adhere to or follow in English). The implication is clear: authority is respected and listened to and power relationship, in sociolinguistic terms, is highly valued. Power relationship is best demonstrated in the use of titles or honorifics when addressing occurs. Power in case of point here is associated with age, education, social class, sex, social positions, and ranks, and family relations, etc.

Power relationship is the predominant norm or value orientation in the Chinese culture, just as individualism is the important value orientation in the Western culture. Each member of the Western society comparatively speaking enjoys independence to dance and equality, which lays the foundation for the establishment of solidarity relationship as the main relationship in the social interactions in the West.

Solidarity is a sociolinguistic term not only referring to the equal and informal relationship, but also the desire for the setting up of equality, intimacy, common interest, sharing, etc. Whatever it may possibly mean, its core notion is equality. The emphasis on solidarity over power on the Western side can best be demonstrated in the use of first names in everyday interaction.

Even words functioning as compliment is more often than not used by American women to achieve solidarity. Solidarity as an embodiment of equality and the result of individualism is no doubt a dominant value in the Western culture.

3. The Norm of Behaving According to One's Status (the Norm of Status Identity) vs. Freedom of Actions

As mentioned above, the interpersonal relationship in the Chinese society is basically asymmetrical, obligatory, and complementary and the harmonious relationship, the ultimate social goal is achieved through the efforts in fulfilling the obligations and responsibilities ascribed to each member of the society. In fact, ever since the ancient time China has long had an operating system of so-called "status identity" which defines the specifics of the status for each member in the society on the one hand in the family and on the other hand in the society and accordingly the obligations and commitment each member must fulfill. Every members appropriate behavior (including what a person says) is thus specifically detailed according to what family and social status an individual has. If everybody knows his or her place, every member behaves as his or her status identity dictates social order or harmony is achieved. If one violates this norm, one says something inappropriate for example, then one may run the risk of losing face and dignity, or even worse, one is breaking social order. This can partly help explain why the Chinese are so much concerned about face and face work and why we say that speech behavior is markings of social status identity and social status, especially in China. This can also help explain why in China what counts in communication is not what you say but who you are and how you say what you intend to say.

In contrast to the system of status identity in the Chinese society, equality and freedom have long replaced the so-called "system of status identity". *Independence Declaration* officially guarantees the rights of equality, freedom, etc. for every member of the society. In fact, the advocacy of individual rights has been existing throughout American history. The people believe in the dignity, indeed the sacredness, of the individual. Anything that would violate (their) own decision, (their) own judgment, (their) right to think for (themselves), (their) lives as (they) see fit, is not only morally wrong, it is sacrilegious. "Relationships are symmetrical rather than asymmetrical—even if they are bound with an institution or organization, the relationship is contractual. That is, the obligation and responsibility are contractual in nature. Or even though Americans get involved, they are also committed to equality and individualism—they can cut free from anybody they are involved and define their own self.

4. The Maintenance of Warm Human Feelings between Self and Others vs. the Practice of Instrumentality and Fair Play

As a result of the strong influence of relationship orientation and the achievement of harmony as the ultimate goal in interactions, the maintenance of ever-lasting relationship based upon good feelings or expressive relationship between self and others has become common practice among the Chinese people. In the Chinese context, the maintenance of good feelings between self and others is in fact sort of social norm dealing with how to get along with others in the society. Good feelings in case of point here can be looked as sort of gift given to those who enjoy happy event or are on joyous occasions, or sort of help offered to those who are in difficulties. When the gift or help is received, the receiver will be indebted and in turn will return as good as they receive. This reciprocation in China develops ever-lasting good interrelationship. Looked at in this way, interactions are an end in and of themselves.

This norm roughly includes the following maxims: ①reciprocation in everyday interactions; ②how to treat people, especially when they are in difficulties and troubles; and ③indebtedness.

(1) The maxim of reciprocation in everyday interactions refers to the exchange of gifts, help, or visits in everyday activities among acquaintances, especially among in-group members. Reciprocation or re-turning as good as one receives helps maintain relationship.

(2) The maxim of the silver rule in treating people is "Do not do onto others what you would not have do onto you." or "Do onto others as you would have them do onto you." People should show concern, sympathy, and empathy for or offer help to those who are in trouble. It is very important that men have the capacity to "measure the feelings of others by one's own". This can help explain why verbalized concern in the Chinese context is not what the Western scholars called "negative politeness or face".

(3) The maxim of indebtedness in reality, as the relationship in the Chinese society is asymmetrical and complementary, and reciprocally obligatory, everybody in the Chinese society is, in different degrees, indebted to other people, who are in turn also indebted. The mutual indebtedness is in fact the extension of the reciprocally obligatory relationship between parents and their siblings in a family. The Chinese saying "Parents raise their children in order to get in return support from them when they are old just as farmers store grain in case famine occurs"(养儿防老，积谷防饥). This leads to reciprocal indebtedness between parents and siblings: parents would do everything they can to meet the need of their children; and in return, children would be expected to do everything they can to meet the need of their parents when they are old. This indebtedness can best be demonstrated in the following poem: "When I behold the sacred Liao wo (a species of grass symbolizing parenthood) my thoughts return/To those who begot me, raised me, and now are tired. /I would repay the bounty they have given me. /But it is as the sky: It can never be approached." The maxim of indebtedness is extended beyond the family relations to almost all other social relations, as almost all the relationships are the extension of family relationships. So much so that when one shows good feelings or gives gifts to others, he or she is actually expecting his goodness to be returned. In fact, "One should not forget the goodness others do to him, even though it is very trivial." has virtually become a cultural standard to measure one's morality.

Influenced by individualism and equality orientation in the Western culture, relationship is not commonly made use of and efforts in the use of silver rule and the practice of the maxim of indebtedness are seldom made. For the Americans, for example, instrumental interaction is highly valued and fair play in social interactions and transactions is regarded as the standard between the strong and the week, the aged and the young, etc. Instrumental relationship and fair play are just as prescriptive of the Western behavior as the norms of the maintenance of good feelings between people in the Chinese culture.

In contrast to the maintenance of interactional closeness between people as an end, the Westerners regard interactions as a means or instrument to another goal. The instrumental relationship is like those between shop assistants and customers, doctors and patients, etc. When interaction takes place, the two sides may possibly don't know each other well. Let alone friendship between them.

The unspoken social rule which people follow in their instrumental relationship is fair play. Fair play is impersonal and objective in nature in that the instrumental oriented people, when interacting with people, should follow the same rule or norm. Put differently, they should be fair and reasonable in dealing with people or what is called in Chinese "equitable treatment to both children and old men in interaction".

Fair play is a curious Anglo-Saxon notion to the Chinese; there was simply no translation for this word—it was reproduced according to its sound into the Chinese culture. In fact it implies the same meaning as equality. The point that was incomprehensible was the inclusion of the other person's weakness inside the rules so that fair play included in it a statement of relative strength of the opponents and it ceased to be fair to beat a weak opponent. It is a rule for persons of every status, for every situations.

The instrumental orientation and the concept of fair play in the West and the hierarchical or asymmetrical relationship orientation in China are so extremely different that the approach of the young, the inferior, the low social positioned, etc. towards the old, the superior, the high social positioned in the American context may incur negative reactions among the Chinese people. The style of directness and confrontation underpinned the assumption of instrumental orientation, fair play, and equality may quite likely make the Chinese annoyed.

The Impact of *Ren* and *Li* and Individualism on Interaction and Communication

The principle of *Ren* and *Li*, the key concept of Confucianism in China and individualism the most dominant orientation actually act shapers of the patterns of interpersonal relationship which in turn affect interactions and communications on both sides. As these principles underlying interpersonal relationships between the East and West are entirely different, the interpersonal relationships and communication patterns, styles they underpin are also entirely different. The following briefly illustrates the differences in terms of interpersonal relationships and communications due to the differences in these principles (see Table 3-2 and Table 3-3).

Table 3-2 Differences in terms of interpersonal relationships

	East	West
Orientation	Relationships	Individualism
Emphasis	Obligations/ responsibilities/ commitment	Human rights/freedom
Purpose	Harmony	Extension of self: e. g. persuasion
Nature	Reciprocal, asymmetrical	Symmetrical
	Hierarchical/vertical	Equal/horizontal
Characteristics	Expressive	Instrumental
	Indebtedness	Contractual
	Other/listener oriented	Self oriented
	Face and face	Less face and face
Work	Interdependent	Independent
	Complementary	Competitive
	Tolerant	Intolerant
	Personally known intermediaries	Professional intermediaries
	Sympathetic and empathetic	Objective
	In-group and out-group distinction	In-group and out-group indistinction
	Personal relationships and public relationships overlap	Personal relationships and public relationships seperated
	Long term and stable relationships	Short term and in-stable relationships
	Whole person oriented	Role oriented
	Personal	Impersonal
	Showing concern	Showing consideration/no imposition
	Making use of relationships	No making use of relationships
	Group privacy	Individual privacy
	Knowing one's place	Equitable, aggressive
	Power, authority/elders	Solidarity

Table 3-3　　Differences in communication patterns and styles

	East	West
Purpose	Harmony	Extending self
Style	Indirect, flexible, implicit, personal, non-assertive, non-confrontational, formal, non-argumentative, ambiguous, self-restraint	Direct, explicit, impersonal, assertive, confrontational, informal, humorous, argumentative, exaggerative, self-exposure, precise
Meaning and context	High context, meaning is sensed (mind reader), or meaning is in the implicit codes, sensitive to contextual cues; e. g., who says is more important than what to say	Low context meaning is in explicit codes, e. g., much information is in the message, or not very sensitive to contextual cues
	Field dependent	Field independent
Attitude to communication	Less talkative, negative attitude to talkativeness and argument	Talkative, positive attitude to talkativeness and argument
Interaction characteristic	Other oriented, inter-dependent	Self and other oriented
	Humble self and respect others, showing concern for others, face and face work	Equality, considerate (no imposition)
	Power	Solidarity
	Low degree of deviation	High degree of deviation
	Allowed from ideal role enactment	Allowed from ideal enactment
Discourse	Cyclical, spiral	Linear, chain-like
	Climaxing	Anti-climaxing
	Emphasis on outcome/result/what	Emphasis on process/how/process of solving problem
	Fewer cohesive derives	Emphasis on the use of cohesion
Nonverbal	Silence is gold	Negative attitude to silence

(JIA Y X. Interpersonal relationship and intercultural communication: East and West[M]//HU W Z. Aspects of intercultural communication. Beijing: Foreign Language Teaching and Research Press, 1999: 505-522.)

Comprehension Check

A. Questions for Discussion

1. How do you understand "Five Constant Relationships are asymmetrical" ?
2. Why is humanitarianism in the Western philosophy symmetrical in nature?
3. Could you list examples to demonstrate the differences in terms of interpersonal relationships? And the differences in communication patterns and styles?

B. Detail Understanding

Match the explanations to the terms.

Term	Explanation
1. *Li*	A. It advocates that men should not go to extremes or should constantly keep themselves in terms of behavior.
2. *Ren*	B. Men should be warm and benevolent to others or love them and respect themselves. Self or an individual must emerge himself into the group or collective.
3. Doctrine of the Mean	C. It is a sociolinguistic term not only referring to the equal and informal relationship, but also the desire for the setting up of equality, intimacy, common interest, sharing, etc. Its core notion is equality.
4. Solidarity	D. It defines almost all the norms or rules for the appropriate conduct and behavior for every social member according to his or her social position.
5. Fair Play	E. "Do not do onto others what you would not have do onto you."
6. Silver Rule	F. It is impersonal and objective in nature in that the instrumental oriented people, when interacting with people, should follow the same rule or norm.

Suggestions for Further Reading

1. GALLAGHER H C. Willingness to communicate and cross-cultural adaptation: L2 communication and acculturative stress as transaction[J]. Applied Linguistics, 2013, 34 (1): 53-73.
2. 胡文仲，孙有中. 跨越文化的屏障—胡文仲比较文化论集[M]. 北京：外语教学与研究出版社，2004.

Unit 4 Verbal Communication

No one when he uses a word has in mind exactly the same thing that another has, and the difference, however tiny, sends its tremors throughout language.

—Wilhelm Von Humboldt

Objectives:

To understand the differences behind words;

To learn culture connotations through words.

Warm-up Activity

Melinda put down the pile of papers on the desk and confided to her colleagues: "I don't think that new person in the Accounting Department is going to fit in. He doesn't seem to be very sociable."

After a moment, her colleague—Tim asked why. Then Melinda explained that she had met the new person downstairs near the water cooler and that she had said the usual greeting and he had merely answered "Hello" and walked off.

She went on to say that the following day, she had taken down some files to the Accounting Department and had seen the new person and had smiled and said "Hello" again as she stopped by his desk. To her question "How's everything?" he had responded "So-so". Then he had looked back at his work.

"I really had to work hard to try to get him talking. I thought he was shy at first but I don't think so. He just didn't want to talk. I've decided he's rude or there's something very wrong with his social skills." Melinda confided to Tim.

Tim tried to be understanding. "That's not the right way to treat someone who's a new person. Do you think he's really concentrating on doing a good job and making a good impression? Maybe he's worried about his new job."

Melinda considered this idea. "Well, even if that's so, he should know how to end a conversation politely. Just walking or looking away isn't acceptable. It gives the wrong message."

Questions for discussion

1. *Why was Melinda offended by the new person's behavior?*
2. *What should the new person have done, even if he did not want to or have time to talk?*
3. *Comment on Tim's conversation with Melinda. Is Tim giving the right message to his colleague?*

Part One

Intensive Reading

Different Connotations of Words

Language is the carrier of culture. Words are the building blocks of a language. Thus differences in Chinese and English cultures are reflected in the words. It is not unusual for the same word to have different connotations.

Different Connotations of Animals

1. Dragon

The Chinese people regard themselves as the descendants of "龙"(dragon). "龙" is a sacred symbol of power and charity. The image of "龙" enjoys high prestige among Chinese people and its cultural implication is taken for granted. In the West, dragon is described as a monster with wings and claws, which is evil and can breathe fire. Many English legends, like *Beowulf*, usually ended up in the victory that the national heroes killed the dragons. Many Chinese parents "望子成龙"(literally, which means expecting one's son to become a dragon), which would sound ridiculous to the English-speaking people.

2. Phoenix

In Western myths, phoenix has the connotation of rebirth. According to the Greek myths, phoenix can live a very long life—some say 500 years. After this period, phoenix would build itself a nest and burn itself. When everything goes to ash, a new phoenix would fly from it. So when someone just suffered a fire, people would wish the building would rise like a phoenix from the relic.

In traditional Chinese myths, phoenix is the head of all birds. In feudal society, it symbolizes the imperial power and auspice. So the character "凤" (phoenix) could be found in many Chinese girls' names.

Phoenix could also be used to refer to rare or precious people or things, for example, "凤毛麟角".

3. Owl

In English, there is a phrase "as wise as an owl". So owl is the symbol of wisdom. In children's literature, owls are always intelligent and serious. When there are disputes among the animals, they would ask for the owl's judgement. In the English nursery rhythm *Mother Goose Fairy Tales*, owls are like this:

A wise old owl lived in an oak.
The more he saw the less he spoke.
The less he spoke the more he heard.
Why can't we all be like that wise old bird?

However, in Chinese, owl is thought as a symbol of omen because it always flies around graveyard at night, sending out sad voice. In the old legend, it is said that someone would die if the owl rest on his house. Owl is related to bad luck and death. So when people hear the cry of an owl, they would worry that something bad will happen. Amazingly sometimes owls in English also have bad connotations. For example, in Shakespeare's *Macbeth*, when Macbeth murdered Dunean, there is a conversation between him and his wife:

Macbeth：I have done the deed. Didn't you hear a noise?

Lady Macbeth：I heard the owl scream and the crickets cry.

4. Whale

Whale is a huge animal，so in English it is a symbol of valuable things. The following examples prove it— "a whale of a chance"(一个极好的机会)，"whale on skating"(滑冰高手)，"a whale at tennis"(善打网球的人). However，in China，people pay little attention to its value but to its huge appetite. "蚕食鲸吞" means that a small country is embezzled by others like a silkworm eating little by little or like a whale swallowing.

5. Cat

In Chinese，"猫"(cat) is a symbol of loveliness and shrewdness. Chinese people love cat because it is a lovely companion and it is a master in catching mice. Some ancient poets wrote poems to prize cats. But in English，cat，in a way，is the embodiment of devil. People detest cat，especially the black cat.

6. Dog

Dog is universally acknowledged as man's best friend for the sake of its faithfulness among the English-speaking people in the Western world. Nowadays，more and more Chinese are inclined to choose dogs as their pets for the same reason. Dog stands for the image of faithfulness and friendship in both Chinese and English. This is reflected in sayings like "Love me，love my dog." in English and "打狗也要看主人" in Chinese. In most cases，dog is a neutral term in its image-making in English. It is preferable to call a person as a lucky dog，a top dog，etc. in English. "To let sleeping dogs lie" means "not to make trouble or disturb others". "Every dog has its day" means "every person will succeed or become fortunate some day". All the phrases do not contain derogatory connotations. But most Chinese phrases with "狗"(dog) are associated with negative implications，such as "狗仗人势" "狼心狗肺"，etc. So dog is given more affirmative attitudes in English.

7. Magpie

In Chinese，"喜鹊"(magpie) is an auspicious bird which brings unexpected good news. It is said that its voice brings good news as the following saying shows "今朝闻鹊喜，家信必有归". What's more，its voice is the forecast of fine weather，such as "鹊声宣日出". It is proved that magpie can bring us good luck，whereas in English，it refers to wordy people. For example，"She kept muttering like a magpie." It is said that people in English-speaking countries feel disgusted towards its voice. Besides, it stands for chaos and disorder. For example, "a magpie collection".

There is an interesting custom of counting magpies in Britain and Ireland. People believe magpies may represent good or bad luck of various forms in a complex manner, depending on the number of magpies present, according to various traditional rhymes. One of them goes like this:

> One for sorrow, two for joy, three for girl, four for boy, five for silver, six for gold, seven for a secret never told, eight for heaven, nine for hell, and ten for the devil's own self.

8. Cricket

In Chinese culture, crickets give the connotation of loneliness and dreariness. Many famous poets used the image of crickets in their works to invoke such feelings. For example, "昨夜寒蛩不住鸣，惊回千里梦，已三更" [(南宋)岳飞:《小重山》]. While in English, crickets are merry and joyous. English people think that those who can hear the singing of crickets on Christmas Eve are the luckiest.

9. Bat

In English there are such phrases as "as blind as a bat", "have bats in the belfry"(异想天开). Bats will cause bad connotations in the Westerners because they think bats are ugly and ferocious. In the myths bats are always connected with "vampires".

But in Chinese culture, bats symbolize auspice, health and happiness because the Chinese character of "bat"(蝠) has the assonance of "福" which means happiness.

10. Chicken

In English, chicken has the connotation of "coward". They would say, "You chicken!"(你这个胆小鬼). But in Chinese, there is no such connotation.

11. Fox

Fox, in both English and Chinese, refers to a common wild animal with a cunning nature. When used in comparison, it is a synonym of "slyness, trickiness, and deceitfulness." On this point, the similarity of cultural connotation of the animal word is beyond our mind. People are very familiar with a series of English and Chinese idioms or sayings. For example, "as cunning as a fox", "as sly as a fox", "a sly old fox", and "露出了狐狸尾巴".

Meanwhile, fox have different connotations in the two respective cultures. For example, in Chinese, the coquettish women are blasphemed as "狐狸精"; a group of evil people who accompany each other are called "狐朋狗友"; the behavior that a person bullies others by evil authority is referred to "狐假虎威"; flattering is known as "狐媚". In English, fox does not have a derogatory meaning to such an extent. It refers to deceitfulness while it also refers to a good-looking or shrewd person. For example, in America, "a fox" is used to refer to a sexy, charming or smart girl; "crazy like a fox" refers to a shrewd person who is not easy to be cheated

Even some people take fox as their name, from which peoples favoritism towards the animal is obviously understood.

12. Peacock

In English, peacock always has derogatory meanings. *Webster's Third New International Dictionary of the English Language* explains it as following: One making a proud or arrogant display of himself. *Collins Cobuild English Language Dictionary* explains that "if you describe someone, especially, a man as a peacock, you mean that he is rather proud of himself and likes wearing attractive clothes and looking good." It shows that peacock usually has a derogatory sense in English. Therefore, "as proud as a peacock" could be heard in their daily life. In Chinese, peacock is said to be vain and conceited. For example, "孔雀开屏，自作多情". On the other hand, peacock is a symbol of good luck. People say that it is auspicious to see peacocks' open the wings.

People of the Dai Minority living in the south of Yunnan province show their hope by peacock dance, whereas, in English, peacocks' prettiness is ignored while their vanity is taken notice of.

13. Tortoise

Chinese people believe that tortoise can live for hundreds of years. So it is a symbol of a long life in Chinese culture. It is the reason for that there are many carvings about tortoise on ancient palaces, temples and other buildings in China. On the other hand, tortoise has a very derogatory meaning. It is a terrible insult for somebody to be called "王八". In English there are no such connotations and tortoise is only a tardy animal.

14. Buffalo

Buffalo has no connotative meanings in Chinese, whereas, in American English, there is an idiom "to buffalo". How it originated has something to do with "west movement". At that time, people in the west part of America hunted a great number of buffalo for the skin then they could get much money from leather trading. However, they found that it was not an easy job to hunt buffalo, so some people complained, "We are buffaloed." It means that they felt helpless. Then it evolves into "threaten" and "menace".

15. Petrel

The petrel in Chinese culture is a bird to be eulogized. The mental image that the term evokes is a small lonely bird winging over the vast ocean, braving storms and flying with stamina and courage. Many young people in their moment of fantasy compare themselves to petrels, struggling to get ahead in the vast world of humanity, braving hardship and adversity, advancing with perseverance and courage. What a blow it is to discover how little respect Westerners have for the bird! A stormy petrel is "a person regarded as a herald of trouble, strife or violence or someone who delights in such trouble, etc."

In English there are also some other animals with connotations which Chinese doesn't have. A "goat" in English refers to a person who always does sexual harassment towards women. "Duck" can be used to refer to a lovely person apart from the denotative meaning. A "unicorn", looking like horse but having only one horn, exists in the Western legend. It refers to something existing in name only.

Different Connotations of Names about People and Place

Every object has a name, but the names of Chinese people and places do not contain the same connotations as those of the English-speaking people and places.

A score of figures in literary works claim their unique images among the native readers generation after generation. "孔乙己" under the pen of Lu Xun is taken for granted as a poor scholar who was shabby, miserable and pedantic. No such image can be linked with the image when the English-speaking people come cross "孔乙己" unless they have read or heard about him before.

On the contrary, the Chinese people might not be familiar with the connotative image of the name "Grandet", one of the most notorious misers, unless they have known something about Balzac's work.

New York is a metropolis in the USA and the city is well known all over the world. But few Chinese people can connect the term "Big Apple" with New York. Shaoxing is not a common city for Chinese people because a great number of famous persons came from Shaoxing in history such as Qiu Jin, Lu Xun, Cai Yuanpei, etc. The Western people who know little about the history of Shaoxing may not place the city in the center of cultural background with its long history and many celebrities.

Different Connotations of Natural Phenomena

Britain faces the sea in the west of Europe, whose climate is conditioned by the sea for its sake. The summer in Britain is as mild as gentle spring breeze due to its location influenced by the maritime climate. That is the reason why in Shakespeare's poem such a line is frequently quoted "Shall I compare thee to a summer's day". Summer in Britain has the connotation of the whole mild climate, which stimulates the English without any hesitation to have a number of sound associative images linked with love. On the contrary, summer in China is too hot for people to endure because the country is mainly influenced by the continental climate. The image of the summer only spurs the Chinese to think about the burning sun high in the sky and people are sweating under it.

From where is the wind blowing? In the history of English literature, a great number of poems sang high praises of the west wind including Shelley's *Ode to the West Wind*. As west wind blows in Britain, the temperature is mild and animating. On the contrary, in China west wind blows in the season of the freezing winter and is always associated with something shabby or sorrowful while "east wind" (东风) seems like the "west wind" in English.

Different Connotations of Plants

Plants are symbols of the natural world and the representative of the beautiful natural surroundings and they are closely related to human existence. There are occasions when one plant word is rich in connotation in one culture while deficient in another. For example, in Chinese culture, the plants "pine, bamboo and plum" remind people of the spirit of being vigorous, tall and straight, the symbol of long life and exemplary conduct and nobility of character and branches and flowers that withstand the frost and defy the snow while English doesn't possess such connotations.

Potato is so favored by the people in the Western countries that it has entered into many English idioms with different connotations. For example, "A couch potato" is someone who spends most of his time watching television and does not exercise or has any other hobbies; "a small potato" is an insignificant figure; "a clean potato" refers to a decent man. In English, you can refer to a difficult subject that people disagree on as "a hot potato". Such potato-related instances are extremely common in English. In Chinese, however, such phrases and idioms are seldom seen.

Daffodils, or yellow narcissus, are merely a sort of flower in Chinese, while in English they are a symbol of spring and happiness. We can see it in many literature works, especially William Wordsworth's masterpiece *I Wandered Lonely as a Cloud*.

The oak has long been considered sacred by many European civilizations. In the Bible, the oak tree at Shechem is the site where Jacob buries the foreign gods of his people. In addition, Joshua erects a stone under an oak tree as the first covenant of the Lord. In classical mythology the oak was a symbol of Zeus and his sacred tree. According to a legend, King Arthur's round table was made from one huge slice of an ancient oak tree. The oak is a common symbol of strength and endurance and has been chosen as the national tree of England, the United States and many other countries. Many famous poets wrote about oaks in their works. While in Chinese literature, the images of the oak are hard to find.

The willow is a famous subject of Chinese culture, particularly painting (pen and ink). When ancient Chinese were seeing their friends off, they would present them with wigs of willow showing that they wanted their friends to stay longer. In English folklore, a willow tree is believed to be quite sinister, capable of uprooting itself and stalking travelers. The ancient Celts believed that the spirit of the dead would rise up into the trees planted above, which would grow and retain the essence of the departed one. Throughout Britain many cemeteries, particularly those situated near rivers, lakes or marshes are often to be found lined with willow trees to protect the spirits in place.

(ZHONG X Q. International communication[M]. Hangzhou: Zhejiang University Press, 2018.)

Vocabulary

mutual *adj.*	having or based on the same relationship one towards the other
embezzle *vt.*	appropriate fraudulently to one's own use
shrewdness *n.*	intelligence manifested by being astute (as in business dealings)
neutral *adj.*	one who does not side with any party in a war or dispute
derogatory *adj.*	expressive of low opinion
affirmative *adj.*	expecting the best
auspicious *adj.*	favorable circumstances and good luck
muttering *n.*	a complaint uttered in a low and indistinct tone
dreariness *n.*	extreme dullness; lacking spirit or interest
ferocious *adj.*	extreme violent
assonance *n.*	the repetition of similar vowels in the stressed syllables of successive words
coward *n.*	a person who shows fear or timidity
blaspheme *v.*	speak of in an irreverent or impious manner
conceited *adj.*	having an exaggerated sense of self-importance
eulogize *v.*	praise formally
stamina *n.*	enduring strength and energy
harassment *n.*	a feeling of intense annoyance
notorious *adj.*	known widely and usually unfavorably
covenant *n.*	written agreement

Exercises

A. Words in Use

Fill in the blanks with the words given below. Change the form when necessary. Each word can be used only once.

neutral	affirmative	auspicious	ferocious	blaspheme
eulogize	notorious	embezzle	derogatory	conceited

1. The publication of my first book was an ________ beginning of my career.
2. After that I ceased to ________, but I cursed my father.
3. That country remained ________ in the war.
4. The oncoming force of the typhoon was ________.
5. I can't give you an ________ reply now.
6. African leaders find it surprisingly hard to ________ development funds.
7. Leaders from around the world ________ the Egyptian president.
8. I thought he was ________ and arrogant.
9. It is an area ________ for drugs, crime and violence.
10. He refused to withdraw ________ remarks made about his boss.

B. Questions for Discussion

1. Can you cite some words possessing various connotations (such as color words) in different language?
2. Have you experienced the culture conflict arising out of the words connotations?
3. What do you think we should do to avoid this kind of culture conflict?

C. Translation

1. How it originated has something to do with "west movement". At that time, people in the west part of America hunted a great number of buffalo for the skin then they could get much money from leather trading. However, they found that it was not an easy job to hunt buffalo, so some people complained, "We are buffaloed." It means that they felt helpless, Then it evolves into threaten and menace.
2. Many young people in their moment of fantasy compare themselves to petrels, struggling to get ahead in the vast world of humanity, braving hardship and adversity, advancing with perseverance and courage.
3. In the history of English literature, a great number of poems sang high praises of the west wind including Shelley's *Ode to the West Wind*. As west wind blows in Britain, the temperature is mild and animating. On the contrary, in China west wind blows in the season of the freezing winter and is always associated with something shabby or sorrowful while "east wind"

(东风) seems like the "west wind" in English.

4. There are occasions when one plant word is rich in connotation in one culture while deficient in another. For example, in Chinese culture, the plants "pine, bamboo and plum" remind people of the spirit of being vigorous, tall and straight, the symbol of long life and exemplary conduct and nobility of character and branches and flowers that withstand the frost and defy the snow while English doesn't possess such connotations.

D. Case Study

Case 1

Mr. Johnson is a sales representative of an American electronic company. He has worked for the company for many years, and has built up some loyal clients who have helped him a lot. Among those clients there is a Mr. Han from Hangzhou, China. Mr. Johnson was assigned by the company to Hangzhou to resolve some technical problems. The first idea that came to his mind was that he should go and see Mr. Han. From what his American colleagues have told him before, Mr. Johnson learned that in China it would be better to bring some gifts if you visit someone. He decided to bring a very special gift to Mr. Han—a new model of electronic clock, which is the new product of the company and sells very well in America. He was very proud of himself for this great idea. But to his surprise, Mr. Han looked offended when he saw the clock. He simply refused to accept it with no explanation. Mr. Johnson was very embarrassed and puzzled.

Questions

1. Why did Mr. Johnson offend Mr. Han?
2. What should Mr. Johnson do to avoid the misunderstanding?

Case 2

Mr. Smith, a very white man, but a very yellow one. He was very red with anger when he found himself cheated by his close friend, but, he said nothing. Last Friday, a black letter day, he had a car accident. He was looking rather green and feeling blue lately. When I saw him, he was in a brown study. I hope he'll soon be in the pink again.

Question

Translate the above short passage into Chinese.

Part Two

Extensive Reading

A Tentative Comparison of First Naming between Chinese and American English

Non-native speakers of English as well as native speakers of English from countries other than America often express their surprise at the wide use or distribution of reciprocal first naming among people in the United States. This change from an address form employed to define intimate relationships within a family of among close friends or business associates to the one used to define general relationships between strangers, between people of asymmetrical age and occupational status, between students and professors, and between young people and their seniors, has been quite a recent development which has naturally stimulated cross-cultural studies of first naming in different countries. My own observation and investigation of Chinese first naming demonstrate that there are more differences than similarities in first naming between the Chinese and American addressing systems. This paper attempts to draw a cross-cultural comparison of first naming between Chinese and American English. My comparison will focus on three areas: form, usage and function.

First Naming Address Forms

First naming address forms in Chinese and American English are quite different because they are derived from dissimilar linguistic systems. Each has a number of distinctive variant forms of its own. The Chinese first naming address forms seem to outnumber the American ones. Yet the fact that they all possess more than one variant form is a significant similarity which is thought provoking and worth exploring. The following is a representation of the first naming address forms in both Chinese and American English.

The American first naming address forms:

(1) one-word first name: Mary, Jane, John, Bill, etc.

(2) compound first name: Mary-Jean, Ervin-Tripp, etc.

(3) endearment first name: "Liz" for Elizabeth, "Jan" for Jane, "Jim" for James, "Dick" for Richard, etc.

(4) generic first name: Jack, Mack, Buddy. etc.

(5) nickname: "Shorty" for a tall man, "Happy" for a person who never Smiles, "Carot" for a red-haired person, "Fatty" for a fat person, etc.

Though I have listed five variant address forms of first name in American English, the frequencies with which they are used in daily life are obviously not the same. It is clear that Numbers (1) and (3) are the most frequently employed ones. It might seem odd for me to include nickname in the American first naming address forms here. This is not so because Robbins Burling (1970) believes that a nickname even when based on one's last name, unquestionably acts as the equivalent of a name. The generic first name in (4) is a special form invented for name is unknown or who is a stranger. In contrast, the Chinese language finds more variant address forms in first naming.

Chinese first naming address forms:

(1) one-character first name: Fang (芳), Xiao (晓), *Ren* (仁), Yi (毅), etc.

(2) two-character first name: Wenli (文莉), Ruifang (瑞芳), Xinghua (兴华), Hongzhi (宏志), etc.

(3) one-character first name + er (儿): Minger (明儿), Lier (丽儿), Fenger (峰儿), Zhonger (忠儿), etc.

(4) two-character first name made by the reduplication of a one-character first name: Qian→Qianqian (倩→倩倩), Fang→Fangfang (芳→芳芳), Ming→Mingming (明→明明), Tong→Tongtong (同→同同), etc.

(5) one-character name made by just keeping the second word of a two-word first name (also but rarely by keeping the first character of a two-character first name): Hongxia→Xia (红霞→霞), Yaoting→Ting (耀庭→庭), Haishan→Shan (海山→山), etc.

(6) two-character first name made by putting A/a before a one-character first name: A-hui (阿惠), A-dan (阿丹), A-long (阿龙), A-gen (阿根), etc.

(7) two-character first name made by putting Xiao (young) before a one-character first name: Xiaoli (小丽), Xiaolan (小兰), Xiaohong (小红), Xiaodong (小东), etc.

(8) two-character surname used as first name: Ouyang (欧阳), Situ (司徒), Sima (司马), Shangguan (上官), etc.

(9) infant name: Maomao (毛毛), Manchang (满场), Guyu (谷雨), Laifu (来福), etc.

(10) nickname: Hongyan-er (红眼儿), Baimao-er (白毛儿), Xianbuzhu (闲不住), Dunang (嘟囔), etc.

Among the Chinese first naming address forms, the most frequently used ones are undoubtedly Numbers (1) (2) and (4). The A+ one-character first name is a form employed mainly in south China. The *Xiao* + one-character first name has 2 restricted usages, too. The infant name, though regarded here as a first name, is found mostly used in Chinese small towns or rural areas before a child goes to school. The nickname is chiefly used among friends or associates.

The First Naming Usage in Both Languages

In the American usage, the reciprocal and nonreciprocal use of first name is regulated or conditioned by a number of factors such as age, sex, occupational status, etc. Robbins Burling (1970) well summarizes the traditional American usage of this particular address form. She says that the most common pattern is for two people mutually to use first names. Americans are even a bit proud at the speed with which they get on "first name basis", though this does not mean that Americans are friendlier than people of other nations, but only that they use first names in situations where many Europeans would continue to use a more formal address form. In situations where the addressee's first name is unknown, Americans may even substitute a sort of generic first name: Mack, Jack, Buddy. Between newly introduced adults, title and last name are generally used symmetrically, but only a small increment of intimacy needs to develop before first names are of first names between casual acquaintances, some people move quickly to do so for their own reasons. Towards this linguistic phenomenon, she has the following observation to make:

> Younger people probably move to first names more rapidly than older people, and those of the same sex move more rapidly than those of the opposite. A common occupation or nationality or any common experience at all, encourages the rapid use of first names.

The nonreciprocal pattern is employed only when people differ markedly in either age or occupational status. Children are often expected to address as Mr. or Mrs. so and so, but they themselves are always addressed by first names. Adults address those who are 15 years older than themselves by title and last name. Though they are often called asymmetrical address may also occur between master and servant, employer and employee, officer and enlisted men, or professor and student. Even after the two people have come to know each other well enough to allow the person of superior rank to use other person's first name, the difference in status can until make it difficult or impossible for the junior-ranking person to reciprocate.

Burling also observes that age alone or occupation alone can be enough to force an asymmetrical address pattern, but when the two criteria are in conflict, the occupational criterion seems to predominate. For instance, in the rare home that still has a servant, an adolescent girl might call the family's middle-aged cook by her first name but be addressed in turn by a title. The navy officer may address the middle-aged enlisted man by his first name, but he can expect a title in return. The same asymmetrical pattern occurs between a young executive and an elderly janitor when they interact verbally. But the nonreciprocal pattern is most common when age and occupational status point the same way.

I believe it is appropriate for us to call this American usage formulated by Burling as traditional because it has now undergone considerable change, although its rules or principles are not entirely outmoded. Nessa Wolfson (1989) noted this rapid change by saying that the American address model proposed by Brown and Ford, elaborated by Ervin Tripp and others has been changing in the direction of ever increasing use of first names between strangers and between people of asymmetrical age and status. It is now quite common to hear employees first naming their bosses, students their professors, and young people their seniors. Another striking change has been taking place in the frequencies with which strangers introduce themselves by first name alone. It has been noticed that service personnel in stores, car agencies, restaurants, and similar places now often identify themselves to clients and customers by giving only their first names. While such usage undoubtedly varies with geographical area and social class, the movement away from title and last name appears wide spread in the United States.

What can be seen through this discussion is that there are actually two kinds of American usage for first naming in operation: traditional and modern. This is a clear indication of a last moving linguistic change, reflecting in one dimension the change of social relationships.

In the Chinese usage are found both symmetrical and asymmetrical patterns of use to occur in verbal interaction. In the Chinese family, relationships that denote solidarity generally encourage the symmetrical use of first name. We find, therefore, in daily interaction husband and wife, brothers, sisters, brother and sister, and cousins reciprocate each other's first name. Husband and wife can do so irrespective of their age difference. Brothers, brother and sister, and cousins can first name each other provided that their age difference is almost minimal or the family allows a nonreciprocal use of first name in spite of the age difference. The symmetrical pattern is also found to occur between lovers or boy and girl friends, close friends, classmates or schoolmates and associates. Lovers or boy and girl friends form a special type of intimate relationship outside the family, which calls for words of affection to keep them constantly close together. When this dyad of people first name each other, age difference does not affect the symmetrical nature of the pattern. Furthermore, they may select the most intimate address form to first name his or her bosom friend. Close friends can address each other by first name on condition that their age difference is not great. As for the relationship between close classmates or schoolmates, close work or business associates age difference does not affect the use of first names. Yet in Chinese society, sex may affect the use of first name. If a man and woman of general relationship first name each other, they may be suspected of having a very intimate relationship.

Generation difference in China was and still is a very important factor in determining the use of address forms. On account of this, elder members of a family such as grandparents, parents, uncles and aunts, etc. can generally first name family members of the younger generation, yet the latter can't reciprocate. Age difference can also force an asymmetrical pattern on members of the same generation within a Chinese family. We find, therefore, elder brothers, elder sisters and elder cousins can first name their younger brothers, younger sisters and younger cousins, but the latter can't reciprocate unless the family allows a symmetrical usage.

There are always exceptions to the rules. One obvious exception is that among brothers, sisters, cousins, close friends, close classmates or schoolmates, close work or business associates, one-character first names are seldom reciprocated because they are generally used by elder members of a family in addressing the younger members or by lovers or boy and girl friends in addressing each other. Even between a husband and a wife, lovers or boy and girl friends one-character first names are seldom exchanged in the presence of others. Here we might saying that setting may affect the use of first names. Besides, between male and female friends or associates first names are generally avoided in the presence of others for fear that doing so might leave on others an impression of intimate relationship between the interactions.

In discussing the Chinese usage, we should not overlook one marked difference between the two addressing systems. Chinese first names, especially the one-character and two-character first names can be followed by other address forms. This is less seen in American English or any other variety of English. Let's look at the following instances.

(1) first name+*xiansheng*

Dezhong	*xiansheng*
Dezhong	Mr.
Mr. Dezhong	

(2) first name+*tongzhi*

Zhihua	*tongzhi*
Zhihua	comrade
Comrade Zhihua	

(3) first name+*xiong* or *di*

Quan *xiong*	Minghua *di*
Quan elder brother	Minghua younger brother
Elder Brother Quan	Younger Brother Minghua

(4) first name+*zi*/*jie* or *mei*

Mei *jie*	Bing *mei*
Mei elder sister	Bing younger sister
Elder sister Mei	Younger sister Bing

This peculiar Chinese usage adds politeness, a new dimension of meaning to intimacy, which shows once again the deferential features of Chinese speech.

The Manipulation of First Names

In both Chinese and American societies, first names are generally used to define personal relationships, especially intimate ones. Chinese researchers have found that first names were employed in China to define only intimate relationships within a family, but were later extended to address people of close relationships outside a family. It seems that the American usage has developed in the same direction. Yet Americans use it far more widely both within and outside a family, whereas Chinese still confine it to intimate relationships. As discussed early on, Nessa Wolfson (1989) observes that in modern America, first names are exchanged symmetrically between strangers and between people of asymmetrical age and status. This is obviously in opposition to traditional American usage. Chinese researchers have not recorded such an extension of the usage. I have myself searched famous writings by renowned authors such as Cao Yu, Lao She, Qian Zhongshu, etc., and have also made keen observations on daily interactions between people, but have failed to see such a change. How do we account for such differences in the two addressing systems? Katherine French (1981) carried out an investigation of this linguistic change in American English and examined the way in which service personnel, often total strangers to their customers, not only introduce themselves by first name, but request that they be so addressed. According to French, the reasons for this usage given by interviewees were that the use of first name was friendlier, that it simplified the interaction since last name are often difficult to understand or remember, and such usage provided the employee with anonymity. Thus, with no manifestation of the difference in status, both participants to the interaction are put on an equal footing. So we see here once again the idea of solidarity is manifested and stressed. As for the Chinese usage which has not changed much, it has its own reasons. Due to traditional Chinese culture, whether inside or outside a family, from ancient times to the present day, personal relationships has been well defined in various ways. The Chinese are well aware of these relationships, and they don't want to confuse them by the misuse of address terms. The Chinese are culturally trained to be deferential. They do not think it appropriate or polite enough to address a person with whom he has no close relationship by first naming him or her in their encounter. Traditional Chinese values teach people to respect the old and repress the young. This also prevents young people from addressing the elderly by first names.

Living in a society, a person has quite complex personal relationships with others, ranging from the general to the intimate. The use of first name address forms in everyday interaction reflects this social reality. One comment made by Robins Burling (1970) proves this to be true:

> ... for those with whom we are most intimate, we can use several alternative names, and in a sense we are not only able to set them off from all other people but give names to their various facets. The alternative names would seem to indicate the variety and complexity of our relationships with these people.

I believe this comment applies to the Chinese usage too. What strikes us as peculiar is that Chinese often manipulate first naming as a powerful and convenient device to achieve personal ends. We find in real life situations an unmarried young lady who has several admirers may address the one man she loves most by first naming him, thus, setting him off from all others as the most intimate friend. The love affairs of young people often witness a gradual development of their relationship demonstrated in the use of the variant address forms. At the beginning of their relationship they often address each other by full name or by full name title such as *tongzhi* (comrade) or *xiansheng* (Mr.), for instance, Xia Hongmei or Xia Hongmei *tongzhi* (Comrade Xia Hongmei). As their relationship deepens in intimacy, they try to show their affection to each other by first dropping the addressee's family name (Hongmei or Comrade Hongmei), then dropping the address term tongzhi (Hongmei), then turning the 2-character first name into a one-character first name (mei). The last variant is the most intimate, showing the shortest distance between the two but the greatest affection for each other. There are also instances when husband and wife, sweethearts or lovers fall out when their relationships deteriorate, they often switch immediately from first naming to full naming in addressing each other, which signals no affection at all but demonstrates the longest distance between them.

(DU X Z. A tentative comparison of first naming between Chinese and American English[M]//Hu W Z. Aspects of intercultural communication—proceedings of China's 2nd Conference on Intercultural Communication. Beijing: Foreign Language Teaching and Research Press, 1999: 207-219.)

Language focus

distribution	*n.*	分配	reciprocal	*adj.*	互惠的；相互的
asymmetrical	*adj.*	不对称的	intimate	*adj.*	亲密的；个人的
variant	*n.*	（词等的）变体；转化	outnumber	*vt.*	数量多于
generic	*adj.*	共有的	symmetrically	*adv.*	对称地；平衡地
increment	*n.*	增加；盈余	occupational	*adj.*	职业的
enlist	*vi.*	支持；赞助	predominate	*vt.*	支配
janitor	*n.*	守卫；清洁工	outmode	*vt.*	使……过时
dimension	*n.*	方面；维度	solidarity	*n.*	团结
irrespective	*adj.*	无关的	dyad	*n.*	一对；二元体
bosom	*n.*	胸怀；内心	interactant	*n.*	互相作用的东西
	adj.	知心的；亲密的			
peculiar	*n.*	特权；特有财产	intimacy	*n.*	亲密
	adj.	特殊的			
deferential	*adj.*	恭敬的；惯于顺从的	anonymity	*n.*	匿名
manifestation	*n.*	表现；显示	footing	*n.*	基础；社会关系

Exercises

A. Text Reading

Decide whether the following statements are true (T) or false (F).

1. ______ The increasing use of first names between people of asymmetrical age and status has led to the change of the American address model.
2. ______ Americans tend to use first names more, which implies that Americans are friendlier than people without using first names.
3. ______ In China, sex may not affect the use of first name.
4. ______ There are actually two kinds of American usage for first naming in operation: traditional and modern.
5. ______ Generation difference in China still affects the use of address forms.
6. ______ Chinese first names can be followed by other address forms, such as Minghua *di*, while the form is seldom used in American English.
7. ______ First names are employed in America only within a family.

8. ______ In contrast to the traditional American usage, first names are exchanged between strangers in modern America.
9. ______ In China, first names are used as a tool to show the intimacy between people.
10. ______ The Chinese think it impolite to address a person with first name if there is not close relationship between them.

B. Terms Understanding

Find the definitions of the following terms in the text. If you cannot find the exact definition, try to use your own words to interpret it.

1. reciprocal pattern
2. nonreciprocal pattern
3. symmetrical pattern
4. asymmetrical pattern

C. Classroom Activities

1. Could you figure out the change of addressing first names in America?
2. Please discuss together to sum up the similarities and differences on first naming between Chinese and American.
3. Work in pairs and exchange views on the meanings of the following proverbs, and discuss the values transmitted. Then try to find out their Chinese equivalents if there is any.
   Proverb 1: Every dog has his day.
   Proverb 2: More is meant than meets the ear.

Part Three

Academic Reading

Politeness in Correspondence Discourse —A Contrastive Study

Abstract

This paper presents a contrastive study of politeness strategies in the written correspondence from potential contributors to editors in English and Chinese. Altogether 36 letters (20 in Chinese, 16 in English) are analyzed in terms of parameters: ①inside addressing; ② opening; ③ self-referring; ④other- referring; ⑤ closing; ⑥pre-signature and ⑦signature/post signature.

Major findings are as follows:

(1) Inside addressing: Chinese letters are complex with plenty of honorifics; English letters, in comparison, are much simpler. In other words, Chinese letter writers pay more attention to the degree of politeness when addressing the editor, while English letters are more concerned with the level of formality.

(2) Opening: Chinese letters, in most cases, open with either a greeting or phatic talk, or even a greeting followed by phatic talk before real business. English letters, all but one, "get down to business" straight away.

(3) Self-referring and (4) other referring: Chinese letter writers denigrate themselves in self-referring or referring to things related to self, meanwhile they elevate the latter or to things related to the latter. This is not found in English. It is typical of Chinese politeness.

(5) Closing: Chinese and English are more or less similar.

(6) Pre-signature: Chinese letters are rich and varied with pre-signature remarks or good-wishes, whereas English letters are almost monotonous.

(7) Signature/Post-signature: Chinese letter writers, in most cases, sign names. If there is post-signature, it is likely to be honorific+other elevating. English letter writers, in contrast, sign names followed by titles or positions (half of the English letters in our data), which would be read as being arrogant or conceited by Chinese receivers.

(8) English indirectness and Chinese phatic talk: Politeness in English letters in partly achieved through indirectness; whereas the core of politeness in Chinese letters is denigrating self and elevating other. Chinese letters also have indirectness, not at the sentential level, but at the discoursal level.

Politeness Studies: A Survey

Politeness has been a focus of interest in pragmatics for decades now. A considerable amount of literature has been accumulating, and there is no sign of receding interest. In 1990 the *Journal of Pragmatics* organized a special issue on politeness to pinpoint landmarks and predict future trends. It seems now that Brown and Levinson (1978, revised 1987) and Leech (1983) provide the two dominating frameworks for politeness studies. The lasted trend of studies is markedly shifting to cross-cultural perspectives with the objective of challenging or amending these two frameworks.

As far as Chinese politeness is concerned, Gu's two papers, one in English and the other in Chinese (1992, 1999) prove to be most cited both at home and abroad. He argues against Brown and Levinson's fact approach and favors Leech's principle and maxim framework. Based on modern Chinese data, he modifies some of Leech's assumptions and puts forward some maxims such as the self-denigration maxim. The address maxim that are claimed to be unique features of Chinese politeness. Gu's research has been reviewed, supported and amended by Chen (1993, 1996), L. R. Mao (1994), Liao (1994), Li Wei and Li Yue (1996).

The Essentials of Gu's Studies

As Gu's studies are adopted as my analytic framework in this paper, it is necessary, for the sake of clarity, to recapture his main findings here. He observes that:

> There are basically four notions underlying the Chinese conception of *limao*: respectfulness, modesty, attitudinal warmth, and refinement. 'Respectfulness' concerning the latter's face, social status, and so on. 'Modesty' can be seen as another way of saying 'self denigration'. 'Attitudinal warmth' is demonstration of kindness, consideration, and hospitality to other. Finally, 'refinement' refers to self's behavior to other which meets certain standards. (Gu, 1990)

He further points out that:

> Underneath the concept of *limao* are two cardinal principles: sincerity and balance. Genuine polite behavior must be enacted sincerely, and sincerely polite behavior by self calls for similar behavior in return by other... (Gu, 1990)

The four essentials are elaborated into politeness maxims. Gu (1990) demonstrates four maxims:

(1) the self-denigration maxim;

(2) the address term maxim;

(3) the tact maxim and the generosity maxim;

(4) the Principle of Balance, and the Principle of Sincerity.

Gu (1992) offers further revision of them and demonstrates altogether five maxims.

(1) The self-denigration maxim: the maxim consists of two clauses or submaxims: ①denigrate self and ②elevate other. This maxim absorbs the notions of respectfulness and modesty.

(2) The address term maxim: the maxim reads: address your interlocutor with an appropriate address term. This maxim is based on the notions of respectfulness and attitudinal warmth.

(3) The refinement maxim: the maxim refers to self's behavior to other which meets certain standards. With regard to language use, it means the use of refined language and a ban on foul language. The use of euphemisms and indirectness is also covered.

(4) The agreement maxim: The maxim refers to efforts made by both interlocutors to maximize agreement and harmony and minimize disagreement.

(5) The virtues deeds maxim: The maxim refers to minimizing cost and maximizing benefit to other at the motivational level, and maximizing benefit received and minimizing cost to self at the conversational level.

Data Collection

Data for this paper consist of 20 Chinese letters and 16 English letters. All the letters were written between the mid eighties and early nineties and written potential contributors to editors seeking publication. They were initially collected by Hu Wenzhong and Mick Short for the joint project by Beijing Foreign Studies University and Lancaster University. They were left unused and were kindly given to me by courtesy of the project coordinator Gu Yueguo with the approval of Hu Wenzhong.

A contrastive study of politeness is made on 7 parameters: ①inside addressing; ②opening; ③self-referring; ④other-referring; ⑤closing; ⑥pre-signature and ⑦signature/post signature.

Main Findings

1. Inside Addressing (see Table 4-1)

Table 4-1 Inside addressing

Chinese Letters	20	English Letters	16
honorific+title+ solidarity/honorific e. g. 尊敬的编辑先生	2	—	—
honorific+publisher+title e. g. 尊敬的出版社编辑	1	—	—

续表

Chinese Letters	
publisher＋honorific e. g. 编辑室合鉴	1
publisher＋title e. g. 编辑室负责同志	1
title＋honorific e. g. 编辑老师	5
title＋solidarity e. g. 编辑同志	8
—	—
—	—
publisher e. g. 出版社	2

English Letters	
Dear＋honorific e. g. Dear Sir (s)	1
Dear＋title e. g. Dear Editor	1
Dear＋title＋surname e. g. Dear Prof. Leech	4
Dear＋honorific＋surname e. g. Dear Mr. Smith	5
Dear＋first name e. g. Dear Elizabeth	4
Dear＋first name＋surname e. g. Dear Liz Mann	1
—	—

Chinese letters seem to be rich with complicated honorifics, which put the receiver in a superior position at the very beginning of the discourse; English letters, in comparison, are much simpler. In Chinese correspondence, the editors and the letter writers are strangers. The latter pay particular attention to the degree of politeness in addressing the editors. In English correspondence, on the other hand, ten letters are between strangers, and six between acquaintances or friends. In the stranger to stranger cases, the addressing terms are very formal, whereas in the acquaintance to acquaintance or friend to friend cases, the addressing terms are very informal. This shows that in English the consideration of interpersonal distance overrides the consideration of formality, hence the use of politeness markers.

It is quite easy to rank the inside addressing of Chinese letters according to its degree of politeness. It appears to be more polite as the arrow goes up in the Table 4-1. The two letters without either honorifics or solidarity markers read rudely in Chinese. The English letters are more easily discussed in terms of formality. They all begin the inside addressing with the honorific "Dear", but from what follows it they can be read either as formal or informal, known or unknown, being distant or less distant in terms of the relationship between the writer and the receiver. But in the English letters the equivalent of the first two Chinese inside addressing, which read as extremely respectful and polite, cannot be found.

2. Opening (see Table 4-2)

Table 4-2 Opening

Chinese Letters	20	English Letters	16
greeting + phatic talk + business	3	—	—
greeting + business	4	—	—
phatic talk + business	7	phatic talk + business	1
business	6	business	15

Chinese letters, in most cases, open with either a greeting or phatic talk, or even a greeting followed by phatic talk before real business. English letters, all but one, "get down to business" straight away. It seems to be customary for Chinese writers to start a business correspondence with some kind of phatic talk to show respect for or to establish a rapport with the receiver, while it is apparently not necessary for English writers.

3. Self-referring (see Table 4-3)

Table 4-3 Self-referring

	sphere of politeness	self-denigration
self	ego identity	普通的
	quality (academic)	水平有限
	quantity	一芥之劳
	psychological state	斗胆
	action	试投，拜读，遵嘱，相扰，相求，请求，恳请，烦请
	writing	拙稿/著/译

Chinese letter writers denigrate themselves in self-referring or referring to things related to self, meanwhile they elevate the letter receivers in referring to the latter or to things related to the latter. This is not found in English. When referring to their work, instead of selling him/herself the Chinese writers tend to use expressions such as my clumsy/awkward/poor work, my limited capacity, my little effort, etc. . It is typical of Chinese politeness.

4. Other-referring (see Table 4-4)

Table 4-4 Other-referring

	sphere of politeness	other-elevation
other	ego identity	寄/呈/率上，谨寄，您（们）
	asking to read	奉阅，恳请审阅
	asking for advice	启导，请教，请指导，给予指导，祈望指教，敬请赐教，不吝指教，赐教，多多指教
	seeking publication	帮助出版，大力支持，鼎力相助
	asking for a reply	敬希复音，祈复，赐复，承蒙惠复，祈望早日赐复，敬请便中来函答复为感
extended other		贵社

It is apparent that the Chinese letter writers do not put themselves on an equal footing with the receiver. Instead they themselves by setting up a kind of inferior to superior relation. It is the inferior (potential author) who is asking favour from the superior (i. e. editor), which is the impression the above self-referring and other-elevating terms project. The receiver is respectfully invited to give guidance and enlightenment as well as favoring the writer with a reply.

5. Closing (see Table 4-5)

Table 4-5 Closing

Chinese Letters	20
willing to provide more information if necessary	7
looking forward to a reply	8
thanking	4
making a plea	1

English Letters	16
willing to provide more information if necessary	4
looking forward to a reply	10
thanking	2
—	—

The closing remarks generally comprises three parts: willing to provide more information, looking forward to a reply, and thanking. This is the only part where Chinese and English are more or less similar.

6. Pre-signature (see Table 4-6)

Table 4-6 **Pre-Signature**

Chinese Letters	20	English Letters	16
Giving good wishes e. g. 此致敬礼 此致祝好 此颂夏安 顺祝夏安 叩颂大安 即颂泰安 谨致编安 顺祝编安 顺颂编安 谨致敬礼 祝撰安 夏安 颂祝	18	Giving good wishes e. g. All best wishes With best wishes Best wishes	4
Thanking e. g. 谢谢	1	Thanking	11
无问候语	1	None	1

Chinese letters are rich and varied with pre-signature remarks or good wishes, whereas English letters are almost monotonous. All Chinese letters, except one, express high respect, best regards or best wishes to the receiver in pre-signature.

7. Signature/Post-signature (see Table 4-7)

Table 4-7 **Signature/Post-signature**

Chinese Letters	20	English Letters	16
full name	14	full name	8
full name+honorific e. g. ×××敬上	5	—	—
title+full name e. g. 系主任×××	1	title+full name e. g. 系主任×××	8

Chinese letter writers, in most cases, sign names. If there is post-signature, it is likely to be "honorific+other-elevating". English letter writers, in contrast, sign names followed by titles or positions (half of the English letters in our data), which would be read as being arrogant or self-conceited by Chinese receivers.

8. English indirectness and Chinese phatic talk

Politeness in English letters is partly achieved through indirectness; whereas the core of politeness in Chinese letter is self-denigrating and other-elevating. The following structures are found in the English letters.

I was wondering whether it would be suitable for...

I wondered if I might get your opinion on...

I wonder if you remember...

Would it be worth...

Could I suggest that...

We would very much appreciate...

I would be most interested in...

I would be happy to send you... should you...

I would welcome your comments on...

If you would like to...

If Longman would be willing to... .

All these are within a sentence boundary. In Chinese letters indirectness is also found. It is not at the sentential level, but at the indiscoursal level. As we pointed out above, most Chinese letters begin either with greeting and/or with phatic talk before the real purpose of writing is conveyed.

Conclusion

The findings in this contrastive study support Gu's view that self-denigration and other-elevation remain unique and at the core of the modern conception of politeness in China. In Chinese correspondence discourse, writers tend to use more politeness devices, which occur throughout the letter, and therefore Chinese letters read more politely at least to Chinese readers than English ones. This type of Chinese letter is more polite than other types of Chinese friendly correspondence since the writer believes that in seeking publication he/she is asking a favour from the receiver, whereas English writers seem to take it as an ordinary business letter, which does not call for special consideration of politeness. It is perhaps this essential difference in the business relationship itself that generates the differing discoursal attitudes.

(LIU D L. Politeness in correspondence discourses—a contrastive study [J]. Foreign Language Teaching and Research, 1999,357.)

Comprehension Check

A. Questions for Discussion

1. Try to demonstrate the differences and similarities on politeness in the written correspondence between English and Chinese.
2. How do you understand "In Chinese letters indirectness is also found. It is not at the sentential level, but at the indiscoursal level" in Part Main Findings 8?

B. Detail Understanding

Fill in the blanks on the politeness in the written correspondence between English and Chinese.

Point	Differences or Similarities	
1. Inside addressing	Chinese	
	English	
2. Opening	Chinese	
	English	
3. Self-referring	Chinese	
	English	
4. Other-referring	Chinese	
	English	
5. Closing	Chinese	
	English	
6. Pre-signature	Chinese	
	English	
7. Signature/Post-signature	Chinese	
	English	

Suggestions for Further Reading

BLAKE R J. New trends in using technology in the language curriculum[J]. Annual Review of Applied Linguistics, 2007, 27:76-97.

丁启红. 委婉语与禁忌语对比研究[D]. 成都理工大学硕士论文，2006.

刘润清. 人际交往·话语得体·语用距离[J]. 外语学刊，2011，(1)：59-62.

Unit 5 Nonverbal Communication

Human beings draw close to one another by their common nature, but habits and customs keep them apart.

—Confucius

Objectives:

To understand the relationship between verbal and nonverbal communication;

To recognize how nonverbal behavior is influenced by culture;

To interpret behavior culturally and communicate nonverbally.

Warm-up Activity

Early during the Suzuki family's stay in the United States, Mr. Suzuki went out after work with several American businessmen. They went to a small restaurant and ordered a pitcher of beer. As is the custom in Japan, Mr. Suzuki filled the glass of everyone at the table but himself. He left his own glass empty. The American men at the table looked at Mr. Suzuki in surprise. One asked if Mr. Suzuki didn't want a drink. Mr. Suzuki smiled and nodded. The men waited for him to fill his own glass. When he did not, they dismissed it and began to talk. Throughout the night, the Americans continued to fill their own glasses or had them filled by Mr. Suzuki. They assumed that Mr. Suzuki did not drink, and left his glass empty.

Questions for discussion

1. *Why did Mr. Suzuki leave his own glass empty?*
2. *What would a Chinese do in similar situations?*

Part One

Intensive Reading

Nonverbal Communication

Differences in nonverbal communication, or body language, are often subtle and can be the source of intercultural misunderstanding. During my first few days at the College of Micronesia, the division secretary was on sick leave. When she returned, I introduced myself and asked "Are you feeling better?" She answered "Yes" nonverbally by raising and lowering her eyebrows. I interpreted her response to mean "What did you say?" So I repeated the question a little more slowly, and again she raised her eyebrows. I asked the question a third time receiving the same nonverbal response. Out of frustration, I finally said, "I hope you are feeling better soon." About a week later, when I learned that raised eyebrows mean "Yes" I realized that the secretary must have thought me dense for repeatedly asking the same question.

Micronesians use the same shake of the head as Americans as a way to say "No". A frown accompanied by a wave of the hand at chest level is an emphatic "No!" or "Stop it!" Micronesians throw their heads slightly back and to the side to indicate "over there". Depending on the context of the question, the response could mean a few blocks away or the next island over. The apparent ambiguity of that particular response was sometimes confusing. Similarly, if I, as an outsider, were to summon a Micronesian by repeatedly curling my index finger upward, the gesture would imply that the receiver had the status of an animal. More than a few times, I had to control my impulse to use that common American gesture.

Much more difficult was remembering that the proper nonverbal gesture for summoning someone in Micronesia is to make a downward movement of the hand from the level of the head to the shoulder. The first time a Micronesian beckoned me in this manner, I thought he was telling me to go away. I stood in utter confusion until he finally asked me to "come here".

Touching as a Nonverbal Code

Cultures differ in the overall amount of touching they prefer. People from high-contact cultures, such as those in the Middle East, Latin America, and southern Europe, touch each other in social conversations much more than people from noncontact cultures do, such as those in Asia and northern Europe. These cultural differences can lead to difficulties in intercultural communication. Germans, Scandinavians, and Japanese, for example, may be perceived as cold and aloof by Brazilians and Italians, who in turn may be regarded as aggressive, pushy, and overly familiar by northern Europeans. Cultures also differ in where people can be touched and in their expectations about who touches whom. Finally, cultures differ in the settings or occasions in which touch is acceptable.

Time

As members of a "doing" culture, European Americans are very concerned with time, compartmentalizing it carefully to avoid wasting it. Micronesia is a "being" culture. Micronesians are more likely to listen to their natural impulses to eat when they are hungry and sleep when they are tired than to the hands of a clock. Cooking, fishing, and other tasks are determined by mood, weather, or ocean tides. In the remote villages and outer islands, much time is spent relaxing and socializing. The men meet to discuss community affairs or play games. The women weave or socialize over a card game. I had difficulty relating to people in the village who appeared to spend a great part of the day just sitting around doing nothing. I would have been bored but, interestingly, the word "bored" does not exist in Micronesian languages.

In city centers, where people are expected to abide by work hours and class times, Micronesians find the transition to schedules unnatural and confining. It is not considered unusual or rude for Micronesians to arrive later than their appointed time. It would, however, be unusual to meet a Micronesian who was in a hurry or anxious over a deadline. Because European Americans typically view time as a commodity, the time issue causes many misunderstandings. It took most of the first semester for me to understand that student tardiness was not a sign of disrespect or apathy.

During the fall semester I was asked to present a communication workshop to local radio announcers. I had very little time to design the workshop, so I gave the support staff the course materials to duplicate and assemble. Two days before the workshop was scheduled I discovered the duplicating hadn't been completed. I expressed my concern about having the materials on time but was assured that they would be ready. I heard indirectly that if I was in such a great hurry I should do the job myself. Surprisingly, the materials were delivered one hour before I left for the radio station.

I arrived at the station ten minutes early and found only one person there. The general manager and three announcers trickled in over the next 20 minutes. As I was about to begin, the electricity shut down, leaving us without air conditioning or lights. The general manager suggested we move the workshop to the college campus. By the time we drove to the campus and settled into a classroom, 15 minutes were left of the scheduled time. I had time only for a brief introduction and an icebreaker activity. I was disappointed that we lost virtually an entire session and that my preparation had been in vain, but none of the participants felt sorry.

Space or Privacy

While the concept of private property does exist, Micronesians tend to be less attached to their belongings than European Americans are. Acquaintances who were Peace Corps volunteers on Pohnpei said this was a frustrating cultural difference that they found difficult to accept. They explained that if they want to keep personal possessions such as hair clips, books, or cassette players for themselves, they would have to put them away in a private place. Their Pohnpeian family's attitude toward such items is one of detachment, which is generally true for most Micronesians. For instance, if something is borrowed and subsequently lost or damaged, the owner will not express anger, because people are much more important than possessions in their culture. In contrast, European Americans tend to react to losing a possession with varying degrees of anger and, depending on the object, may perceive a loss almost as a loss of part of oneself.

The issue of privacy was a challenge for me in Pohnpei. As a typical European American, I highly value my privacy, but the concept of privacy is strange in Micronesian cultures because togetherness is the norm. Although most Micronesians have been exposed to American cultural patterns and accept them, they still do not fully comprehend the need for "quiet time" or privacy. Being alone is generally associated with strong emotions, for instance, avoiding an individual or group to keep from expressing strong anger toward others or hiding because of feelings of sadness or great shame. Micronesians may also think that someone desiring solitude is mad or "physically sick and wants to be alone".

The day I moved into my two-bedroom bungalow, the landlord sent his son over to make some repairs on the house. His three sisters followed him over, walked into my living room, tied up the curtains to let the breeze in, and sat down for a chat among themselves. They were as relaxed and natural as if they were in their own home. I, on the other hand, didn't quite know what to do. Should I offer them something to drink? Make small talk? Try to entertain them in some way? The young women were fully engaged in their conversation in Pohnpeian language, so I retreated uncomfortably to my back room to work until everyone was ready to leave. On other occasions, the children in the neighborhood would pile onto my back porch to watch the video playing on my TV. They seemed as interested in what I was doing as in the plot of the film. After some time, I noticed my boundaries relaxing, but I was never fully comfortable with the territorial differences. The most disturbing violations of my privacy were when the young men in the neighborhood looked into my windows at night. The nocturnal habits of a single *menwai* (outsider) woman were apparently entertaining.

I moved back to California in 1990, when I accepted a teaching position at San Joaquin Delta College in Stockton. The first day on campus I met a visiting professor who had been a Peace Corps volunteer in Micronesia. He encouraged me to teach intercultural communication because, he said: "it's an important course, great fun, and a forum for Micronesian tales."

(MARIE V. Living in paradise: an inside look at the micronesian culture [M]//LUSTIG M W, LOESTER J. Among US: essays on identity, belonging, and intercultural competence. Boston: Allyn & Bacon Incorporated, 2005.)

Vocabulary

ambiguity *n.*	an expression whose meaning cannot be determined from its context
summon *vt.*	call in an official matter, such as to attend court
beckon *vt.*	signal with the hands or nod
aloof *adj.*	remote in manner
pushy *adj.*	marked by aggressive ambition and energy and initiative
compartmentalize *vt.*	separate into isolated compartments or categories
abide *vt.*	put up with something or somebody unpleasant
commodity *n.*	articles of commerce
tardiness *n.*	the quality or habit of not adhering to a correct or usual or expected time
apathy *n.*	an absence of emotion or enthusiasm
duplicate *n.*	something additional of the same kind
vi.	make or do or perform again
assemble *vt.*	get people together
trickle *vi.*	run or flow slowly, as in drops or in an unsteady stream
detachment *n.*	the state of being isolated
solitude *n.*	a state of social isolation
bungalow *n.*	a small house with a single story

Exercises

A. Words in Use

Fill in the blanks with the words given below. Change the form when necessary. Each word can be used only once.

summon beckon pushy abide duplicate commodity compartmentalize tardiness assemble trickle

1. He made himself unpopular by being so __________.
2. The prices of the __________ are quite stable this year.
3. I've heard the residents of the Infernos will __________ a Diety of Fire to

honor any hero who brings them the Grail.

4. Fundamentally speaking, the accumulation of difficult employment in these years is caused by the slowness and __________ of enterprise innovation.
5. The old woman, seeing that I hesitated to enter, began to __________ to me repeatedly with her hand.
6. Water flowed in a very thin __________ over pebbles.
7. He cannot __________ to stay in one position for long.
8. If the fire alarm goes, staff should __________ outside the building.
9. It occurred to us that we were merely __________ their research.
10. Life today is __________ into work and leisure.

B. Questions for Discussion

1. It is common that Chinese students of the same gender often touch each other while they are talking. How might Western people interpret this behavior? What is the cultural difference behind?
2. Nonverbal message can also contradict verbal message. What might happen if your nonverbal message contradicts your verbal message?

C. Translation

1. Similarly, if I, as an outsider, were to summon a Micronesian by repeatedly curling my index finger upward, the gesture would imply that the receiver had the status of an animal.
2. European Americans are very concerned with time, compartmentalizing it carefully to avoid wasting it. Micronesia is a "being" culture. Micronesians are more likely to listen to their natural impulses.
3. The issue of privacy was a challenge for me in Pohnpei. As a typical European American, I highly value my privacy, but the concept of privacy is strange in Micronesian cultures because togetherness is the norm.

D. Case Study

Case 1

Mark had recently moved from Denmark to Sydney to work as a salesperson for a large Australian company. After three weeks, he was invited to join a local club. During the first few weeks at the club, Mark would either stand in the corner talking with someone or sit on a sofa listening to other people talk and chat. As time went by, he came to know most of the club members and seemed to enjoy talking with them. One day, at an evening party, one of the female members approached him. Mark immediately showed his interest by talking about the atmosphere of the party. At first, the conversation between them seemed to go quite smoothly, but as it progressed, the lady seemed to step further and further away from Mark as he had been gradually moving closer to her. The lady obviously seemed uncomfortable. As Mark was about to ask her questions regarding Australian social customs, another man standing nearby directed a glance toward the lady. She excused herself and went to talk with that man, leaving Mark standing alone and wondering why their conversation had come to such a sudden stop.

Question

Why did that woman suddenly stop talking with Mark and turned to another man?

Case 2

David Li had just started working for the foreign-owned company. He was sitting at his workstation but had not been given any assignment that he should be doing at that moment. He was relaxing and waiting and then thought he would take the opportunity to have a look around. He poked his head into several offices just to see what there was to be seen.

Suddenly Mr. Parker came up to him and angrily asked him what he was doing. David Li was embarrassed. He laughed and quickly started to move back toward his workstation. This did not seem to satisfy Mr. Parker who started to talk rapidly and angrily. Hoping to calm him down, Mr. Li smiled and apologized, trying to explain that he was trying to learn more about the department. However, Mr. Parker got even angrier. Finally, another worker came by and calmed him down, but as Mr. Parker left he still looked angry. Mr. Li sighed—he knew he had made a bad start, but still didn't understand why.

Questions

1. Why Mr. Parker became even angrier while Mr. Li smiled and apologized?
2. What suggestions can you give Mr. Li?

Part Two

Extensive Reading

Culture and Politeness

The Notion of Face

Politeness is a universal phenomenon in human communication, which in most cases is expressed and realized through language. In the study of language and politeness, Penelope Brown & Stephen Levinson (1978) first formulated the politeness theory which considers politeness as the expression of the speakers' intention to mitigate face threats carried by certain face threatening acts towards another person. With data from different cultures, a conceptual framework has been suggested based on the notion of "face". For this reason, the theory of politeness is also called "the face theory".

In sociolinguistic studies, face is usually given the following general definition: "Face is the negotiated public image, mutually granted each other by participants in a communicative event." (Scollon & Scollon, 2000) This implies that in interpersonal communication, shared assumptions and the negotiation of face are the two important aspects in the process of communication. It can be noted that while there is much negotiation of face in any form of interpersonal communication, participants must also make assumptions about face before they can begin any communication. Before we talk to someone, we often make significant assumptions about what kind of person the other person is and what kind of person he or she would like us to think of him or her as. For example, we often find it difficult to address other people appropriately. You may call the president of a university by his official title, his title as a professor, a teacher, a workmate or even by simply using his name, depending on the shared assumptions about your relationships. Many aspects of linguistic form depend on the speakers making some analysis of the relationships among themselves. The choice of terms of address is one of the first of these recognized by sociolinguists. The study of face in sociolinguistics arose out of the need to understand how participants decide what their relative statuses are and what language they use to encode their assumptions about such differences in status, as well as their assumptions about the face being presented by participants in communication.

We can also notice that in people's assumptions about the participants in communication and their negotiation of the relationships, they often do not have to figure out everything from the beginning every time they talk to someone. In communication, most people would make certain assumptions about their relationship with the other participants and the face that they tend to claim for themselves and are willing to give to the others involved in the communicative situation. To start with such unmarked assumptions, the participants would continue to undertake certain amount of negotiation of their relationship during the process of communication. For example, if a person wants to ask a rather large favor of another person, he or she is likely to begin with the assumed relationship, but then he or she will begin to negotiate a closer or more intimate relationship. If such a closeness is achieved then he or she is likely to feel it is safer to risk asking for the favor than if their negotiations result in more distance between them.

To further elaborate on Brown & Levinson's theoretical framework, two aspects of peoples feelings are involved with face. The first is the desire of the individual not to be imposed on what the researchers called "negative face", while the second "positive face" is the desire of the individual to be liked and approved of. (Brown & Levinson, 1987, 2007) As an illustration to the two kinds of faces, we may imagine a conversation between two acquaintances, one of whom is suffering from a bad cold. In this situation, if one fails to express his/her concern over the illness, he/she may offend the other person's positive face which requires sympathy or empathy, while one may offend the negative face of the person suffering from illness through intimate suggestions on how to deal with the illness. Therefore, in deciding how much to take another persons feelings into account, we have to consider various factors such as the social status of the participants involved, the social distance between the speakers and the gravity of the threat we are about to make to the other's face.

Although politeness is a universal concept, it is culturally defined because what is considered polite in one culture can sometimes be inappropriate or simply strange in another culture. For example, in the above case, both Chinese and American would normally show their concern over the others' illness, but their preference for the positive or negative politeness strategies may be different. Chinese tend to offer detailed suggestions to the treatment of illness, which is considered appropriate in the Chinese cultural context as an expression of concern over others' welfare. However, such an act may be considered as an offence to others' privacy, or a threat to the negative face in the American cultural context, which normally requires an expression showing empathetic understanding of others' illness. This also suggests that different cultures may have different preference of politeness strategies.

Politeness Strategies

Through the explanation of the notion of face, we may claim that politeness is the manifestation of respect for another's face through speech in communication. This is usually accomplished by politeness strategies that we use to show our concern for others involved in the interaction, even when we may perform an act of threatening his/her face. There are two major types of politeness strategies in communication, i. e. positive politeness and negative politeness strategies.

Positive politeness strategies involve the intention of the speaker to let the addressee know that he or she is liked and approved of. For example, compliment is often used by native speakers of English as a strategy to show positive politeness. In the English native speaking context, people tend to compliment the addressees on their accomplishments, appearances, or other attributes, as a form of positive evaluation to express positive politeness to the other participants in communication. Other possible ways to show positive politeness can be the use of signals to tell the addressee that they can become friends or members of the same "in-group". Such strategies can show similarities in viewpoints and aims, as well as giving gifts, showing interest in the other, and being friendly and cooperative, etc. Negative politeness, on the other hand, involves the speaker's wish not to disturb or to interfere with the addressee's freedom. This can be exemplified by a show of deference, indirect strategies in making requests and the strategies of using apologies and other forms of remedial work to maintain the addressee's independence.

In contrast to the politeness strategies used in communication, there is a possibility that a speaker may not have any attempt to take the feelings of the addressee into consideration. The speaker in this case may just simply make a direct statement or a direct request. In Brown & Levinson's terminology, such a way of speaking is referred to as "bald on record". This suggests that the speaker is attempting to speak clearly and unambiguously without any consideration of the addressee's "face wants". The motivation for speaking "bald on record" may be due to an emergency that requires an unambiguous statement or the indifference of the speaker to the feelings of the addressee, or other possibilities that would induce such a type of speech. (Brown & Levinson, 1987, 2007)

Brown & Levinson (2007) believe that most relationships between people are relatively stable. They therefore suggest that the degree of threat to other's face involved in the speech act is the most common reason for the change in level of politeness and the selection of an appropriate politeness strategy. For instance, if the speaker is about to ask a very minor favor, the degree of face threatening will be low and the level of politeness will not be great. However, if the speaker is to ask the addressee for a big favour which involves considerable effort, the threat to the other's face is inevitable and the level of politeness will be great.

It is also assumed that apart from differences in the degree of threat to the other's face, politeness levels between people are relatively stable in any society. The general level of politeness in a particular relationship is quite constant and could therefore serve as an index of social closeness and the relative power relationship between the interlocutors. Through using politeness as a social strategy, the members of a culture are able to judge the social relationships between the interlocutors. For example, negative politeness can be seen as a strategy more often used by those who are less powerful than the addressee, while the use of positive politeness is a sign of social closeness between the speakers in communication. In this sense, a study of the politeness strategies used in a community will enable us to understand the relationships between individuals as well as the way a particular society is structured.

It is pointed out that although the principles of politeness in human interaction are universal as suggested by Brown & Levinson's theoretical framework, but what counts as polite may differ from culture to culture. In other words, the patterns in the realization of politeness are culturally specific. However, Brown & Levinson's theoretical framework has been a very useful contribution to the study of language in society. The notion of positive and negative face has proved fruitful in many respects in the study of cultural patterns of politeness strategies across cultures. For example, Chinese culture in general has been described in many studies as having a preference for the positive strategies in politeness, contrasting to the American and other western cultures which tend to prefer negative politeness strategies in handling interpersonal communications. For interpreters who are involved in intercultural communication, this theoretical framework also provides them with a useful tool for the observation of the cultural differences among their clients and for helping them resolve possible miscommunications among them.

(CHEN J P. Translation and intercultural communication[M]. Beijing: Foreign Language Teaching and Research Press, 2012.)

Language focus

sociolinguistic *adj.* 社会语言学的
intimate *adj.* 亲密的
impose *vt.* 强加；欺骗
empathy *n.* 移情
manifestation *n.* 表现；显示
exemplify *vt.* 例证；例示
terminology *n.* 术语
induce *vt.* 诱导；引起
interlocutor *n.* 对话者；谈话者
encode *vt.* 编码
elaborate *adj.* 详尽的
acquaintance *n.* 熟人
gravity *n.* 重力；庄严
compliment *n.* 恭维；称赞
remedial *adj.* 治疗的；补救的
unambiguous *adj.* 不含糊的；清楚的
index *n.* 指标；指数
fruitful *adj.* 富有成效的；多产的

Exercises

A. Text Reading

Decide whether the following statements are true (T) or false (F).

1. ______ Participants do not have to make assumptions about face before they can begin any communication.
2. ______ In interpersonal communication, shared assumptions and the negotiation of face are the two important aspects in the process of communication.
3. ______ Although the notion of face could be applied universally to the anal-

ysis of politeness in all cultures, the degrees of which "negative face" and "positive face" are adopted tend to be culturally specific.

4. ______ There are two aspects of people's feelings are involved with face. The first is called "negative face", while the second is "positive face".
5. ______ In the Chinese cultural context, positive politeness strategies are only adopted in interpersonal communication.
6. ______ Patterns in the realization of politeness differ a lot in various cultures, which suggests that different cultures may have different preference of politeness strategies.
7. ______ When politeness is analyzed as a social strategy, people can get to know the way a particular society is structured through observing and analyzing the politeness strategies used in society.
8. ______ People have to figure out everything from the beginning every time they talk to someone.
9. ______ The selection of an appropriate politeness strategy largely depends on the degree of threat to others' face involved in the speech act.
10. ______ Politeness levels between people are not stable and constant in any society.

B. Terms Understanding

Find the definitions of the following terms in the text. If you cannot find the exact definition, try to use your own words to interpret it.

1. face theory
2. negative face/politeness
3. positive face/politeness
4. "in-group" membership

C. Classroom Activities

1. Compare Chinese and American cultures and discuss how you would describe the respective cultures in terms of their "negative face" and "positive face" orientations.
2. In the Chinese cultural context, positive politeness strategies are usually adopted in interpersonal communication. However, negative politeness strategies are also used in certain contexts. Try to find examples to illustrate the positive and negative strategies used in the Chinese cultural con-

text considering the factors of "in-group" and "out-group" membership in communication.

3. Discuss the relationship between social relation and politeness with reference to the Chinese social-cultural context.

Part Three

Academic Reading

Perspective on Nonverbal Intercultural Communication

During the last decade, anthropologists, linguists, psychologists, psychiatrists, sociologists language teachers, and communication specialists have begun to awaken us to the urgent need of understanding what is called "silent language". That is, these scholars have demonstrated how gestures, body motions, practices due to attitudes toward time and space, and general social behavior all communicate a great deal. Rooted deeply in cultural conventions, a virtual "hidden dimension" in communication between people of different countries—these nonverbal cues must be exposed and appreciated more than they now are.

Now let us look at nonverbal cues ①expressed in body motion and gestures, ②stemming from general habits in communicating.

Nonverbal Cues Expressed in Body Motion and Gesture

At the outset it should be clearly understood that modern research has strongly emphasized that body motions and gestures are learned. That is, they are culturally determined. Most studies prior to World War Ⅱ were based on a single culture, and they assumed that the same gestures were present, with the same meaning, in other cultures as well. The studies assumed that gestures were "natural", especially in the expression of certain emotions. If natural, then of course they would be universal. But contemporary scholars have concluded that "there is no 'natural' language of emotional gesture, and that our gesture language which is meaningful to us is as unintelligible to another culture as our verbal language is". Earlier studies also asserted or implied that body movements and gestures were biological, instinctive, and inherent characteristics of a certain race or nationality. These traits would thus not be subject to modification and change. But this has been disproven. Studies of immigrants have revealed how gestures are modified and changed to conform to the gestural patterns of the new homeland, just as the spoken language is changed. Just as they exhibit "foreign accents" in their speech, first and second generation immigrants usually retain some vestiges of past gestural habits and thus develop what is called "hybrid gestures". Following generations, however, thoroughly adopt the new gestural habits just as foreign accents disappear.

1. Body Posture

Mankind's body postures are legion. One authority has asserted that the human body is capable of adopting about one thousand different "steady postures". For instance, although you are accustomed to sitting in a chair when resting, about one-fourth of the world population has learned to rest in a squatting position. Most Westerners look on this as a rather improper, primitive, and childish position. Our children squat very naturally, but through verbal admonishments and constant examples we teach them to forgo this highly comfortable position for the sitting posture. Furthermore, many people in other lands do most of their sitting on the ground and floor (frequently on mats), and hence when they sit in chairs they tend to curl one or both legs under them, which to some Westerners seems strange and perhaps primitive. Sitting on one's heels with knees resting on the floor is a formal sitting position of Japan, and is one position of prayer for the Moslem.

Positions of prayer have vastly differing connotations depending upon whether one is a member of the "in-group" or not. When a devout Moslem prostrates himself and a devout Christian kneels, they feel they are engaging in acts symbolizing humility and appropriate submission to a deity. But to a person outside of these religious frameworks, such motions may connote a primitive and even pagan gesture of appeasement to some wrathful God, and thus an affront to the dignity of man.

Westerners stand up to show respect, which they say is the "natural" thing to do. But some Polynesians sit down. The erect, stiff Prussian posture connotes arrogance to many people, but to a German it conveys respect.

When an American puts his feet up on his desk, it signifies a relaxed, informal attitude, many times a sort of tribute to the person with whom he is conversing. But to some Latin Americans and Asians, this connotes rudeness and perhaps arrogance.

2. Movements of the Body or Torso

Movements of the whole body or parts of the torso can communicate different messages in different cultures. The impression we may receive from vigorous African dance movements or intricate Oriental dance gestures may be quite different from the impressions received by members of those cultures.

The slow saunter of the American cowboy and the small rapid steps of a Chinese woman quickly illustrate that people walk differently, and that the type of walk may connote different things to different people. In England and parts of South America a male commonly clasps his hands behind his back when he walks, but to Americans this may connote an aristocratic, haughty attitude. Male friends in parts of the Middle East, Asia, and South America commonly walk arm in arm or holding hands, which to an American may connote effeminate behavior.

In parts of South America a slight bow is a common courteous gesture of greeting, especially when one does not stop to converse. An Oriental who has to leave a gathering will usually bow before departing, which communicates his apology. Similarly, members of the British House of Commons when entering or leaving the chamber will stop and bow toward the speaker, thus communicating not only an apology for interrupting the proceedings but also a general respect for the Crown. Some in the Middle East bow to show respect for someone. To an American, the bowing gesture connotes formal, aristocratic, quaint movement that he considers rather irksome, fastidious, and undemocratic.

Some Mediterranean, Middle East, and South American males embrace as a common form of greeting by placing the head over the other person's right shoulder and then over the left, together with gentle pats on the back. Most Northern Europeans and Americans think this to be too emotional and possibly effeminate. Kissing in public is rather common in America, whereas in Asia it is considered highly indecent. Furthermore, instead of bringing the lips into contact to show mutual affection, some people, like the Eskimos and Polyne sians, rub noses.

3. Movements of the Head and Facial Expressions

Movements of the head and facial expressions may communicate different messages in different cultures. For instance, an educated Englishman may lift the chin slightly when conversing, as a poised, polite gesture. But to an American it may connote arrogance or snobbery. "Turning up his nose" has become a meaningful American idiom.

We may think that nodding the head up and down for affirming something, and shaking it from side to side for negation, are "natural" things to do. But other cultures employ other gestures to say "yes" or "no". A Malayan tribe says "yes" by thrusting the head forward, whereas Ethiopians say "yes" by throwing the head back, and "no" by jerking the head to the right. Some Arabs and Italians indicate the negative by lifting the chin, whereas this means "yes" to the Maori in New Zealand. The Arab communicates a minimal negation by merely raising the eyebrows, whereas that means "yes" in some Borneo tribes, who would lower them to indicate negation. In different parts of India and Ceylon, affirmation may be communicated by throwing the head backward and slightly turning the neck, by bending the head down and to the right, or by turning the head rapidly in a circular motion. Some inhabitants of northern Japan communicate negation by passing the right hand back and forth in front of the chest, and indicate affirmation by bringing both hands up to the chest, and then waving them downwards with palms up.

The Japanese smile and laugh does not necessarily mean happiness or friendship. As a carefully cultivated act of social duty and etiquette, it is employed in a large number of circumstances and may among other things, suggest shyness, embarrassment, discomfort, wonder, or surprise. In some areas of Asia and Africa laughing or smiling suggests weakness. Hence, teachers never smile in the classroom lest it impair discipline.

4. Use of the Eyes

Different cultures have developed a variety of uses for the eyes in the communicative process. We are familiar with the American admonition to maintain good eye contact with one's audience. But some cultures teach their young people, especially girls, that to look someone in the eye, especially an older or more important person, is disrespectful and highly improper. Hence, one should lower one's gaze accordingly. For example, recently a very expressive girl from Indonesia, studying at an American university, told me that because of this emphasis in her culture, the most difficult thing for her in American public speaking classes was to learn to look at her audience.

On the other hand, in a conversational situation, Americans do not practice such rigorous eye contact as Britons and Arabs do. The educated Briton considers it part of good listening behavior to stare at his conversationalist and to indicate his understanding by blinking his eyes, whereas we Americans nod our head or emit some sort of grunt, and are from childhood taught not to stare at people. One writer has asserted that the "Arabs look each other in the eye when talking with an intensity that makes most Americans highly uncomfortable". Furthermore, the Arab has grown so accustomed to facing the person with whom he is conversing, but he finds it awkward and feels it is impolite, for instance, to talk when walking side by side. Thus he may dance ahead in order to achieve eye contact. Americans make more use of eye movements in general, while other cultures make more use of hand and arm motions.

5. Hand and Arm Motions

The use of hand and arm motions for communicative purposes varies to a remarkable degree between cultures. The following contrasts have been suggested:

> Gesture among the Americans is largely oriented toward activity; among the Italians it serves the purposes of illustration and display; among the Jews it is a device of emphasis; among the Germans it specifies both attitude and commitment; and among the French it is an expression of style and containment.

Some, like Americans and Northern Europeans, look on frequent and vigorous gesturing as too emotional, immature, and rather vulgar, and thus use them rather sparingly and with restraint. On the other hand, those inhabitants of Southern Europe, the Middle East, and South America, view gestures differently and use them much more frequently and with much more energy. The familiar adage that if an Italian has his arms amputated, he would be speechless, rather meaningfully depicts his reliance on gesture. Recently when judging twenty-five contestants in a high school oratory contest, I noted that only one student used arm and hand movements with grace and ease and meaningful reinforcement of the verbal message. He proved to be an exchange student from Italy! The Arabs, writes one observer, have obtained such an eloquence of gesture that often words seem superfluous in conversation. At the other extreme would be those who use hand and arm gestures very sparingly, like some Indian tribes in Bolivia. Because of the cool climate, they keep their hands under shawls or blankets most of the time, and hence rely more on facial and eye expressions.

When an American clasps his hands over his head, it signifies, usually with pride and occasionally a touch of arrogance, that victory over some foe has been achieved. A prize fighter, for instance, so signals after having been designated the victor. But to the Russians, this is a symbol of friendship. Thus, when Khrushchev came to the United States a few years ago and was photographed making that gesture, millions of Americans were irritated at what they interpreted to be an arrogant signal of confidence in the eventual victory of Communism over America and capitalism. But the gesture was meant to communicate a spirit of friendship. In Colombia, a similar gesture but with clasped hands level with the face means "I agree with you". To clap the hands together is a familiar Western habit to communicate approval, but to many in the Orient it is used primarily to summon an inferior person, such as a servant.

Shaking hands is a gesture of friendship widely used in many cultures, but some Indian tribes in Bolivia have taken it as a challenge to wrestle and have obliged accordingly! Latin Americans shake hands more frequently, more vigorously, and continue it longer than North Americans do. The latter omit it occasionally as a sign of informality, but Latin Americans may interpret its omission as discourtesy. Of course, shaking hands is done with the right not the left hand. One origin of such a practice is that it symbolized a peaceful gesture, in that the right hand was the hand which held weapons, and these would have to be set aside in order to shake hands.

But the right hand has been glorified throughout the centuries for other reasons as well. In Moslem countries and some other Oriental countries, to touch anybody with the left hand is an obscenity, for a main function of the left hand is to aid in the process of elimination of body wastes, whereas the right hand is used for the intake of food. Hence, the left hand is unclean and the right is clean. To offer something in the left hand to a Moslem would be an insult of the most serious type.

This pragmatic origin of the prestige of the right hand has been stressed by religious literature and practices. In the *Old Testament*, the right hand has always held more favor. The right hand is associated with strength, goodness, honor, guidance, sustenance, safety, pleasure, and salvation. The *New Testament* has of course retained this glorification of the right hand, for on the Judgment Day the saved shall be on the right hand of God and the damned on the left. The ascended Christ is metaphorically seated on the right hand of God. This image is repeated in basic liturgical statements of faith of the institutional church, such as The Apostles Creed and the Gloria in Excelsis. In a Christian marriage ceremony the participants are instructed to join, not their left, but their right hands. The *Koran*, the Moslem holy book, likewise associate the right hand with favorable connotations. The Buddhists also glorify the right hand.

One only needs to observe the shape of school desks, the contours of handles of kitchen utensils, and the placement of levers on machines to realize how completely dominant righthandedness is in our own Western culture. Thus, it is not surprising that the right hand has been so prestigious that it is only in the last generation or so that parents in the Western world have finally ceased the cruel and laborious practice of forcing their left-handed children to eat and write with their right hands. According to some theorists, this forced shifting of handedness has been a contributory cause of stuttering and other nervous insecurities.

A number of other gestures with hands and arms vary considerably between different cultures. In some parts of the world, members of the same sex greet each other by grasping forearms. In many parts of the world a slap on the back is a familiar form of greeting, although this may be interpreted by some people as too informal, aggressive, and even discourteous. In parts of the Middle East males may greet each other by grasping, raising, and kissing right hands. We may greet someone by boisterous wave of the arm, but Hindus and Buddhists do so with a graceful and dainty placing of the palms together with fingers pointing skyward, which communicates not only a "hello" but also a sort of "peace be with you".

When departing or when refusing some food or drink, some Arabs will place their right hand over their heart to indicate sincere regret. In parts of Asia, an individual gives an article with both hands, not just one, and receives an article in the right hand, with the left hand supporting the right elbow to demonstrate proper respect and gratitude. Raising the thumb to the nose is a recognized disrespectful vulgarism in the Western world, but in South India a similar gesture with the thumb higher on the bridge of the nose is a sign of respect. The American thumb gesture in hitchhiking is absent from many cultures, for as one source contends, it would originate only "in a country where total strangers are welcomed as passengers". Latin Americans customarily call a waiter by sharply rapping on the table or striking a glass with a ring or a utensil. North Americans would consider this somewhat aggressive and rude and would call the waiter by raising the hand slightly or catching his eye. A Portuguese will communicate his approval of something by tugging at an ear, whereas in Colombia, a similar motion indicates anticipation of some punishment, such as a child expecting a parental scolding. American male teachers who serve in the Orient are cautioned not to touch the girl students, for it is considered a virtual obscenity for a man to touch a woman.

In parts of South America one would indicate the size of an animal by extending the arm, palm down, but to indicate the height of a human, one would keep the palm vertical. Not to distinguish between these gestures for animal and human would be a grave error, which North Americans customarily commit since they have no such separate gestures. Likewise, we frequently point at humans and animals with the same kind of hand and index finger gesture, but in parts of Asia it would be extremely rude to point at people, for this is only done toward animals. This involves another adjustment for American teachers abroad who are accustomed to calling on students by pointing at them.

The specific use of fingers has a variety of messages in different cultures. Some Arabs will demonstrate friendship by placing index fingers side by side. In Jordan, friendship may also be symbolized by locking little fingers, and enmity is demonstrated by extending the second finger and inviting to lock. But in neighboring Syria and Lebanon, according to some observers, the meaning of those symbols seem to be reversed. The familiar Roman thumbs-up gesture still symbolizes in Britain good fortune or success, but in parts of India the same gesture is so offensive that to make it could actually cause a fight. In the United States we admonish a small child not to do something by shaking the index finger forward and backward, whereas in South America the finger would move from side to side. In America we indicate in jest that someone is mentally unstable by making a circular motion with an index finger near the temple, whereas in France the same message is conveyed by a similar motion in front of the forehead.

Nonverbal Cues Stemming from General Habits in Communicating

The general manner of communicating orally in interculture communication situation can lead to unfortunate misunderstandings. If unclear communication and needless friction are to be avoided or reduced, members of different cultures need to understand the varying habits and manners of others, and what these practices mean and do not mean.

1. Degree of Expressiveness

Different cultures have considerably differing habits in the amount of expressiveness. This is rooted in the varying habits of child rearing and in varying attitudes toward people of different ages, classes, and stations in life. In the family setting, for instance, most Americans encourage their children to enter freely into dinner table conversation and other family discussions and to participate early in decision making. By contrast, in Asia and elsewhere, children are taught to be silent in the presence of elders and, for instance, are usually separated from them when eating. The children certainly are never to disagree verbally with the parent, or with older brothers and sisters, for that matter. In parts of India, even an adult would not enter into the decision-making discussions if his aged parents were still in the family circle. It is not surprising, therefore, that many foreigners look upon American young people as brash, immodest, and rude, possessing no proper respect for parents or older siblings. On the other hand, Americans may look upon young people of other cultures as being too reticent, too quiet, too unresponsive, too lacking in self-confidence, which may be interpreted erroneously as inferiority.

In many countries a student would very seldom ask a question in class, for to do so would not only suggest that he is uninformed but that he is implying that the teacher has been unclear, which would be highly disrespectful. In America most teachers encourage the student to ask all kinds of questions. It is a mark of a good teacher to draw out questions and a mark of a good student to ask numerous, meaningful questions. American teachers abroad thus have to realize the lack of questions or lack of recitation from their students does not mean that the teacher is being ineffective or that the students are ignorant and lethargic, for they are merely being respectful.

2. Degree of Intimacy of Address

In parts of Asia or in other lands where strict social hierarchies are firmly entrenched, a person younger than, or in a lower class than, the person with whom he is communicating should manifest an appropriate humbleness and choose language appropriately. Specific labels should precede the person's name to indicate the appropriate status of the person spoken to and relationship between the conversation. Titles and educational degrees should be carefully acknowledged. In order to ascertain the proper relationship, an Asian, for instance, is likely to ask a foreigner a number of questions, such as how old is he, what is his occupation, how much does he earn, or is he married. To an American these questions seem much too personal and inappropriate. But they are meant to be a respectful endeavor to determine how to address the visitor.

Americans are quick to get on a first name basis with everyone. But to the British and others this is considered too personal, too pushy, too rude. They are offended and irritated with what they feel is aggressive egalitarianism. The British would use the first name only when speaking to a servant, gardener, or people on the low social ladder, but not for a person of equal rank, unless they are very intimate friends. Americans misinterpret the reticence to adopt first name labels as unfriendliness.

3. Degree of Emotion and Animation

Different cultures have decidedly varying attitudes and practices in relation to how much emotion and animation an individual should display in a communication situation. When discussing gesturing, the Northern European and North American attempt to control and suppress their emotions greatly. This is based on the cultural premise that this demonstrates maturity, disciplined behavior, and emotional stability. On the other hand, this behavior is viewed by others, such as the Russians, Mediterranean peoples, and Latin Americans, as lacking in frankness, friendliness, and sincerity, as hiding something and gesturing an air of superiority. Many foreigners misinterpret American lack of excitement in conversation or public speaking as a lack of interest or concern.

However, quite the reverse is true in a gift exchanging situation. Some Asians and South Americans do not normally show gratitude for a gift and do not open it in the presence of the giver, whereas Americans tend to express gratitude profusely and usually open the gift immediately in the presence of the giver. This communicates that the recipient is so grateful that he can hardly wait to open it. The American interprets the other practice as showing lack of enthusiastic appreciation.

Women speak more excitedly than men in America. But in many cultures it is just the reverse. For instance, in Arab societies, the men manifest more animation than the women.

4. Degree of Frankness

Cultures vary considerably in the degree of frankness expected. The English, for instance, with their long heritage of open, direct, and frank confrontation in parliamentary debating and in the heckling of public speakers, are more likely to be more sharp and blunt than most people, including the Americans. Britons hit hard and expect to be hit hard in return. This was freshly illustrated for me recently when a British colleague in a faculty committee meeting stirred considerable animosity by his frank, sharp, and unambiguous statement of his views on the topic under consideration. When told later of the reactions of some of the committee members, he was shocked, for he thought he had expressed himself rather mildly and circumspectly.

Most Asians would be far more reticent than Americans to engage in a sharp exchange, and tend to couch their remarks very carefully so as not to hurt the feelings of, or embarrass, the other person. This results in rather heavy use of euphemisms and ambiguity. It has also been asserted that some Asians are less able than some Westerners to separate the criticism of issues and the criticism of the person holding those views. Thus, criticizing their views means you are really criticizing the person. Peace Corps volunteers are learning that the common American frankness and open criticism create in the recipient a strong embarrassment, loss of face, and possible hostility.

5. Degree of Intensity and Persistency

Different cultures have developed varying habits in relation to the use of intensity and persistency in certain communicative situations. For instance, a normal unstressed English "no" may be interpreted by an Arab to mean "yes", for a real negation, to the Arab's way of thinking, would be emphasized much more. Likewise in some cultures a mild, hesitant "yes" is interpreted as a polite refusal. A Filipino expects to be asked more than once when invited to a dinner, until he "reluctantly" accepts. A single invitation would be considered an affront, being interpreted to mean that he really is not sincerely invited. Likewise, he will usually wait until the hostess has asked him two or three times before he will approach the prepared feast. An Arab likewise considers it polite to refuse some proffered food several times and then finally to accept it. But when an American says "no, thank you" to the hostess' offer of food, he usually means it, and that ends it.

6. Degree of Volume

Different habits between cultures regarding the degree of volume in communication situations need to be understood. Some, like the Arabs, like to be bathed in sound, as it were. Thus, conversation tends to be loud, and the volume on the radio and phonograph is turned up. Some foreign students in American college dormitories cause some unintentional ill feeling by keeping their radios very loud. In many countries where radios are not so plentiful, and where warmer climate permits open houses, it is an act of thoughtful and kind neighborliness to keep the volume high in order to permit neighbors to listen. To Americans, such loud volume is interpreted as thoughtless imposition on anothers' privacy. In interpersonal conversation, on the other hand, many in the Orient and elsewhere speak more softly than Americans, and would interpret the loud volume of an excited American as connoting aggressiveness, loss of self-control, or even anger.

Summary

In today's jet dominated world, it is becoming increasingly urgent that the peoples of the earth learn not only each other's languages but also each other's nonverbal habits in communication. Many nonverbal cues are transmitted by body motions and gestures. In different cultures many similar gestures transmit different messages. In other instances the same message is sent by different motions and gestures, thus creating unfortunate misunderstandings. Furthermore, nonverbal cues stem from general habits in communicating, which may differ considerably between cultures. Varying degrees of expressiveness, intimacy of address, animation, frankness, persistence, and volume in different cultures need to be recognized.

It is clearly apparent that man on this shrunken globe must become aware of these culturally determined differences, and accordingly act with greater enlightenment. But this, of course, will not solve all problems in human relations. That all cultures have cues for expressing animosity as well as affection only demonstrates that animosity exists to be expressed. But through greater clarity of communication we can surely hope for, and confidently expect, a reduction of unintentional offensiveness and an increase in mutual understanding.

(ISBISTER K. Building bridges through the unspoken: embodied agents to facilitate intercultural communication[M]//PAYR S, TRAPPL R. Agent culture: human-agent interaction in a multicultural world. London: Lawrence Erlbaum Associates, 2004: 233-244.)

Comprehension Check

A. Questions for Discussion

1. Can you use some examples to explain "*Body movements and gestures were biological, instinctive, and inherent characteristics of a certain race or nationality*"?
2. Do you agree with the notion that "*By contrast, in Asia and elsewhere, children are taught to be silent in the presence of elders and, for instance, are usually separated from them when eating. The children certainly are never to disagree verbally with the parent, or with older brothers and sisters, for that matter*"? Why or why not?
3. Will all problems in human relations be solved if we become aware of these culturally determined differences?

B. Detail Understanding

Figure out the countries or areas matching to the nonverbal connotations.

Countries or Areas	Nonverbal Connotations
1.	Sitting on ones heels with knees resting on the floor is a formal sitting position.
2.	When people puts his feet up on his desk, it signifies a relaxed, informal attitude, many times a sort of tribute to the person with whom he is conversing.
3.	It's common for male friends to walk arm in arm or holding hands.
4.	Raising the eyebrows communicates a minimal negation.
5.	It is considered awkward and impolite to talk when walking side by side.
6.	Clasps the hands over one's head is a symbol of friendship.
7.	Raising the thumb higher on the bridge of the nose is a sign of respect.
8.	Friendship may be symbolized by locking little fingers, and enmity is demonstrated by extending the second finger and inviting to lock.
9.	Loud volume is interpreted as thoughtless imposition on anothers' privacy.

Suggestions for Further Reading

1. HINKEL E. Language learning and language culture in a changing world [J]. Applied Research in English, 2012, 1 (2): 45-56.
2. 范杏丽. 不同文化背景下的非语言交际对比[J]. 华中科技大学学报（社会科学版), 2000, 14 (2): 122-124.
3. 黄悦. 跨文化交际中的非言语交际行为研究[D]. 大连：辽宁师范大学, 2012.

Unit 6 Intercultural Business Communication

Live together like brothers and do business like strangers.

—Arab Proverb

Objectives:

To understand the role of culture in business communication;

To know what intercultural business communication is;

To tell what intercultural business communication can do in today's global business world.

Warm-up Activity

Walther Habers worked for many years as commodities trader in Rotterdam. On a business trip to Milan, he waited almost two hours for his 10:00 a. m. appointment. When the Italian commodities buyer finally came out to meet him, it was time for lunch. Two hours later, after lunch, Habers walked back to the office for the meeting. By this time Habers was inwardly furious. He would miss his afternoon appointments. Being well traveled, he understood that time was treated differently in Mediterranean cultures, but this was his first experience "in the thick of it". Although he eventually made the sale, Habers swore he would never again "allow such a waste of time". The buyer from Milan, however, was never aware of any problem and thought the transaction was a great success.

Question for discussion

Identify problems and misunderstandings caused by different time systems.

Part One

Intensive Reading

Intercultural Design of Advertising and Trademark

The design of advertising and trademark is the sign of products. Intercultural design of advertising and trademark consists of language effect and cultural effect. Therefore, from the perspective of cross-cultural communication, intercultural design of trademark and advertisement should be consistent with the custom and culture of the two languages.

Design Affected by Cultural Differences

Generally speaking, if we pay enough attention to the difference between Chinese and English design of advertising and trademark, we may find that Chinese people tend to be more indirect and prefer the use of modifiers, while English people prefer to use direct and concise expressions.

1. "You" Attitude

The design of Chinese advertising and trademark usually adopts the "I" centered attitude and emphasizes the publicity of their products and services. However, the design of English advertising and trademark focuses on "you" attitude. Usually they concern more about the cultures for which the product is intended, and their selling point is how the products are able to do for the customers and how the advertising would make people feel. Coca Cola, for instance, boasts "tastes good and makes you happy", while The Ford Motor Company has chosen a translation that means "happy and unique or special". These tactics in selling products attract Chinese customers, because they believe those things are good sign and could bring them good luck.

You may find out that the successful intercultural design of advertising should not only consider culture, history, values, but also norms and traditions when promoting the product into another foreign target market. Mcdonald varies its offerings by selling beer in Germany, wine in France, mango milk shakes in Hong Kong, China and mutton pie in Australia.

2. Individualism

Many societies, like the United States, consider individualism positively and regard it as the basis for creativity and achievement; some others consider it with disapproval. The design of Chinese advertising and trademark thinks highly of the public feelings, while the design of English advertising and trademark cares more about individuality.

Chinese culture focuses on the unity, while Western culture values the individualism and characteristic, which also reflects in the advertising, such as Nike's "just do it", and "I can". The success of nike's advertising is partly because the brand boasts personal pursuance, effort and individuality.

You may point out that Nike is also quite popular in China. Yes, we can not deny the fact that China as a society is collectivist. However, to fulfill the social needs, culture must continuously evolve to reflect the best interests of a society. It is common that more and more youth groups feel at ease to accept foreign ideas. Thus, in the design of cross-cultural advertising and trademark, the advertisers should also be aware that culture is dynamic.

3. Blind Faith

The design of Chinese advertising and trademark values people's physiological need and tradition, and at the same time, the design of English advertising and trademark pays attention to people's spiritual life and creativity. Language is the carrier of culture and people's spiritual life. Having been strongly influenced by the doctrines of Buddhism, most Chinese regard death and the loss of fortune as very unpleasant topics. When the famous foreign brand of men's accessories "Goldlion" first appeared in the Chinese market with the name "金狮", it was not sold well. Because the name sounds very close to "今死" "金失" and "尽输" in some Chinese dialects. And then "Goldlion" was translated in another way. The source brand name was taken apart into "gold" and "lion". The first part was literally put into "金" to be faithful to the original, while the latter adopted the method of semantic transliteration and was put into "利来", meaning "bringing profit". From then on, "Goldlion" has achieved great success in Chinese market.

It is well-known in China that "黑猫" is a famous brand name of mobile sprayer. However, when translating into English, "Black Cat" is not proper for the countries where people generally believe in Christianity. Since some Christians regard black cat as a taboo image and the word "cat" always implies the meaning of "a mean and unpleasant woman".

Color, even the same one, symbolizes variously from country to country, and symbols in different cultures also influence people's purchasing behavior. Companies should be particularly sensitive to the choices of color in the international advertising.

Just like pink is associated with femininity in the United States, yellow is considered the most feminine color in some other parts of the world. People in many Latin American countries disapprove of purple because people in these countries usually relate purple with death; by contrast, purple signifies elegance and quality in China.

4. Different Concerns

Most Chinese learners of English mistake the writing of English ads for the translation of Chinese ones. Being unfamiliar with the style of advertising English, they cannot but resort to translation of the original Chinese version into English. Such ads might impair the images of the advertisers and our country if they appear in the international market. For when shoddy English reaches customers, they may judge the products or services to be shoddy too. English ads of this kind should be eradicated, or improved, or rewritten. Look at the following corrected version of an erroneous ad:

> Longyan Salted Crisp Peanuts are specially prepared with the imported advanced equipment and superior technology. It is extremely popular in China, and some Southeast Asian countries.

Although this improved ad is grammatically correct, it cannot hit its goal. It is not likely to secure the attention of any potential foreign buyers, because it is colourless. Note that advanced technology is given excessive emphasis in this ad. This may appeal to potential Chinese buyers but probably not to people of English-speaking countries. What is valued in their food ads is generally the products' natural flavor and freedom from pollution. Therefore, cultural differences should also be taken into consideration in our composing of English ads. For this purpose, therefore, a market research and a study of the target audience should be conducted before we write English ads.

On this basis, we can recompose the Longyan Peanuts ad as the following:

Give me Longyan Peanuts.
Or let me go nuts.

Why are Longyan Peanuts so popular at home and abroad? The crack lies in our state-of-the-art technology. The cutting edge innovations. Together with the traditional recipe. They are unrivalled. Next time, when your kids nag for some nuts, easy-to-crack, give them Longyan Peanuts.

Longyan Salted Crisp Peanuts
Savour the epicurean delicacy flavour
Oh-so-good-to-be-alive

This version is undoubtedly far more effective than the previous one because it embodies some background information and linguistic devices. The parody in the headline will immediately conjure up in the reader's mind the familiar line by the famous American poet Patric Henry, "Give me liberty, or give me death". Meanwhile "peanuts" rhymes with "nuts" and therefore helps enhance the attention value and memorability of the ad. It is often the case that people may feel more comfortable to accept the familiar things. Western people with the cultural background of knowing Patric Henry's poem, or even the rhythm of the parody previously may be easier to understand the ad and memorize the product.

The Problems in Trademark Translation and Their Solutions

A trademark is a distinctive sign which identifies certain goods or services as those produced or provided by a certain entity or person. Trademarks can be distinctive words, phrases, logos, symbols, slogans or other things that identify the source of the product and make it distinctive. Trademarks can consist of letters, numbers, sounds, smells, colors, or even product shapes used to promote and distinguish the product in the marketplace. Trademarks allow companies and businesses to distinguish their products and to prevent consumer confusion among products, and protect the meanings they've chosen to identify their products or services.

The translation of the trademark is a very practical translation action with high commercial value. It also transmits the culture from the SL (source language) to the TL (target language).

1. The Problems of the Culture in Trademark Translation

As translation is between two or more languages and different languages contain and convey different cultures, the cultural dissimilarities are the most important barriers in cross-cultural communication such as the trademark translation. Chinese trademarks have cultural characteristics.

Many translators are not aware of the cultural differences and don't pay attention to the possible barriers.

In Chinese, "喜鹊" has the meaning of "reporting the coming of spring and happiness". In English "magpie"(喜鹊) gives us the association of jaw and prolixity. Almost for the same circumstance, in Chinese, "凤凰" represents "lucky and beauty", while in English, "phoenix" means rebirth. It gives them the feeling of waking up from death. "White Elephant" translated from "白象", is regarded as rubbish in Western countries. Another example, "dragon" is always the symbol of riches, honors, power, authority and luck in the several thousands years' history in China. It is one of the most respectable animals to the Chinese. There are many Chinese idioms and stories about dragon. All the things linked with dragon are good and righteous. However, most Westerners consider dragon as the embodiment of evil and disaster. Suppose we Chinese people don't know the culture difference between us and Western countries, and we use "White Elephant" or "Dragon" as the trademark of some of our products which will be exported to foreign countries, what kind of effects will we get? It will surely cause great embarrassment or even losses.

2. Take More Negative Translated Trademarks for Example

"蓝天"—Lamp. In Chinese it is a commendatory term or at least a neuter one, and is widely used as trademarks by various products. When exported to foreign countries, it was translated into "Blue sky". However, in the international market, its sales were very bad, because the blue sky means being worthless in English.

"金鸡"—Alarm clock. Its translated version is "Golden Cock". At the first sight of this version, many foreigners could not help laughing, because cock has a very vulgar meaning and is a very strong slangy word. So there are few people who bought this kind of clock. If the word "Rooster" replaces it, it would be much better, because "Rooster" can be accepted easily and in the meantime expresses the meaning that this alarm clock is as timely as a rooster to wake you up.

"芳芳"—Lipstick. It is translated as "FangFang". In China "芳芳" is a beautiful name indeed, which are used to name girls. But in English "fang" means a dog's long sharp tooth or a snake's poison tooth. Who dares to buy this kind of lipstick? What about the free translation "Fragrance" or the transliterated version "FunFun"?

"西子"—Fancy soap. It is translated as "Shitze", which is pronounced like "Shits". "Shits" in English is a very negative word. Who would like to use the soap whose name is sound like shits for washing?

"卡卡"—Biscuit. It is translated as "KAKA". When the products arrived Russia, the Russian loaders got shocked to find that all the boxes are printed with "KAKA", because in Russian, "KAKA" refers to shit!

"马戏"—Playing cards. It is transliterated as "MAXIPUKE", which turns out to be a funny English trademark, indicating "to puke maximally"!

"大白兔"(Rabbit)—Candy. It is associated with "insecurity or a person who plays a game badly".

"乌鸡白凤丸"—"Black Cock White Phoenix Pills", together with an introduction of the product: "Black Cocks Provide the Vital Tonic for Women." The translator of this brand must have not realized that he/she is actually destroying the image of the famous brand!

"宜而爽"—Textile products. It is translated as "A Natural Fit and Comfort". A well-known brand of napkin "心相印" is translated as "Mind Acts upon Mind". Although both their meanings are closely equivalent to those of the original ones, the trademarks are too long to be good trademarks.

Transliteration, the usual method in English-Chinese trademark translation, often brings customers a kind of foreign style, indicating high quality of products. When those trademarks first occur in the market, they might inspire customers' curiosity. Since they are easy to read and remember, they became popular in China. However, having come across too many trademarks with a "foreign style", customers will become less interested in them. Nowadays, we have too many trademarks transliterated with such Chinese characters as "特" "斯" and "克", for instance, "赛特" "飞亚特" "阿尔法特" "迪斯" "真维斯" "高斯" "伊莱克斯" "别克" and "星巴克".

3. Some Examples of Successful Translated Trademarks

The meaning of a trademark includes two parts：referential meaning and associative meaning.

A well-translated trademark should not only sound pleasant，but also convey beautiful "referential and associative meaning" to customers.

The most successful example is "可口可乐"(Coca Cola). The translated version not only imitates alliteration like the original one，but also helps to arouse favorable associations of customers. The translated version has become even more successful than the original trademark. Another example is "可伶可俐"(Clean&Clear) which also achieves satisfactory effects through the similar method.

The formal beauty of a translated trademark mainly refers to its pleasant pronunciation. Different pronunciation may arouse different psychological reactions.

Many English-Chinese trademark translations sound beautiful and clear in terms of pronunciation，for instance，"派克"(Parker)，"柯达"(Kodak)，"夏普"(Sharp)，and "捷安特"(Giant).

A cosmetic brand "Relvon" is rendered as "露华浓"，which is cited from a famous classic Chinese Tang poem by Li Bai："云想衣裳花想容，春风拂槛露华浓". The translated trademark not only sounds similar to the original trademark in pronunciation，but also indicates that the cosmetic will bring beauty and elegance to women. Another brand of detergent product called "Safeguard"，is translated into Chinese as "舒肤佳"，ingeniously indicating the feature of the product. In fact，many foreign trademarks are good examples，such as "飘柔"(Rejoice)，"高露洁"(Colgate)，"奥妙"(OMO)，"锐步"(Reebok)，"雪碧"(Sprite)，"潘婷"(Pantene)，"雅芳"(Avon)，"玉兰油"(Oil of Olay)，"汰渍"(Tide)，"席梦思"(Simmons)，"奔腾"(Pentium)，"固特异"(Goodyear)，"佳洁士"(Crest)，and "强生"(Johnson's). All those translations bravely break the bound of the original meaning. They cleverly combine phonetic transcription and semantic manipulation by exploiting the advantage of Chinese characters to fit the different features of different products.

Some Chinese trademarks are also well translated in the similar way. "瑞鹊"，a brand of plastic utensil has its English name called "Richway"，which not only avoids possible unfavorable association aroused by literal translation， but also brings customers good blessings. Some other Chinese trademarks are also well rendered. For instance, "雅戈尔" is translated as "Youngor", "方正" as "Founder", "万家乐" as "Macro", "海信" as "Hisense", "美的" as "Midea"(a clever combination of "my idea"), "华帝" as "Vantage", "格力" as "Gree"(looking similar to "agree"), "西冷" as "Serene" and "回力" as "Warrior".

Sometimes, according to different aesthetic values of different translators and various product features, the same trademark can be translated into different versions. For example, the trademark "Best" have several versions like "百思特" "百德" and "倍舒特" which are the trademarks for pagers, hot water heater and napkins respectively. "超级"(the brand of a kind of oatmeal) and "优博"(the brand of a kind of milk powder) are the different renderings of "Super". Another example is "Welcome", which is translated as "卫康" and "胃康" respectively for the different products of contact lens and toothpaste.

Sometimes, translators will change the original meaning of trademarks in translation according to Chinese psychology and logic. For instance, a famous French perfume called "Poison", is rendered into Chinese as "百爱神". "Goldlion" is not literally translated as "金狮", because in Chinese, "金狮" sounds the same to "金失", which means to lose money. It is translated as "金利来", which turns to mean to earn more money.

The English trademark of "宏基" is "Acer", which is a newly coined word. It breaks the traditional rules in trademark translation and fully exploits the advantage of English language. Since "A" is the first letter in the alphabet, the trademark initiated by "A" often occurs in the beginning part of product list, thus can easily draw the attention of customers. "Acer" looks similar to "Ace", so it would easily arouse the association of "outstanding" and "excellent".

"Legend"(联想), "Serene"(西冷), "Frestech"(新飞), "MAXAM"(美加净), "Skyworth"(创维), "Shinco"(新科), and "Gree"(格力) are all examples of successful trademark internationalization.

(张春柏. 商务英语写作[M]. 北京:高等教育出版社,2001.)

Vocabulary

tactic *n.*	a plan for attaining a particular goal
transliteration *n.*	a transcription from one alphabet to another
femininity *n.*	the trait of behaving in ways considered typical for women
impair *vt.*	make worse or less effective
eradicate *vt.*	destroy completely, as if down to the roots
erroneous *adj.*	containing or characterized by error
conjure *vt.*	bring into existence
trademark *n.*	a formally registered symbol identifying the manufacturer or distributor of a product
righteous *adj.*	characterized by or proceeding from accepted standards of morality or justice
vulgar *adj.*	lacking refinement or cultivation or taste
slangy *adj.*	expressed in slang
alliteration *n.*	use of the same consonant at the beginning of each stressed syllable
render *vt.*	give something useful or necessary

Exercises

A. Words in Use

Fill in the blanks with the words given below. Change the form when necessary. Each word can be used only once.

tactic	impair	eradicate	conjure	vulgar
erroneous	righteous	femininity	render	slangy

1. A walk in the fresh air soon __________ her headache away.
2. __________ punishment is a thousand light years away from revenge.
3. The team won the game thanks to Jeff's fabulous spot __________.
4. She kept her __________ even in greasy overalls.
5. Loud noise would __________ your hearing.
6. Two doctors __________ the help at the accident.
7. The government has a fundamental interest in __________ racial discrimina-

tion in education.

8. In fact, hacker culture values informal, __________ and humorous language used with precision.
9. We must oppose these __________ trends of thought.
10. The vice premier led a __________ life in his hometown after he resigned.

B. Questions for Discussion

1. Do you think unawareness of cultural differences in advertising is a serious problem? Why or why not?
2. Discuss why the following marketing strategies don't work:

   (1) A soft drink was introduced into Arab countries with an attractive label that had six-pointed stars on it.

   (2) Pepsodent tried to sell its toothpaste in Southeast Asia by emphasizing that it "whitens your teeth".

   (3) One company printed the "OK" finger sign on each page of its catalogue and wanted to sell the products in Latin America.

C. Translation

1. The design of advertising and trademark is the sign of products. Intercultural design of advertising and trademark consists of language effect and culture effect.
2. The design of Chinese advertising and trademark usually adopts the "I" centered attitude and emphasizes the publicity of their products and services. However, the design of English advertising and trademark focuses on "you" attitude. Usually they concern more about the cultures for which the product is intended, and their selling point is how the products are able to do for the customers and how the advertising would make people feel.
3. The design of Chinese advertising and trademark values peoples physiological need and tradition, at the same time, the design of English advertising and trademark pays attention to peoples spiritual life and creativity.
4. A trademark is a distinctive sign which identifies certain goods or services as those produced or provided by a certain entity or person. Trademarks can be distinctive words, phrases, logos, symbols, slogans or other things that identify the source of the product and make it distinctive.

D. Case Study

Case 1

Mountain Bell Company tried to promote its telephone and services to Saudis. Its ad portrayed an executive talking on the phone with his feet propped up on the desk, showing the soles of his shoes.

Question

This ad didn't work. Can you explain why?

Case 2

There is a well-known foreign brand of beverage in China, that is, Coca Cola. The Chinese meaning of "Coca Cola" is "古柯", which is a kind of tropical shrub. At first, when we heard this name, nobody wanted to drink it. Cocaine, an illicit drug, is refined from Coca's leaves. But nowadays it has made a great profit in the Chinese market. Why? Mostly because they advertised the brand as "可口可乐".

The newly designed trademark not only eliminate customers' fear, but also is coincident with the pronunciation. What's more, it has a good and significant tasty meaning. "Cola" is translated into "可乐", which accords well with the Chinese nation's traditional deep love for a lucky name. We Chinese always attach importance to the name's meaning: we usually try our best to get a good name that contains many active meanings. "可乐" is undoubtedly the best choice. And as a whole, "Coca Cola" is an alliteration, and "可口可乐" also sounds harmoniously. They are easy to read loud and remember. Whenever we hear the name "可口可乐", we will get a cool feeling. So we can say this brand is a successful trademark.

Questions

1. What does "可口可乐" mean in Chinese?
2. Can you explain the brand Sprite in a similar way?

Part Two

Extensive Reading

Cultural Influences on Context: The Business Setting

There is a well-known saying that everyone has to be someplace. This article is about those place-settings where communication events occur. Communication is not devoid of external influence: all human interaction is influenced to some degree by the social, physical, and cultural settings in which it occurs. This is known as the communication context.

Generally, when we communicate with members of our own culture, we have internalized the cultural rules that govern the behavior within the context, and we are able to communicate without giving much thought to those rules. But when we are engaged in intercultural communication, we must be aware of how our culture influences the communication context; otherwise, we may encounter a variety of surprises. We start here by discussing the relationship between communication and context, and then we examine how it functions in the business setting.

Culture and the Business Context

Many countries are not directly tied to an international system of economic interdependence, and most countries have at least one asset within their borders that is needed by another country. No country is completely self-sufficient. As a result, never before in history has the business arena portrayed such global qualities. Many of our products, from the cars we drive to the clothes we wear, are manufactured by foreign companies. Even Tropicana apple juice contains concentrates from Austria, Italy, Hungary, and Argentina.

The increase in globalization is a result of growth in U. S. and foreign multinational industries since the 1960s. Multinational corporations increasingly participate in various international business arrangements. Joint ventures or "cooperative arrangements between two or more organizations that share in the ownership of a business undertaking" are quite common. Licensing agreements in which one company grants to another company the "rights to trademarks, patents, copyrights or know-how for a fee" are also common. A joint venture between a U. S. multinational corporation and a company in Peru to manufacture chemicals, rayon, acetate, and other fibers results in a licensing agreement in which the local partner pays a royalty for process and product technology as well as profits earned.

Turnkey projects are "contracts for the construction of an operating facility that is transferred to the owner once it is finished and ready for operations". An example of a turnkey project can be found in the Bechtel Corporation, which builds many oil refineries and gasoline processing plants throughout the world.

Subcontracts have also become commonplace. An example of a subcontract can be found in the maquiladora plants along the border between United States and Mexico. Finally, management contracts have also increased dramatically over the last decade. In management contracts, one company provides another company with managerial expertise for a fee. For instance, a U. S. multinational corporation has entered into a management contract through a joint venture in Thailand to produce appliances. The multinational corporation provides production, technical, and marketing management for five years for a fixed fee.

These numerous international business arrangements often result in individuals from one culture working not only with, but for individuals from another culture. The most successful firms in the global arena will be companies whose employees not only understand world economics and global competitiveness but also have the ability to communicate effectively with international counterparts. International managers are expected to be competent and cosmopolitan, but often they are not. This challenge exists because even a seemingly universal concept like "management" can be viewed differently from culture to culture. We now turn our attention toward the views various cultures hold regarding management and managers.

Cultural Views toward Management and Managers

Dominant managerial values in the United States include achievement and success, belief in hard work, pragmatism, optimism, puritanism, rationality, impersonality in interpersonal work relationships, equality of opportunity, acceptance of competition, and individualism. This set of values is not cross-culturally consistent.

In Germany, the manager is not a cultural hero. In fact, Germans do not have a strong concept of management. The reason for this is that Germany has historically honored the worker who possesses exceptionally high occupational skills and qualifications. As such, Germany has an apprenticeship system that culminates in a skill certificate recognized throughout the country. The highly skilled and responsible German workers do not necessarily need a manager, American-style, to motivate them. They expect their boss or meister to assign their tasks and to be the expert in resolving technical problems. Germany has one of the world's lowest rates of personnel in leadership and staff roles. As such, managers are usually vice president or department heads. Their dominant values include a strong sense of professional calling and pride in work, a tendency toward an authoritarian leadership style, and a paternalistic commitment to the country's welfare. From a German perspective, effective managers are self-confident, energetic, open-minded, and particularly competitive.

As was the case with the Germans, the Japanese do not share a strong sense on management. For them, the key component of the organization is the "worker group". This worker group can expect lifelong employment and advancement according to seniority. A Japanese manager's constituency is his or her employees. Instead of growth, an important focus for Japanese managers is keeping men in good-paying jobs in order to maintain social stability. Because of this system of lifetime employment that focuses on the worker group, the Japanese are to a large extent controlled by their peer group rather than by their manager. Manager-section chiefs or department heads value groupism, harmony, acceptance of hierarchy in work relationships, sense of obligation, and debt of lower level personnel to superiors, and consensual decision making.

Management style in France also differs from the style in the United States. Whereas in the United States it is assumed that managers and employees have a fair contract between themselves, in France each class is honored in what has been labeled a stratified society. That is, managers act in very superior roles. In France, employee not only accept rigid role positions, but expect them. That is, subordinates are aware of their place in the societal hierarchy. They do, however, feel honor toward their own class. The French value this high power differential. Additional values include individualism and authority based on absolutism. Because French managers or cadres are well paid, have attended the best schools, and come from well-established families, they tend to have an elitist approach to management. This elitism is very different from the perspective in mainland China. Hofstede summarizes the Chinese view:

> Overseas Chinese American enterprises lack almost all characteristics of modern management. They tend to be small, cooperating for essential functions with other small organizations through networks based on personal relations. They are family

> owned, without the separation between ownership and management typical in the West, or even in Japan and Korea. Decision making is centralized in the hands of one dominant family member, but other family members may be given new ventures to try their skill on. They are low-profile and extremely cost-conscious, applying Confucian virtues of thrift and persistence. Their size is kept small by the assumed lack of loyalty of non-family employees, who, if they are any good, will just wait and save until they can start their own family business.

Chinese business values also emphasize kinship, interpersonal connections, respect for elders, and hierarchy. These values are a result of three decades of Communism, which stresses a collectivistic society. Despite a recent move to a market economy, factories and larger businesses in China still reflect past collectivistic characteristics. For example, in the collectivistic society, the government provides jobs for all as well as cradle-to-grave social welfare for workers and their families. This system in China is known as "the Iron Rice Bowl".

Because of the impact of social history, business management in China is affected by interpersonal connections. In business management, a group relationship is manifested in interpersonal connections (*guanxi*), which overpower the formal organizational structure in many cases. Business contracts are often specified in legal terms but implemented relying on trust and relationships between the parties involved.

We see yet another difference in managerial approaches when we look at Mexico and Latin America. The Mexican and Latin American managerial style has often been characterized as autocratic and paternalistic. Despite the fact that these countries are in a rapidly changing business transition, causing higher level employees to be less accepting of autocratic management, the autocratic style stands in sharp contrast to the egalitarian concept of management in the United States.

As a result of this authoritarian but honorable business system, dominant managerial values include centralized decision making among a few top-level managers, the self-presentation of status by executives, and a delicate balance between maintaining formal respect in the hierarchy and portraying informal sensitivity toward workers' dignity.

From this examination of various cultural views regarding management styles and managers, you can appreciate how a business procedure, often thought of as universal, differ from culture to culture. Because of the cultural diversity in the global economy, you may soon find yourself employed by an organization that transacts business with people from many different cultures. You may find yourself managing, being managed by, or co-managing with members of other cultures. Your ability to succeed in these situations will very much depend on your skills as an intercultural business communicator. With this in mind, we now move from broad cultural views of management to differences in business protocol, negotiation, and views toward women.

Culture-Specific Business Practices—Business Protocol

In most parts of the world, correct protocol is essential. To introduce you to some of the variations in protocol, we start with the elements that help initiate business relationships: appointment seeking, greeting behavior, and gift giving.

1. Appointment Seeking

The protocol for orchestrating an initial contact and appointment to conduct business can range from making a telephone call to using a "go-between" or an emissary. The manner in which the initial business contact is made and the amount of advance notice between the contact and appointment are key factors to consider when doing business with another culture. A few examples will clarify this point. In EI Salvador and much of Latin America, including Mexico, appointments must be made a month in advance by mail or telephone and then followed up one week before the meeting. In the Latin American culture, you should establish your contacts as high up in the organization as possible.

When doing business in China, it is important to establish contacts before you invest in a trip. Arranging appointments can be assisted with local Chinese businesses and government officials. To do business in Saudi Arabia, you must have a sponsor act as an intermediary, make appointments, and arrange meetings. In Italy as well, strong contacts who can represent you and make appropriate introductions are preferred. Even with such a representative, it is important that your initial contact be written in Italian.

The date you plan your business trip is also of major importance when dealing with another culture. For example, in China, many businesses close the week before and the week after the Chinese New Year. In Saudi Arabia, no business is conducted during Eid al-Fitr—the three-day festival of Breaking Fast at the end of the month of Ramadan. In Japan, business is not conducted during New Year's holidays, Golden Week, April 29 to May 5, and Obon, in mid-August, because many people travel to the graves of their ancestors. In Israel, the Jewish holy day, the Sabbath begins at sunset on Friday and ends at sunset on Saturday. Therefore, the business week runs from Sunday through Thursday. Conducting business on the Sabbath would be highly inappropriate.

2. Greeting Behavior

Once a meeting has been arranged, it is important that the greeting protocol of the host culture be observed. Americans tend to be informal and friendly. Both men and women shake hands on meeting and leaving. A small kiss on the cheek or a hug is appropriate between women or between men and women who have known each other for a long time. First names generally are used with the exception of senior persons or formal situations. Business cards are exchanged in business settings but not in social settings. However, the greeting behaviors typical to North Americans are uncommon in many cultures. For instance, in Saudi Arabia, greetings involve numerous handshakes and tend to be expressive and elaborate. Saudi men often embrace and kiss on both cheeks. Saudi women are rarely present for business meetings, but when they are, an introduction is unlikely. Titles are very important for Saudis and are always used. Business cards are routinely exchanged and are printed in both Arabic and English.

China offers a contrasting example. Here, Westerners normally receive a brief handshake on meeting, but a more common form of greeting is a nod or bow from the shoulders. Chinese greetings are formal and use titles and last names. First names are used only among close friends. Again, business cards are translated into standard Chinese and are routinely exchanged. In Finland, firm handshakes are the normal greeting for men and women. And it is customary for women to be greeted first. So important is a firm handshake to the Finnish that even children are encouraged to shake hands. However, hugs and kisses are reserved for greetings with close friends and family. Introductions include first and last names or a title and a last name. As a final example of cultural variations in greeting behavior, in India, the traditional greeting is the Namaste, formed by pressing the palms together, fingers up, below the chin. A slight bow may be added to show respect.

3. Gift Giving

An old adage in the United States says, "Be ware of Greeks bearing gifts." Most Americans view gift giving in the business setting as a form of bribery, but for many cultures, gift giving is a standard part of business protocol. As such, it is important to know not only the views concerning gift giving, but also what gifts are appropriate for the culture with which you will be doing business.

Examples of gift giving in Japan can illustrate this point effectively. Gifts are very common in the Japanese culture. Business gifts absolutely must be given at midyear and at year end. They are often given at first business meetings. It is also a standard practice to bring flowers, cakes, or candy when invited to a Japanese home. The ceremony of gift giving is more important to the Japanese than the gift itself, although modest and elaborate gifts are prevalent. It is appropriate to allow your Japanese business colleagues to present gifts first, and then match your gift with the same quality as theirs. Do not expect gifts to be opened directly in front of you because this may be construed as a sign of greed. You should not open gift in front of your Japanese business colleagues, but instead open them when you are alone and thank them later. The paper the gift is wrapped in is also very important to the Japanese. Rice paper is ideal; paper that Americans consider appropriate is distasteful to the Japanese. Although items made by well-known manufacturers are usually good gifts, you should avoid giving knives and scissors because these items symbolize the severance of the relationship. A clock also is an inappropriate gift because it reminds the recipient that time is running out. To give a clock as a gift is equivalent to saying, "I wish you were dead!" Gifts with even numbers of components are also highly inappropriate in Japan, particularly in numbers of four, which could be considered the equivalent of the inauspicious number 13 in the United States. As the preceding example indicates, the rules for gift giving in Japan are very different from the rules for gift giving in the United States. Even when visiting a home in the United States, it is not customary to bring a gift, although a small token of flowers, a plant, or a bottle of wine is appreciated. Instead of gifts, letters of thanks are standard in the United States.

We have covered only a few elements of business protocol to make the point that business practices differ from culture to culture. This introduction to variations in protocol should amplify the importance of knowing and acting on the business practices that are acceptable in the culture in which you will be doing business. With such differences in protocol, there are also numerous variations from culture to culture in negotiation strategies. We now turn our attention to this important matter.

Culture-Specific Business Practices—Negotiation

A major difference in cross-cultural negotiation is the pace at which negotiations are conducted. North American, Australian, Swiss, British, and Singapore negotiators value rapid negotiations, whereas other cultures such as China, Japan, much of Latin America, and Africa prefer slower negotiations. The pace of the negotiation process is but one example of cross-cultural negotiation differences. Direct versus indirect communication is often problematic in business dealings as well. In negotiations with many cultures, a "yes" really means "no". In some cultures, personal relationships take priority over the product or service, and therefore business does not begin until friendships are established.

Decision making, "top down" versus group decisions, risk taking versus prudence, and individual values versus collective values also complicate the negotiation process. In order that you understand these differences, we first turn our attention to some specific strategies for negotiation. Next, we consider what forms of evidence are acceptable for various cultures. Finally, we examine societal trust as a negotiation variable.

1. Strategies

Americans grow up believing in the motto "He who hesitates is lost". Therefore, most Americans conduct business at a lightning speed. It is not uncommon for contracts to be signed during the first business meeting. These rapid contracts are facilitated by the fact that middle managers have the authority to make quick decisions without consulting the "boss" or conferring with the group. Sales forces are taught to "close the deal" as rapidly as possible. Brief small talk often precedes the business interaction, but the "bottom-line", short-term rewards, and financial arrangements quickly become the focus. In most instances, whether the business person is a man or a woman is largely irrelevant. Prior contacts are helpful but not necessary because a person's last successes are deemed more important. Business cards are exchanged, but generally only when the parties wish to do business in the future. Communication is usually indirect, informal, competitive, and at times argumentative.

In much of Latin America, business negotiations are conducted at a much slower pace than in the United States. There is even a proverb that states, "To a hurried demand, a leisurely reply." In Argentina, it may take several trips to accomplish your goal, partly because it takes several people to approve each decision that is made. Personal relationships are so important that if you do not have a contact or intermediary, you may well never get an appointment. For this same reason, Argentines prefer to deal with the same representative for each transaction, or the whole negotiation process begins again from scratch.

In Mexico, too, relationships are important, and a great deal of time is spent building rapport before business proceeds. Mexicans are very expressive, and interactions often involve loud exchanges. These exchanges should not be taken personally, since embarrassing one's counterpart is generally avoided. Success in much of Latin America is tied to appearances. Business executives dress fashionably and expect their counterparts to embody this same aura of success.

Negotiation in Eastern Europe is also different from that in the United States. In Poland, Hungary, and Russia, the time it takes to negotiate business usually depends on whether or not the government is involved. When it is, negotiations proceed at an unhurried pace. However, when you deal with entrepreneurs, transactions can progress rapidly. Business cards are important and are given to everyone with whom you come into contact. Business laws in Eastern Europe are in a state of flux; therefore, having a legal representative present is often a good idea. Direct, factual communication is important to Russians. Negotiations are often spirited and dramatic, with the Russian negotiator insisting the deal is over and storming out of the room, only to return to the negotiation table a short time later.

In Western Europe, negotiations also progress in a different manner. For the French, business is a very formal issue, and any appearance of a casual attitude will derail the transaction. Their eye contact tends to be so intense that even North Americans may feel intimidated. French negotiators are often reserved. In Germany, business is also conducted very formally with great attention to order, planning, and schedules. Because of this slow methodical process, it is virtually impossible to speed up a business transaction. Humor, compliments, and personal questions are not a part of German negotiations. Instead, business may begin immediately after an introduction. It is important to be well prepared when conducting business in Germany. It is better to be silent rather than offer an uneducated opinion. Although the Dutch are also straightforward and efficient in negotiations, business is conducted at a slower pace than in the United States. The Dutch are not hagglers, so they tend to place importance on the "bottom line". Humor is downplayed, but personal integrity is very important.

Swedes are also very serious about business. They show little emotion during negotiation and expect the same from you. Consensus is important to Swedish negotiators and they tend to avoid confrontation. They may cut off a discussion abruptly if they think it will lead to an argument over a sensitive topic. In conversations, Swedes do not appreciate exaggeration or superficiality. However, silence is a part of their language pattern, so they expect interactions to be filled with long pauses. The Swiss value detail, precision, hard work, thrift, and a focus on the task at hand. Virtually every culture in Western Europe values education and longevity. As a result, it is important to include college and university degrees above the Bachelor's level and your company's founding date on your business card.

In the Middle East, business transactions have a different flavor as well. In Israel, a strong sense of fatalism pervades the business environment. This possibly is due to the fact that neighboring countries have been hostile to Israel and have frequently attempted to destroy it. As a result, successful business deals in Israel must promise an immediate return. Long-term guarantees are rarely selling points. Israelis are confrontational and emotional in their negotiating style. Interactions are conducted at very close distances, and physical contact is common among men, but not with women. Face-saving and the avoidance of shame are crucial to both Saudis and Egyptians.

Despite many commonalities, each culture has its unique negotiation style. For example, in South Korea, you may be asked the same question repeatedly because Koreans are trying to make sure they are correct in their decisions. In Japan, it is important to incorporate the words "I am sorry" into your vocabulary, not as a form of ingratiation but as a form of politeness. In Indonesia, there is such a great deference to superiors that subordinates will tell them exactly what they want to hear rather than the truth. The superior will then be told the truth later in private by means of informal channels. In China. all collateral materials should be printed in black and white because colors have great significance for the Chinese. Hong Kong China negotiators, perhaps because of their Western exposure, tend to be more direct and quick-paced.

2. Sources of Truth

The French have a saying: "Only truth is beautiful." It is also relative, for an important part of the negotiation process is determining what form of truth is acceptable and/or believable. That is, there are many different kinds of truth in the world, and the source of "truth" for a culture can heavily influence business transactions. Whereas many cultures, including the United States, rely on the accumulation of objective facts, other cultures may trust subjective opinions, religious beliefs, and/or mysticism. For successful business negotiations to occur, it is important to understand the form of evidence or truth the culture you are doing business with prefers.

In much of Latin America, decisions are often based on subjective data that are usually influenced by the Catholic church or political affiliations. Facts are accepted only if they support subjective feelings. Faith in the Catholic church as a source of truth often results in a strong sense of fatalism among people in Latin America. This sense of fatalism extends into business transactions. Proverbs such as "If your trouble has some remedy, why worry? And if it has no cure, again why worry?" and "Tomorrow is another day" reflect this outlook.

In Eastern Europe, countries are shifting from subjective faith in a communistic ideology to a reliance on more objective facts and reasoning. Western Europe has traditionally relied heavily on analytical, objective facts as the focus of evidence. The locus of these facts is based in ideologies of democracy in

Germany and the social welfare state in Sweden. However, in Switzerland, the segments of the population that are not German or French rely on subjective feelings based on faith in nationalism and utopian ideas.

Middle Eastern countries tend to value their religious faith as the primary source of evidence and truth. For instance, in Israel, subjective faith in Judaism and the success and security of the nation are prominent influences. In Egypt and Saudi Arabia, faith in Islamic ideas forms the basis of all truth. Objective facts may support Islamic ideologies for many Egyptians, but for most Saudis, objective facts seldom overrule their faith.

In South Korea, decisions are often based on nationalistic ideologies, and one's feelings are supported by the ideology of the group and wholeness. In Hong Kong China, reliance on some objective facts is becoming common. Chinese philosophy, which is founded in ideologies of universal order and harmony, has an impact on business. That is, ancient beliefs and religious practices are very much a part of Chinese business dealings today. Two such ritualistic practices are reliance on the lunar calendar and the use of "diviners" or a "*feng shui*" man to determine auspicious dates and arrangements for meetings, opening new offices, moving, and so forth. It should be clear by now that criteria for defining truth are culture-bound.

3. Trust

Another variable that confounds cross-cultural business negotiation is the issue of trust. We have alluded to the fact that establishing trust before conducting business is very important in several cultures, but it is also necessary to consider the trust level of the society as a whole in determining the potential for successful business negotiations.

Trust or social capital has a profound impact on business from the transaction itself to the entire economic growth. Cultures can be placed on a continuum of high trust to low trust. For example, cultures such as Germany, Japan, and the United States are high-trust oriented in their business dealings. They have a marked proclivity toward association with other cultures. Their trust in dealing with other cultures has allowed them to create large, private business organizations. It is no accident that the world's best-known brand names come from countries that are also good at creating large organizations. In contrast, in low-trust societies like China, France, and Italy, the reluctance to trust non-kin has resulted in many small family businesses.

The cultures of the world are becoming dependent on one another. As a result, the most useful kind of social capital is often not the ability to work under the authority of a traditional community or group, but the capacity to form new associations and to cooperate within the terms of reference they establish. It appears that social capital or trust needs to be factored into cross-cultural business issues.

Culture-Specific Business Practices—Women

The role of women in international business is another area of particular importance in cross-cultural communication. As you might suspect, that role is directly linked to the values of each culture. Women constitute a large proportion of the world's workforce and therefore demand our attention. Comparing attitudes toward women in the international business setting helps us understand how women are perceived and treated in various cultures.

Because of the male-dominated business environment in Eastern Europe, it is extremely rare to find female negotiators. On the other hand, Western Europe is less chauvinistic. Sweden has one of the highest percentages of women in the world's workforce. In France and Italy, women can effectively negotiate, but they should expect gallant and often flirtatious behavior from males. The Dutch, at least by American standards, are somewhat chauvinistic, but American women can negotiate successfully in this male-dominated society. In Spain, macho and chauvinistic attitudes toward women prevail, and only certain roles are appropriate for women in business. Germany is one of the most difficult business environments for women.

Israel is the most favorable country in the Middle East for businesswomen. Although there are male-dominated values, women have considerable influence inside and outside of the home. Nonetheless, strict behavior codes dictate what a business-woman can and cannot do. For instance, foreign women should not offer to shake hands with an Israeli. Even in the exchange of business cards, a woman must place the card on the table for the man to pick up rather than touching him. Egypt tends to be less sex segregated than the remaining Middle East countries, improving the possibility of successful negotiation by women, but their presence in the business environment is a rarity. Saudi Arabia is one of the most difficult countries in the world for women to engage in business.

Hong Kong China is the most favorable place for women to negotiate. Women are even part of many important negotiating teams. Taiwan China, Thailand, Singapore, and Japan also offer somewhat favorable business environments for women; however, Japanese men are still uncomfortable with women in positions of power. In South Korea, it is rare to have women participate in business. In South Korea, men have higher social status than women. Korean women may even open doors and allow men to pass through first.

Although global changes are taking place to improve the role of women in business settings, women from these countries who have the opportunity to conduct business internationally often find that they are considered "foreign executives" who are expected to be very good at what they do or else their firms would not have sent them abroad. With the realization that many of the qualities sought after in the international manager—communication skills, ability to establish rapport, listening skills, sensitivity, and interpersonal abilities have been traditionally viewed as a part of the female role in many cultures, there may slowly come a concomitant increase worldwide in women in the international business arena.

We should be aware of the important influence culture has on the conduct of business. Therefore, we implore you to heed the words of President John F. Kennedy: "The greater our knowledge increases, the greater our ignorance unfolds."

(SAMOVAR L A, PORTER R E, STEFANI L A. Communication between cultures[M]. 1st ed. Beijing: Foreign Language Teaching and Research Press, 2000.)

Language focus

asset *n.* 资产；有利条件	portray *vt.* 描绘；扮演
expertise *n.* 专门知识；专家的意见	pragmatism *n.* 实用主义
apprenticeship *n.* 学徒期；学徒身份	culminate *vt.* 使达到顶点
paternalistic *adj.* 家长式作风的	constituency *n.* 选民；支持者
hierarchy *n.* 等级制度	consensual *adj.* 在双方同意下成立的
rigid *adj.* 严格的	subordinate *n.* 下属
absolutism *n.* 专制主义	elitist *n.* 优秀人才；精英
thrift *n.* 节俭	kinship *n.* 亲属关系

protocol *n.* 协议；礼仪
emissary *n.* 使者；间谍
bribery *n.* 贿赂
rapport *n.* 关系；亲善；一致
affiliation *n.* 从属关系
allude *vi.* 暗指
gallant *adj.* 勇敢的；华丽的
orchestrate *vt.* 精心安排
intermediary *n.* 仲裁者；调解者
prevalent *adj.* 流行的；普遍的
fatalism *n.* 宿命论
utopian *adj.* 乌托邦的
proclivity *n.* 倾向
flirtatious *adj.* 轻浮的

Exercises

A. Text Reading

Decide whether the following statements are true (T) or false (F).

1. ______ Apart from the necessary understanding of world economics and global competitiveness, the employees of companies in the global arena should also have the ability to communicate effectively with international counterparts.
2. ______ Japanese do not have a strong concept of management.
3. ______ When visiting a home in the United States, it is a standard practice to bring a small token of flowers.
4. ______ Japanese place importance on the direct, factual communication.
5. ______ The sense of humor is very important for the Dutch.
6. ______ While American managers emphasize supervisory style, decision making, and control mechanism, the Japanese are more concerned with communication process, interdepartmental relations, and paternalistic approach.
7. ______ The source of evidence and truth in one culture may not be the source of evidence and truth in another.
8. ______ Many Latin Americans are far more impressed with affect and emotion than logic.
9. ______ Asian countries generally rely on objective interpretations as the source of evidence or truth.
10. ______ Women are also part of the global economy in the workforce.

B. Terms Understanding

Find the definitions of the following terms in the text. If you cannot find the exact definition, try to use your own words to interpret it.

1. communication context
2. turnkey projects
3. subcontracts

C. Classroom Activities

1. Demonstrate that how business protocol differs among cultures.
2. Discuss in group about some recent observations in advertisements that reflect diversity.
3. Work in pairs and exchange views on the meanings of the following proverbs; then try to find out their Chinese equivalents if there is any.

   Proverb 1: The nail that sticks up gets hammered down.

   Proverb 2: The squeaky wheel gets the grease.

Part Three

Academic Reading

Cross-Cultural Influence on Management of Multinational Corporations

With the development of high technology, the number of multinational corporations is growing steadily and their business fields are expanding. Therefore, more and more executives and technicians will be working in multicultural environments. Because of this, the global manager must create new paradigms to meet the demand of the management. If they are to operate effectively in a complex world market, cross-cultural education, training and development will become necessary for those in management positions.

This paper aims to present the cross-cultural impact on the management of the multinational corporation. Firstly, the necessity and importance of cross-cultural study for the global manager will be analyzed theoretically and illustrated with examples. Secondly, the benefits and advantages of cross-cultural research in managing and marketing will be explained. After that, the author introduces some of the skills and competencies of intercultural communication associated with effectiveness in multicultural environments. And finally, the approaches of gaining the skills and competencies will be presented.

Our world is becoming a global village. Thanks to technological advances that transcend time and space, we will increasingly communicate with and perhaps live next to those who are not cultural replicas of ourselves. With the development of cross-cultural communication and business transactions, the world is becoming smaller and smaller in a sense. Meanwhile, the space for business is growing bigger and bigger. Today multinational corporations have sprung up like mushrooms in many parts of the world, and people of different nationalities work together. Multinational corporations, known as the global company, see the world as one market. It minimizes the importance of national boundaries and manufactures and markets its goods wherever it can do the best job. Many executives and technicians working in multicultural environments may be puzzled by the following questions:

(1) What do I have to know about the social and business customs of country X ?

(2) What skills do I need to be effective as a negotiator in country Y?

(3) What prejudices and stereotypes do I have about the people in country Z?

(4) How do these influence my interaction and can we cooperate harmoniously?

Because of this situation, our conception of reality changes as we create a new image of our species, its place and purpose in existence. Global managers must create new paradigms (a paradigm is a conceptual model that influences our basic way of perceiving, valuing, thinking and action, a particular version of reality). Effective management of the global corporation depends on far more than the managerial function and international business. There are also other factors which may influence the management of the world corporation and these factors go far beneath the surface, reaching far into cross-cultural communication. So the study of cultural influences on managing the multinational corporations will do much to increase understanding between the global managers and their staff and hence facilitate the management.

This paper will first analyze the necessity of cross-cultural study for global managers. Then it will explain the benefits and advantages of cross-cultural research in managing the world corporation. After that, it goes to the skills and competencies of intercultural communication associated with effectiveness in a multicultural environment. Finally, it will introduce some of the approaches of gaining the skills and competencies.

The Importance and Necessity of Cross-Cultural Study for Global Managers

Culture teaches us what to value and what to fear, which behavioral signals to watch for from others and which to send, which word to use and which to avoid. It guides everything from our method of reasoning and our choice of mates to our working patterns.

Culture can be divided into material aspect—the products, people's art and technology, and non-material aspect—people's customs, beliefs, values and patterns of communication. All of the customs, beliefs, values, knowledge and skills that guide a nation's behavior among shared paths are part of their culture. The multinational corporations have their subsidiaries in different countries and these subsidiaries will be affected by the culture of the community that surrounds them. The managers anticipate that other people will act as they do and their standards for behavior have pretty much the same meaning around the world. But this is usually not the case. So when the managers and technicians work in another culture, they find themselves in situations for which they are unprepared.

Each country has its own folkways, norms and taboos. When doing business abroad, the seller must examine the way consumers in different countries think about and use certain products before planning a marketing program. There are often surprises. For example, the average Frenchman uses almost twice as much cosmetics and beauty aids as does his wife. The Germans and the French eat more packaged, branded spaghetti than do Italians. If the global manager knows nothing about matters like these, the marketing plan must be a failure.

Business norms and behavior also vary from country to country. Here are some examples of different global business behavior:

South Americans like to sit or stand very close to each other when they talk business, in fact, almost nose-to-nose. The American business executive tends to keep backing away as the South American moves closer. Both may thus end up being offended.

In face-to-face communications, Japanese business executives rarely say "No" to an American business executive. Thus, Americans tend to be frustrated and may not know where they stand. Americans come to the point quickly. Japanese business executives may find this behavior offensive.

Not surprisingly, interaction among people of different cultures is often filled with uncertainties and even difficulties. Such differences can have serious consequences. Usually, the case of the serious problem is not due to personality factors but due to the ineffective communications or misunderstandings of the verbal and non-verbal communication systems. Cultural differences are barriers and impede communication and interaction. In order to overcome these barriers, one should understand the cultural differences between one's own and another. What's more, management of the multinational corporation is not an isolated subject. It has close connections with cultural elements. When people communicate with one another, there must be assumptions about the process of perceiving, judging and thinking and reasoning patterns. When the assumption is correct, there is ease of communication. But when they are incorrect, misunderstanding and miscommunication arise and these of course would affect the management.

Intercultural Study Benefits the Management of Multinational Corporations

Knowledge about cultures, both general and specific, provides insight into the learned behaviors of groups. It helps the learner to gain awareness of what makes a people unique. The factors are its customs and traditions, its values and beliefs, attitudes and concepts, hierarchies and roles, time and space relations, and verbal and non-verbal communication processes. Information gained in cross-cultural studies will enable managers to become more cosmopolitan, to cope more effectively abroad, to reduce stress and resolve conflict more readily in the international business area.

Now with the open-door policy, many enterprises have involved in international trade. Those engaged in the import-export trade, depending on their understanding and skills in the cross-cultural relations, could either advance or hamper their sales and exchanges. Transcultural studies benefit employees as the following:

(1) Facilitate adjustment and productivity in a foreign country or at home with minority cultures.

It's known that the policy of China's opening out has attracted many foreigners to invest in China. We have set up joint ventures, contractual joint ventures and solely foreign-owned enterprises in our country. Sometimes there are disputed and clashes between the foreign manager and Chinese employees. Some of the disputes arose from the misunderstanding caused by cross-cultural communications. And if the foreign managers knew more about Chinese managing culture, there might not have been such disputes.

(2) Foster interaction, good will and customer relations, as well as business and profits.

In a competitive society, the global manager should function like an intercultural researcher seeking various ways to establish good relationship with his customers. The partner's behaviors are strongly affected by cultural, social, personal and psychological factors. But the cultural factors exert the broadest and deepest influence on them.

(3) Improve human relation skills with foreigners, minorities or ethnic group representatives.

Human relation skills with foreigners are concerned with their cultures. One example will illustrate this: In China, business is discussed over lunch or dinner in the businessman's home. He will invite his foreign partner to his home. But in India, to discuss business at home or at any social function is a violation of hospitality rules.

(4) Offer better understanding of both domestic and international markets.

To be successful, good market research project requires as much careful planning as a well-designed product. Market researches include cultural differences in a foreign market. For example, orange juice is not a breakfast drink in France; Middle Easterners prefer spicy toothpaste; people in the Philippines prefer black shampoo for their blackhair; the Japanese like rice and tuna for breakfast. These cultural differences will help you make a successful marketing decision.

(5) Provide insight relative to organizational culture and personal behavior.

Intercultural study offers us better understanding of the culture in which you are going to work. For example, one aspect of American culture is that people must work hard to accomplish their objectives (Puritan ethnic). We can see this from the corporate culture of Microsoft.

Complaining about how hard you work is like complaining about the weather in Seattle. Everyone has to overwork. Microsoft deliberately understaffs its product team because it saves money, helps communication and encourages the fighting spirit.

(6) Help one to gain a better sense of self and cultural heritage for more effective intercultural interactions.

In order to create cultural synergistic solutions to management problems or to transfer management techniques to another culture, a global manager must know his culture and management practice to manage the corporation effectively.

In a word, cross-cultural study offers better international relationships, which are bound to be enhanced when management, sales, and technical personnel can deal with cultural differences within the world market place.

Skill Required in Managing Multinational Corporations

Management of multinational corporations is not an isolated subject. Global managers function within four basic intermeshing systems: the technical system, the economic system, the political system and the cultural system. Very often the cultural system has been the least amount of consideration of the four in sofar as it relates to management practice and philosophy across different cultures. When these differences result in miscommunications and misunderstandings, they can of course affect the management.

Persons from the same culture but with a different educational background and experience often find communication difficult, let alone the communication between persons from different cultural backgrounds. Chinese managers communicating with employees from other cultures experience greater difficulties than in communication with employees from their own culture. This is because the management system is different in each country. Managers of different nationalities are shaped by the system to which they belong. If one knows the culture of the other person, then it is possible to make tentative predictions about the other's behavior.

Generally speaking, we, Chinese people, are rarely self-centered when working with others. We view with contempt the individual who tries to display personal attributes. This is because we Chinese people are more oriented to the collective. But individualism is popular among American employees. Microsoft encourages individuality, and there are plenty of eccentric characters on the staff.

Different beliefs, values and attitudes lead to different management styles. In some of the most successful American companies, such as AT&T, IBM and P&G, creating heroes is one aspect of the cultural management. The created heroes would inspire the staff by the successful routine duties. But one aspect of the Chinese cultural management is to lay emphasis on collectivism, as the Chinese saying goes, "when everyone adds fuel, the flames rise high." So collectivism is promoted among the Chinese people.

In American companies, all levels of management are open to qualified individuals. An office boy can rise to become a company president. Many people may consider this an American Dream. But this affects the management in its employment practices and promotion. A factory worker who reaches a dead end and sees himself stuck in the same job year after year may take out his aggressive feelings in fighting management or he may leave. But in Chinese companies, especially in those state-owned ones, education and backgrounds are the primary vehicles for employment practice and promotion. For a Chinese employee, a job at a certain post may be lifelong.

The above different management cultures may cause problems for the global managers. P. R. Harris and R. T. Morans, in their book *Managing Cultural Differences*, establish an approach to solving the problem of cultural differences in management techniques—Comparative Management. When we discuss international management style systems, we may ask questions such as "How do they do this in China?" "How do they make effective decisions in the USA?" We look at the two management systems and make comparisons between the two and very often we attempt to discover which system is better. In this case, there are two basic ways to approach the interaction. One is using a cultural dominance model—one cultural system dominates the other within the company, but the organization structure and management techniques are either of them. Another approach is called "Cultural Synergy". An analysis of the cultures is made in terms of similarities and differences between the two instead of making a choice from these two, and the manager would produce integrative solutions from both cultures. The integrative solutions can meet the maximum needs and requirements of the company.

Ruben, in his book, also suggested some skills for the global managers and the skills should be associated with effectiveness in a multinational environment. He refers to the skills as abilities which are universal and common sense. They are respected in mutual culture, tolerance of ambiguity, impersonal relationship with employees, avoidance of hasty judgment, personalizing one's observations, empathy and persistence. Those skills are required for effective management in a different culture. We can develop them in terms of world culture, as they grow beyond particular cultures while cherishing and respecting one's own culture.

Cross-Cultural Training in the Management of Multinational Corporations

In the last two decades, Business English has attracted increasing interest and awareness but cross-cultural training in business is deficient. In fact, time and money are wasted in case of inadequacy of cross-cultural training for management in multinational environment. So far as I know, few multinational corporations in China provide this kind of training for their expatriate employees. Usually pre-departure training which is not specially set for cross-cultural training is provided for those who are going abroad on business. Actually cross-cultural training, education and development are essential for those in management positions, especially for the multinational corporations that acquire subsidiaries abroad and send representatives to work in multicultural settings.

What is cross-cultural training? Cross-cultural training, according to Brislin and Pederson, is designed to teach members of one culture ways of interacting effectively with minimal interpersonal misunderstanding, in another culture. This is a general definition and can be applied to most cross-cultural orientation. Specific training objectives must be developed according to specific needs and purposes of the organization.

In an effort to provide a framework for the categorization of cross-cultural training programs, James Downs, who is in the Peace Corps in America, lists the four models for training as: the Intellectual Model; the Area Simulation Model; the Self-Awareness Model; and a new training trend called the Cultural Awareness Model. I have tried these in my training and they have received good results.

The intellectual model consists of lectures and reading about the host culture. It is assumed that an exchange of information about another culture is effective preparation for living or working in that culture. Now there are wide accesses to these trainings such as books, magazines and audio/video cassettes which can offer useful information for the host culture.

The area simulation model is a culture-specific training program. It is based on the belief that an individual must be prepared and trained to enter a specific culture. It involves simulation of future experiences and practice functioning in the new culture. I have given this culture-specific training to the students. They were given the following situations:

They are all attending an international conference and meeting people who come from many different cultures. They stand up, walk around the room, and talk to other conference participants. They can talk about anything they like. However, they need to follow some rules, and everyone's rules are different:

Culture A: People pause for a long time before they speak, taking time to think about what they are going to say. When they do speak, they speak very slowly.

Culture B: People use their hands a lot when they are speaking. They also speak very loudly to show they are interested.

Culture C: It is rude to look people in the eye when they are listening or speaking, so they try to avoid eye contact as much as possible.

Culture D: People like to stand very close to one another. They also like to touch each other a lot.

Culture E: People do not move their hands, faces, or bodies when they are speaking. They also speak very quietly.

Culture F: People speak very fast. They also like to stand a long way away from the person they are talking to.

After this stimulation, they discuss the cultural differences in social distances and touching, gestures, the way in which people speak and eye contact.

The self-awareness model is based on the assumption that understanding and accepting oneself is critical to understanding a person from another culture. For example, an American manager must identify and understand what is American about America, what common cultural traits are shared by Americans, and what values and assumptions are the foundations for their management practices. Awareness of such cultural influences is essential for any manager who seeks to transfer management concepts or technology. Depending on cultures, there must be an overlap of values in a specific area, and therefore the problems related to transferring ideas will be minimal. Cultural systems might influence management. Sensitivity training is a main component of this method.

The cultural awareness model assumes that for an individual to function successfully in another culture an individual must learn the principles of behavior that function across cultures.

Although different in methods and assumptions, each training program's purpose is to train individuals to interact and communicate effectively in other cultures.

The Canadian International Development Agency conducts a pre-departure program for the global managers, and their training aims to instill the seven skills mentioned in the previous part, with the internationalization which must be more effective transfer of skills and intercultural communication.

Another strategy offered by the American Management Association is to educate the managers with the following eight concepts: Cosmopolitanism, Intercultural Communication. Cultural Sensitivity, Acculturation, Cultural Management Influences, Effective Intercultural Performance, Changing International Business and Emerging Odd Culture.

The above concepts are the key factors in managing the world corporation. They ought to be part of any program of cross-cultural education, training and development. The multinational corporation must be equipped with this awareness in order to survive the superindustrial age in this modern world.

Conclusion

A new century with peace and development as its theme will start. An era is drawing nearer and nearer in which all the information will be jointly shared by all the people in the global village through information highway or networks; all the natural resources including raw materials will be much fully protected and more rationally utilized and redistributed; all the creative work and efforts will be much more respected and the creators will be paid according to their capacity, energy and contribution to human beings. In this situation, the number of multinational corporations is growing steadily and their business fields are expanding, which requires their management to be more effective and their managers to be much more qualified for their positions and responsibilities. To global managers, reeducation of cross-cultural communication becomes a necessity. Their original knowledge and experiences have to be refreshed and bettered so that they could follow the advancing era. One book or two cannot provide all the information they need in the future; a short period of experience in one or two cultures can help them in their work. They have to enrich themselves in their practice. Only practicing in the cross-cultural communication can the global managers obtain more valuable experience and skills to meet their needs.

(GAO H L. Cross-cultural influence on management of international business: Proceedings of the 2013 International Conference on Information, Business and Education Technology (ICIBET 2013), Beijing, China, March 14-15, 2013[C]. Paris: Atlantis Press, 2013: 530-533.)

Comprehension Check

A. Questions for Discussion

1. List some examples to interpret the statement: "*All of the customs, beliefs, values, knowledge and skills that guide a nation's behavior among shared paths are part of their culture.*"
2. What are the benefits of the intercultural study?
3. What do you know about "hospitality rules"? Can you give some specific cases?

B. Detail Understanding

Match the terms and their definitions.

Term	Definition
1. Cross-Cultural Training	A. It is a culture-specific training program. It involves simulation of future experiences and practice functioning in the new culture.
2. The Self-awareness Model	B. It is designed to teach members of one culture ways of interacting effectively with minimal interpersonal misunderstanding in another culture.

续表

Term	Definition
3. The Intellectual Model	C. The self-awareness model is based on the assumption that understanding and accepting oneself is critical to understanding a person from another culture.
4. The Cultural Awareness Model	D. It consists of lectures and reading about the host culture. It is assumed that an exchange of information about another culture is effective preparation for living or working in that culture.
5. The Area Simulation Model	E. It assumes that for an individual to function successfully in another culture an individual must learn the principles of behavior that function across cultures.

Suggestions for Further Reading

1. SAMOVAR L A, PORTER R E, STEFANI L A. Communication between cultures [M]. Beijing: Foreign Language Teaching and Research Press, 2000.
2. 乔·瓦拉治，葛儿·麦考夫. 如何与老美共事[M]. 华经，译. 北京:机械工业出版社，1999.
3. 居伊·奥立维·福尔，杰弗里·Z 鲁宾. 文化与谈判——解决水争端[M]. 北京:社会科学文献出版社，2001.

Unit 7 The Wisdom of China

Observe good faith and justice toward all nations. Cultivate peace and harmony with all.

—George Washington

Objectives:

To understand the values that form the foundation of people's thinking;

To introduce the literature and your favourite writers in China.

Warm-up Activity

The following are some quotes from Chinese and foreign poets. Read them carefully and find out their views about man and nature.

泥融飞燕子，沙暖睡鸳鸯。 ——杜甫

人鸟不相乱，见兽皆相亲。 ——王维

一松一竹真朋友，山鸟山花好弟兄。 ——辛弃疾

We cannot command nature except by obeying her. —Francis Bacon

How I do love the earth. I feel it thrill under my feet. I feel somehow as if it were conscious of my love, as if something passed into my dancing blood from it. —James Russell Lowell

The sky is the daily bread of the eyes. —Ralph Waldo Emerson

Part One

Intensive Reading

Chinese Wisdom and Belief

As one of the four oldest recorded civilizations in the world, China has a long history without being interrupted. From ancient times till now, Chinese people, consisting of people of the Han nationality and other ethnic groups, have been living on the vast land, creating and developing her unique culture. Culturally, indigenous Confucianism and Taoism, have influenced the thought, literature of Chinese people over the centuries, which have shown their lasting charm for thousands of years.

Confucian Thought on Heaven and Humanity

Confucius (551-479 BC), known in China as Kongzi, is a great thinker, educator and founder of Confucianism. His words and life story were recorded by his disciples and their students in *The Analects*.

1. Confucius on Heaven: the Source of Everything

Much of Confucian thought on Heaven and people represents universal human values. This is perhaps why Confucian thought in the 21st century still retains the interest of not only the Chinese but also people in other parts of the world.

In the Shang (1600-1046 BC) and Zhou (1046-256 BC) dynasties, the prevalent concept of "Heaven" was that of a personified god, which influenced Confucius. Generally, however, Confucius regarded "Heaven" as nature. He said: "Heaven does not speak in words. It speaks through the rotation of the four seasons and the growth of all living things." Obviously, Heaven equaled nature, in the eyes of Confucius. Moreover, nature was not a lifeless mechanism separate from humans; instead, it was the great world of life and the process of creation of life. Human life was part and parcel of nature as a whole.

Confucius' equation of Heaven with the creation of life was an innovative idea in his time. The natural process of life creation was the "way of Heaven". This idea was later developed in *The Book of Changes* (*Yijing*), as it stated

"Continuous creation of life is change."

In the natural process of creation of life, Heaven had its inner purpose in creating all things as well as protecting and improving life. Heaven had originated humanity, and humans were obliged to accomplish this purpose. In other words, humans were born with a sense of "heavenly mission", and this was the meaning of human life.

Confucian "Heaven" also had a certain sacred element, which was related to its being the source of life. Thus Confucius required people to hold Heaven in awe. He said that a person of virtue must "respect his heavenly mission", listen to and live out the purpose of Heaven by caring for and improving life.

Under the influence of Confucius, the ancient Chinese developed a sense of awe and belief in Heaven. To them, Heaven was the highest sacred being, with its profound mystery never to be fully understood by mortals. It was not a supernatural, personified deity, but was the world of ever-generating life. As the most intelligent of all beings, humans should take to heart the purpose of Heaven by cherishing life. If one remained "ignorant and disrespectful of one's heavenly mission" by killing or maiming life, one would be punished by Heaven.

In the 21st century, the Confucian caveat of "standing in awe of the ordinances of Heaven" still holds true, as human society begins to pay greater attention to ecological civilization. Humans should indeed listen to the voice of nature, respecting and loving it as the world of life. This is our sacred mission and gives value to all human life.

2. Confucius on the State of Life

Before Confucius, only the nobility had the right to education. He was the first figure in Chinese history to initiate private education. According to historical records, Confucius taught for many years and trained 3,000 disciples. A total of 72 of them excelled in the "six arts", i. e., ritual, music, archery, driving, calligraphy, and mathematics. The great educator, Confucius has been admired by later generations as the "sage of sages".

Confucius believed the basic goal of education was to cultivate "persons of virtue", who should have sound character and uplifted minds. Such persons should be able to shoulder important social responsibilities and to make contributions to society. Confucius regarded lofty ideals, great virtue, love of people, and the "six arts" as the general principles of education. Of these, virtue was the most important. His students were involved in a variety of professions, including politics, trade, education, diplomacy, ritual ceremony, and classifying ancient books. Whatever they did, they all wanted to improve their learning of the humanities and to enhance their virtue.

Confucius emphasized aesthetic education. He said: "Studying *The Book of Songs* (*Shijing*) inspires the spirit and helps one appreciate beauty. Studying *The Book of Rites* (*Zhouli*) enables one to behave properly as a person of enlightenment. Studying music lifts the spirit and helps one to enjoy life." He also said: "Simply knowing the highest standard of virtue (i. e., love for people) is not as good as setting it as one's goal. Setting it as one's goal is not as good as enjoying the practice of it."

Under the influence of Confucius, Chinese thinkers of later generations all believed that students and scholars should not only increase their knowledge, but also and more importantly, broaden their minds and enhance their spiritual ethos. In other words, they should continually seek the greater meaning and value of life. Many modern scholars think the theory on the perspective on life is the most valuable feature of Chinese philosophy.

Laozi's Philosophy of Non-action

Laozi's work, known as *Classic of the Way and Virtue* (*Dao De Jing*), consists of just over 5,000 Chinese characters. It became the basis of Daoism, the school of philosophy parallel to Confucianism in ancient China. The thought of *Laozi* formed the foundation of Daoism, the most influential indigenous school of religion in China. It has also exerted a direct impact on the characteristics, trends of thought and aesthetic sensibilities of the Chinese nation. Today Laozi still plays a role in the development of Chinese thinking.

Laozi was first introduced into Europe possibly as early as in the 15th century and has been one of the most translated philosophical works of ancient China. Many of Laozi's enlightening views are based on his philosophy of naturalness and non-action.

1. Naturalness and Non-action

"Naturalness" is an important concept of Laozi's philosophy. It refers to a natural state of being, an attitude of following the way of nature. Laozi emphasized that everything in the world has its own way of being and development: birds fly in the sky, fish swim in the water, clouds float in the sky, flowers bloom and flowers fall. All these phenomena occur independently and naturally without following any human will, and humans should not try to change anything natural. Laozi admonished people to give up on any desire to control the world. Following the way of nature is the way to resolving conflicts between humans and the world.

"Non-action" is another important concept of Laozi's philosophy. It is the guarantee of "naturalness". Laozi said, "*Dao* or the Way acts through non-action," by which he did not mean that one should do nothing and passively wait for something to be achieved. Neither did he deny human creativity. What he meant is that human enterprises should be built on the basis of naturalness, not on any attempts to interrupt the rhythm of nature. Human creativity should be in compliance with the ways of nature.

Laozi said, "Great ingenuity appears to be stupidity." This is the essence of "naturalness" and "non-action". "Great ingenuity" refers to the highest level of ingenuity, arising so naturally that it does not resemble ingenuity at all. Ingenuity can be achieved through human effort, but "great ingenuity" is superior to ordinary ingenuity. To Laozi, resorting to deceit is true futility and would accomplish just the opposite result. Those who intend to play tricks are not genuine and therefore are not natural.

2. The Philosophy of Non-contention

On the basis of "naturalness" and "non-action", Laozi proposed the view of "overcoming the strong by being weak". The era Laozi lived in was replete with endless wars. Therefore, war was an important theme for philosophers, and anti-war thinking was the norm. Even the great strategist Sunzi advocated "winning a war without fighting it", not to mention the great thinker Confucius, who strongly championed a government based on love.

According to Laozi, war springs from humanity's bloated desires. Conflict arises out of people's struggles to satisfy their desires, and conflict escalates into war. Therefore, Laozi's philosophy is based on non-contention. To him, human striving and competitive strife is the root cause of decline; desiring nothing is the natural way of life.

Laozi said: "The greatest virtue is like water." He compared his philosophy of "non-contention" to water, to distinguish it from the law of the jungle.

He said, "Water nourishes everything but contends for nothing." To Laozi, humans tend to seek higher positions while water always flows to lower places. Driven by desire, humans like whatever they think is superior while despising whatever they think is inferior. Yet water always flows downward. As the source of life, water nourishes all living things on Earth.

No life can exist without water. Water contributes to the world without regard for gain or loss. Remaining low, level and tranquil, water embraces and reflects everything under heaven. The way of water is completely different from the way of people with avid desires.

But the philosophy of Laozi is by no means weak. On the contrary, it is full of strength. According to Laozi, water accumulates great strength in its weakness and quietude. Its strength can break down all barriers in the world. He said, "Nothing in the world is weaker than water. Yet nothing is stronger than water when it comes to breaking something strong." Water is a typical example of the weak winning over the strong. Water is invincible because it desires nothing and contends for nothing.

Remaining weak is not only the way to prosperity, but also the way to preserving life. Laozi regarded fragility as the symbol of life. He explained this with a comparison between life and death: when a person is alive, his body is fragile; when he dies, his body becomes hard and rigid. The same is true with plants: living plants have supple leaves and lovely flowers, while dead plants become dry and hard. Laozi uses these examples to show that the way of the weak is the way to preserving life.

3. Returning to a Newborn State

Laozi saw the world as a madding crowd of vanity. He chose to live a simple, quiet life, and to keep his mind undisturbed in the face of temptation. He said he would rather remain a "newborn baby".

This does not mean Laozi wanted to remain childishly ignorant. He believed that sages—people with the highest virtue, all resembled newborns. The highest level of one's cultivation was to return to the state of a newborn baby.

When human beings come into the world, they gradually acquire external knowledge and accept social norms, along with the growth of their bodies, step by step, and their originally pure minds become tainted with chaotic colors. As humans mature, they become more and more hypocritical. The process of acculturation is the process of losing one's true self.

To Laozi, civilization is to a certain degree a departure from the "true self". The development of human culture is a process of "decoration": clothing as decoration of the body, houses as decoration of the way of living, language as decoration of communication, and state politics as decoration of human organization.

Such "decorations" often turn into bloated desires. Desire-driven human beings fight and deceive one another, leading to war. Laozi made a comparison between the laws of nature and the laws of the human world. Nature takes from the surplus to make up the deficit, such as the wind leveling and the water washing away earth and stones. The human world is just the opposite, i. e. , robbing the poor and oppressing the weak.

Bloated desire has damaged the external world as well as poisoned the human mind. Laozi said, "Beautiful colors blind the eyes, complex music harms the ears, rich flavors numb taste, while riding and hunting madden the mind." Desire disturbs peace of mind. If immersed in a sea of desire, in the end humans would be submerged.

（叶朗，朱良志. 中国文化英语教程[M]. 张桂萍，编 . 陈海燕，章思英，译 . 北京：外语教学与研究出版社，2010.）

Vocabulary

disciple *n.* someone who believes and helps to spread the doctrine of another

rotation *n.* the movement of something through one complete circle

sacred *adj.* which is believed to be holy and to have a special connection with God

awe *n.* the feeling of respect and amazement

maim *vi.* injure or wound seriously

caveat *n.* a warning against certain acts

indigenous *adj.* people or things belong to the country in which they are found

admonish *vt.* warn strongly; put on guard

compliance *n.* acting according to certain accepted standards

ingenuity *n.* the power of creative imagination

futility *n.* uselessness as a consequence of having no practical result
replete *adj.* fill to satisfaction
escalate *vi.* increase in extent or intensity
strife *n.* lack of agreement or harmony
avid *adj.* excessively desirous
invincible *adj.* incapable of being overcome or subdued
fragility *n.* quality of being easily damaged or destroyed
chaotic *adj.* lacking a visible order or organization
surplus *adj.* more than is needed, desired, or required
numb *vt.* making sb. or sth. unable to feel or react
submerge *vt.* cover completely

Exercises

A. Words in Use

Fill in the blanks with the words given below. Change the form when necessary. Each word can be used only once.

sacred	indigenous	admonish	submerge	maim
fragility	surplus	escalate	compliance	strife

1. Hippos are unable to ________ in the few remaining water holes.
2. The owl is ________ for many Californian Indian people.
3. The local war ________ into a major conflict.
4. My joy is in your freedom, not your ________.
5. I'm wondering if there is something, also, that comes out of ________ New Zealand culture.
6. Money is a major cause of ________ in many marriages.
7. Separately, he did also ________ Syria for blocking access to the site and withholding documentation.
8. Norway's budget ________ has fallen from 5.9% in 1986 to an expected 0.1% this year.
9. One of the biggest differences I see between Western and Chinese parents is that Chinese parents assume strength rather than ________.
10. Old drivers are more likely to be seriously injured because of the ________ of their bones.

B. Questions for Discussion

1. After reading the passage, have you got any insight into our chinese-style interpersonal relationship?
2. Please demonstrate the differences between Confucius and Laozi.
3. Write an essay about water and philosophy within 150 words. Your essay should cover the following three points:
   (1) Laozi's philosophy of water;
   (2) Your own experience with water;
   (3) What you have learned from water.

C. Translation

1. In the Shang (1600-1046 BC) and Zhou' (1046-256 BC) dynasties, the prevalent concept of "Heaven" was that of a personified god, which influenced Confucius. Generally, however, Confucius regarded "Heaven" as nature. He said, "Heaven does not speak in words. It speaks through the rotation of the four seasons and the growth of all living things." Obviously, Heaven equaled nature, in the eyes of Confucius.
2. Confucius believed the basic goal of education was to cultivate "persons of virtue", who should have sound character and uplifted minds.
3. "Naturalness" is an important concept of Laozi's philosophy. It refers to a natural state of being, an attitude of following the way of nature.
4. Laozi saw the world as a madding crowd of vanity. He chose to live a simple, quiet life, and to keep his mind undisturbed in the face of temptation.

D. Case Study

The following are classical lines by Laozi for which two English versions are given. Appreciate and compare the two versions. Then tell which of them you prefer.

Case 1

知人者智，自知者明。

今译：了解别人的人智慧；了解自己的人高明。

(1) Knowing others is wisdom; Knowing one's self is insight. (Wang Rongpei et al.)

(2) To understand others is to have knowledge,
To understand oneself is to be illumined. (Arthur Waley)

Case 2

知足不辱，知止不殆，可以长久。

今译：知道心满意足就不会蒙受侮辱，知道适可而止就不会遭遇危险，这样才可以得享长久安全。

(1) The contented man meets no disgrace. Who know (knows) when to stop runs into no danger. He can long endure. (Lin Yutang)

(2) Who is content needs fear no shame. Who knows to stop incurs no blame. From danger free long live shall he. (James Legge)

Part Two

Extensive Reading

Chinese Classical Literature

China has a long and rich literary history, but to many westerners, Chinese literature remains an enigma. Many of Chinese classics are unavailable in translation, as much of china's literary heritage has been untranslatable, despite scholarly efforts.

For over 3,000 years, Chinese literature has encompassed diversified genres (类型) and forms such as mythology (神话), poetry, essay, fiction and drama. It rivals the literature of other countries in the world.

Chinese classical literature refers to literary works from the days before the Qin dynasty to the year of 1919, and is virtually an unbroken strand enduring dynastic changes. Long before the written language appeared, there was an oral tradition of fables and legends. Some of them are still kept in some ancient books as precious heritage of Chinese literature. Over 3,000 years, there has emerged a great variety of excellent works in terms of poems, essays, novels, dramas and so on.

The Book of Songs* and *The Songs of Chu

Poetry, one of the earliest artistic forms, originated from folk songs before the existence of written Chinese. Its content evolved out of people's everyday life, and reflected their labour and entertainment. *The Book of Songs* and *The Songs of Chu* are regarded as the two peaks of China's earlier literary history.

The Book of Songs is a collection of China's 305 oldest poems from the early Western Zhou Dynasty to the middle of the Spring and Autumn Period, and is regarded as the earliest realistic literature in China. As the starting point of Chinese literature, *The Book of Songs* has provided a deep insight into all aspects of social life of the Zhou Dynasty and truly reflected the rise and fall of the Chinese slave society. It has always been worshipped by scholars and has become a cultural gene. In the light of their rhythms, the works can be divided into three sections:

(1) *Feng*（风）or folk ballads (consisting of 160 ballads from 15 regions);

(2) *ya*（雅）or dynastic hymns (consisting of 105 songs, most of which are for entertaining slave owners at feast);

(3) *song*（颂）or sacrificial songs (consisting of 40 songs for sacrificial ceremonies attended by slave owners).

Many poems in *The Book of Songs* portray love stories, social customs and realities in the remote antiquity（上古时期）of China.

The Songs of Chu follows *The Book of Songs* as an important poem collection from ancient China with far-reaching influence. *Chu Ci*（《楚辞》）, as the book's Chinese name indicates, is derived from the songs of the southern state of Chu during the Warring States Period. It pioneered romanticism in Chinese poetry.

Qu Yuan, who furthered the development of poetic styles, is regarded as the first writer to have his name associated with his work in the history of Chinese literature. He was exiled from the State of Chu during a period of sudden unrest in that state. Unable to realise his ideal, he wrote such immortal masterpieces as "Sorrow After Departure"（《离骚》）, "Ask Heaven"（《天问》）, "Nine Elegies"（《九章》）, and "Nine Songs"（《九歌》）. He drowned himself in the Miluo River（汨罗江）out of disappointment, sorrow, and anger.

Qu Yuan was not only famous for his many immortal poems; he was also a true patriot. His love for his country and its people are revealed naturally in his poems. During the Han dynasty, Qu Yuan was established as a heroic example of how a scholar and official who was denied public recognition suitable to their worth should behave.

The Book of Songs is the fountainhead of realism and *The Songs of Chu* romanticism. Later Chinese literature was extended and developed based on these two creation modes.

Prose of the Pre-Qin Times

The prose in the pre-Qin times includes historical prose and philosophical prose.

1. Historical Prose

There are four main representative works of historical prose:

(1) *The Book of History* (《尚书》), the most ancient collection of Chinese prose writings with fragments of disconnected and diverse individual official papers;

(2) *The Spring and Autumn Annal* (《春秋》), the earliest chronicle (编年史) in China with concise and meticulous (细腻的) language;

(3) *Zuo's Commentary* (《左传》), the first comprehensive historical account of the major political, social, and military events of the Spring and Autumn Period;

(4) *Intrigues of the Warring States* (《战国策》), another historical work recording the history of each of the states in the pre-Qin times.

2. Philosophical Prose

During the Spring and Autumn and Warring States periods, Chinese society was undergoing radical changes, and various schools of thought, such as the Confucian School, Mohist School, Taoist School, and Legalist School, all strived to put their ideas into practice by writing books and expounding their theories. Some famous pieces of philosophical prose are:

(1) *Dao De Jing* (《道德经》), written by Laozi, is regarded as the scripture of Taoism. It centres on Tao, the principle underlying and governing all things of existence.

(2) *Mozi* (《墨子》), written by Mozi, is known for its extensive and effective methodological reasoning.

(3) *Mencius* (《孟子》), written by Mencius, makes full use of the expressive power of spoken language in forging an eloquent verbal style.

(4) *Zhuangzi* (《庄子》), written by Zhuangzi, has established the model of an exuberantly (丰富地) imaginative form that defies classification.

(5) *The Analects of Confucius* (《论语》), compiled by the disciples of Confucius, records the sayings and behaviour of Confucius in the form of cate-

chism (问答教学).

Literature in the Han Dynasty

The most notable achievements of the literature in the Han dynasty are its *Hanfu* and *Yuefu* folk songs.

Hanfu emphasises elaboration and description, and is the combination of poem and prose. The most outstanding *Hanfu* writers include Jia Yi and Sima Xiangru. *Yuefu* folk songs are mostly written in five-character lines, although some are in seven-character or multi-character lines. They reflect the reality and life of the working people.

With natural and simple language, these folk songs are colourful narrative expressions and lyrics. Stories in the folk songs are vivid and lively by making use of figurative speech and personification. The most outstanding work is "Southeast the Peacock Flies"(《孔雀东南飞》), which is one of the longest ballads at the end of the Eastern Han dynasty.

Literature in the Wei, Jin, Southern and Northern Dynastics

Chinese literature was most notable for its literary criticism in these dynasties. Also during this period, the stories recording spirits and anecdotes (志人志怪小说) became a genre.

The "Three Caos" (三曹: Cao Cao, Cao Pi and Cao Zhi) and the Seven Masters of the Jian'an Period (建安七子: Kong Rong, Chen Lin, Wang Can, Xu Gan, Ruan Yu, Ying Yang, Liu Zhen) were outstanding literary figures during the Jian'an period. Their poems spoke to the spirit of the time and invoked an ambience of heroism and sadness.

The emergence of Tao Yuanming made the link between Chinese poetry and art. Using plain words in an artistic and profound way, he perfected descriptions of nature, and his style was followed by poets long after. His masterpiece "The Peach Blossom Spring"(《桃花源记》) is eulogized by later generations because it describes the secluded and ideal life people pursue.

Tang Poetry

The Tang Dynasty saw the continued development of Chinese poetry. The development of poetry in the Tang Dynasty can be classified into four stages, namely, Early Tang, High Tang, Middle Tang, and Late Tang.

The four preeminent (杰出的) poets of the Early Tang Period, Wang Bo, Yang Jiong, Luo Binwang, and Lu Zhaolin, regarded as the "Four Literary

Eminences", were the pioneers of the Tang poetry. Their poems, in a refined language, boast beautiful tonal patterns and rhyme schemes. The lines written by Wang Bo "Friendships across the world, make near neighbours of far horizons" (海内存知己，天涯若比邻) help wipe away the lingering sorrow of departure and have become a famous saying to express friendship in later years.

A whole generation of literary giants appeared during the High Tang Period when society enjoyed prosperity and stability. Li Bai and Du Fu are regarded as the representatives of the Tang poets. Li Bai, the "Immortal of Poems" (诗仙), greatest romantic poet in Chinese literature. In his poems, imagination, as long been considered the exaggeration, diction and sonorous (洪亮的) rhythms are blended effortlessly. Du Fu, the "Sage of Poems" (诗圣), has been regarded as the greatest realistic poet in Chinese literature. As mirrors of the times, his poems faithfully and profoundly reflect the social realities of the Tang Dynasty in decline, like a poetic historical account.

The other poets in this period can be grouped into two categories: frontier poets (边塞诗人) represented by Gao Shi and Cen Shen, and pastoral poets (田园诗人) represented by Meng Haoran and Wang Wei. The two categories reflect the alternative paths of the life of scholars, either taking up an official post or living in seclusion. The frontier poems depict the frontier scenery, military life, and soldiers' homesickness, passionate patriotism, and devotion to the state.

In the Middle Tang Period, numerous poets produced many excellent poems, which forcefully exposed the social corruption of their times. The outstanding poet Bai Juyi followed Du Fu and wrote poems reflecting the reality of society. His poetic treasures are satirical and allegorical poems. His most popular poems are the romantic narrative ballads "Song of Eternal Sorrow"(《长恨歌》) and "Song of a Pipa Player"(《琵琶行》).

With the deterioration of the government in the Late Tang period, the poems reflected, more and more, the hopeless and helpless feelings of the people. Poets turned to the theme of nostalgia for the former splendour of old times. The most talented of these were Li Shangyin and Du Mu. Some of their works are about beauty, but some are about disconsolation caused by the lack of opportunity to give full play to their talents.

Song *Ci* Poetry

Poetry typical of the Song Dynasty is known as *Song ci* poetry. Instead of regulated poetry, *Song ci* poetry could express more refined and delicate feelings with irregular metre.

In the Northern Song Dynasty appeared two major *ci* styles. One style is called the "Soft and Tuneful School"(婉约派) represented by Liu Yong, Li Qingzhao, Yan Shu and Ouyang Xiu. Most of their poems are about love and parting, and reflect elite literati taste and the sophisticated aristocratic lifestyle of leisure and luxury. Li Qingzhao, as the greatest poetess in China, also rose to prominence in this period. She expressed her motion in simple and plain language. Her famous *ci* poem, "Slow Slow Song"(《声声慢》), expressed her intense grief and woe (悲痛) over the loss of the country and her husband.

The other style is called the "Powerful and Free School" (豪放派) represented by Su Shi, Xin Qiji and Lu You. with his extraordinarily vigorous style of poetry, Su Shi brought innovations to *ci* and helped broaden its scope, elevate its status and set up the school.

Yuan Dramas in the Yuan Dynasty

Yuan dramas, including *sanqu* and *zaju*, were popular in the Yuan Dynasty.

Sanqu mainly expresses one's emotions in two categories—*xiaoling* (小令) and *santao* (散套). Ma Zhiyuan's "Autumn Thought"(《秋思》), a *xiaoling*, enjoys great popularity. He sketched a picture with only 28 words showing the wilderness of a strange land and expressing his loneliness and sadness.

Zaju originated from the comic performance in the Song dynasty and evolved into the drama in the Yuan dynasty. Important *zaju* writers were Guan Hanqing and Bai Pu. Guan Hanqing, the most highly-reputed dramatist, wrote the masterpiece tragedy "The Injustice to Dou E"(《窦娥冤》). Guan exposed the social injustice of that time.

Fiction in the Ming and Qing Dynasties

In the Song dynasty, *huaben* (话本), the earliest novels written in colloquial language started to appear. By the Ming and Qing dynasties, novels proliferated as a lively and free literary form.

The Ming and Qing dynasties saw the publication of the Four Classical Novels: *Romance of the Three Kingdoms* (《三国演义》), *Water Margin* (《水

浒传》), *Journey to the West* (《西游记》), and *A Dream of the Red Mansions* (《红楼梦》). They have been celebrated for centuries for their rich historical and cultural significance.

Romance of the Three Kingdoms by Luo Guanzhong is recognized as the earliest chapter-by-chapter historical novel in China. Based on history books and folk legends, the book describes the rise and fall of the three kingdoms of Wei, Shu and Wu, and the complex political, military, and diplomatic struggles during that period. One main theme the writer wants to advocate is brotherhood. The basic expressive technique of *Romance of the Three Kingdoms* is realism, but the plot arrangement and the portrayal of historical figures are full of romantic colour. The novel is written in clear, concise and vivid language.

Water Margin by Shi Nai'an tells the story of the rebellion of the 108 heroes at the end of the Northern Song Dynasty. It is the first novel to deal with the subject matter of peasant revolts in China. During the peasant uprising, the rebellious heroes execute justice in the name of Heaven by killing the rich and relieving the poor (杀富济贫，替天行道). At the end of the novel, the rebels at Liangshan, led by Song Jiang, accept amnesty (招安) and surrender to the government. Shi Nai'an was skilled at revealing the inner world of characters through their behaviour and language. His expressive technique originated from storytelling scripts. He was also able to portray each character's appearance and personality. He revealed the characters' dispositions and resistance to oppression through describing their different life experiences.

Journey to the West by Wu Cheng'en is an outstanding romantic work full of fantastic tales. It is generally recognized as a masterpiece about deities and spirits. The novel tells of the Tang Dynasty monk, Xuanzang, assisted by his three disciples: the Monkey King, the Eight-Commandment Pig, and Monk Sha, who was overcame 81 adversities and defeated various monsters and demons before finally reaching India. Wu Cheng'en illuminated the intelligence, bravery, and loyalty of the Monkey King, the piety of Monk Xuanzang, the straightforwardness and good nature of the Eight-Commandment Pig, and the kindness of Monk Sha. Some fantastic and thrilling tales from the novel are still popular with the children of China today.

A Dream of the Red Mansions by Cao Xueqin reached the pinnacle of classical Chinese novels. It has long been acknowledged as the greatest novel in Chinese literature. The writer was born into a noble and powerful family, which was later reduced to poverty from extreme prosperity. His novel describes the prosperity and decline of a large feudal family. The central thread of the novel is the tragic love story between Jia Baoyu and Lin Daiyu. Instead of just telling the love story, it taps the social origins of the tragedy through probing deeply into the characters' minds and complicated relationships. The plot of the novel is ingeniously arranged. Its narratives use mature colloquial language, plain but elegant, explicit but expressive. The novel is really a panorama of feudal society and has been considered an encyclopedia of Chinese literature.

Besides the Four Great Classical Novels, "*Three Volumes of Words*"(三言) and "*Two Volumes of Slapping*"(二拍) belong to townsfolk literature during this period. They are vernacular novelettes (短篇小说) from the Ming Dynasty. They are regarded as model illustrations of Chinese feudal society. Containing many descriptions of daily life of townspeople, they are called the "worldly novels".

Strange Tales from a Scholar's Studio (《聊斋志异》), a collection of about 490 Short stories, is written by Pu Songling in a simple but elegant style. It inherits the traditions of the mystery tales (志怪小说) in the Wei and Jin Dynasties and the tales of marvels in the Tang and Song Dynasties. Many stories contained in the collection are about the love affairs between men and foxes, ghosts or demons, which demonstrate youths' yearning for breaking away from the feudal ethical codes and for free marriage. Pu Songling's characters are well-rounded and adeptly portrayed. The language is fluent and vivid; the plot is intricate; and the structure is tight.

The Scholars (《儒林外史》) authored by Wu Jingzi is China's first colloquial and satirical novel. The novel portrays a group of feudal scholars and directs criticism at the eight-part essay and imperial civil examination system. Its 56 chapters are a series of separate episodes with no single hero through the whole book. The structure shows internal harmony and balance. Wu Jingzi's character portrayal style is simple yet insightful. *The Scholars* is not only the first book to create a variety of images of numerous scholars and intellectuals, but also the first to openly challenge the idea of making academic studies only for the sake of taking official positions. It occupies an important place in the history of Chinese fiction and has exerted great influence on later Chinese satirical novels.

Following the Hundred Days Reform in 1898, supporter called for revolutionary poems and novels to arouse peoples political awareness. Some writers created novels to denounce the feudal system which was the cause of so much dissatisfaction among the people. Many works voiced opposition to the foreign invasion and exposed evils of the day. Novels flourished during this period. The most renowned are *Exposure of the Official World* (《官场现形记》) by Li Baojia, *The Travel Records of Lao Can* (《老残游记》) by Liu E, and *Flowers in a Mirror* (《镜花缘》) by Li Ruzhen.

Beginning with primitive mythology, Chinese classical literature developed with *The Book of Songs*, *The Songs of Chu*, the prose of the pre-Qin times, *Hanfu* and *Yuefu* folk songs of the Han dynasty, the literary criticism in the Wei and Jin dynasties, the Tang poetry, the Song ci poetry, the Yuan dramas in the Yuan dynasty and the Ming and Qing novels. The literary achievements at the end of the Qing dynasty are mainly poems and novels.

(廖华英. 中国文化概况[M]. 修订版. 北京:外语教学与研究出版社, 2015.)

Language focus

enigma *n.* 谜
exile *vt.* 放逐;流放
elaboration *n.* 详细阐述
seclusion *n.* 隔离;隐居
nostalgia *n.* 乡愁
refine *vt.* 精炼;改进
colloquial *adj.* 口语的
brotherhood *n.* 义气
piety *n.* 虔诚;孝顺
panorama *n.* 全景;全景画
encompass *vt.* 包含
eloquent *adj.* 雄辩的;有口才的
ambience *n.* 气氛
allegorical *adj.* 寓言的;讽喻的
splendour *n.* 显赫;辉煌
literati *n.* 文人
proliferate *vt.* 使……扩散
deity *n.* 神
pinnacle *n.* 高峰
marvel *n.* 奇异的事物

Exercises

A. Text Reading

Decide whether the following statements are true (T) or false (F).

1. ______ *The Songs of Chu* is regarded as the earliest realistic literature in China.
2. ______ *The Songs of Chu* is the fountainhead of realism and *The Book of Songs* romanticism.
3. ______ *Intrigues of the Warring States* is the first comprehensive historical account of the major political, social, and military events of the Spring and Autumn Period.
4. ______ *Yuefu* folk songs reflect the reality and life of working people.
5. ______ *Song of Eternal Sorrow* was written by Bai Juyi in the Late Tang Period.
6. ______ *Zaju* came into existence from the comic performance in the Song Dynasty and developed into the drama in the Yuan Dynasty.
7. ______ *Records of the Grand* by Sima Qian is recognized as the earliest chapter-by-chapter historical novel in China.
8. ______ *The Scholars* authored by Wu Jingzi is China's first colloquial and satirical novel.
9. ______ *Exposure of the Official World* is the revolutionary novel to arouse people's political awareness.
10. ______ *Strange Tales from a Scholar's Studio* is based on the traditions of the mystery tales in the Wei and Jin Dynasties.

B. Terms Understanding

Find the definitions of the following terms in the text. If you cannot find the exact definition, try to use your own words to interpret it.

1. Hundred Days' Reform
2. *Three Volumes of Words* and *Two Volumes of Slapping*
3. Eight-part essay
4. Imperial civil examination system

C. Classroom Activities

1. What's the contemporary literary form in the West in the time of Tang Dy-

nasty in China?

2. Compare the works of Shakespeare with them of Guan Hanqing.
3. You are a member of a reading club joined by both Chinese students and international students. It's your turn to introduce one of your favourite writers in China. Your introduction should cover the following points:
   (1) the time he/she lives;
   (2) his/her life experiences;
   (3) his/her style of writing/influences;
   (4) his/her representative works.

Part Three

Academic Reading

Economic Prosperity and Sustainability in China: Seeking Wisdom from Confucianism and Taoism

Introduction

As the most populous country in the world, China is enjoying unprecedented economic growth, but this development has caused serious degradation of the country's physical environment. The resulting environmental problems are particularly aggravated by China's greatly expanding urbanization and ageing population. China is seeking a balanced economic developmental strategy model. It examines the influences of population change and economic growth on the environment with the purpose of providing insights and lessons for achieving a better quality of economic growth and sustainability. Changes need to be made to ease the double burden of restoring the deteriorating ecosystems and improving people's quality of life. We refer to Confucian and Taoist teachings to help support the arguments put forward.

Confucius (551-479 BC) was an educator and philosopher who founded and operated a private school. More than 2,500 years ago, he advocated the unity of humankind with nature and other ideas to encourage the harmonious relationship between human activities and the natural environment. Nowadays, Confucian ideas are influencing the basics of life in China and other East

Asian countries. It can be said that Confucius' thought aligns very well with what has become the basic concept of modern sustainability in the West.

In 1988, 74 Nobel Prize winners appealed in Paris: "If human beings want to live in peace and prosperity in the 21st century, they must look back 2,500 years ago and seek the wisdom of Confucius." Building current civilization's ecological awareness must be achieved through seeking the wisdom of Confucius and Lao Tzu, the two most famous Chinese philosophers. There were many differences between these two influential Chinese philosophers in terms of both their ways of thought and approach to life. Lao Tzu saw life on earth within its context in the wider cosmos and within the view that there is interdependence between all things animate and inanimate. While Confucius also spoke of the importance of this interdependence in terms of harmony, he focused on the ethical standards for people to live together. He introduced a way for people to learn to become more human and developed a code for effective leadership. Both Lao Tzu and Confucius referred to the *Dao*, which means the truth or the way. Jaspers (1957) states: "it is often held that Lao Tzu conceived the *Dao* as beyond good and evil, while Confucius moralized the *Dao*." It could be said that Lao Tzu focused on our spiritual well-being and our connectivity with Earth and the universe, while Confucius focused on the ethical governance and management of a nation.

Is the Concept of Sustainability New to China?

Aitken (1908) argued that Confucius grew up at a place where the natural environment—the mountains, rivers, land, heaven, sun, moon and stars—was held as sacred. This connective and high respect for nature would have been the same for Lao Tzu as their lives were almost in the same period. Lao Tzu taught many ways of maintaining the connectivity with nature including bringing animal movements into ritualistic dances. Confucius accepted all that to be natural; even in the appreciation of nature, he prescribed an order.

The wisdom that both gave to China and to the world is relevant today, as we struggle to address ways to mitigate global climate change and as we address the mismatches between systems that we need to comply with for economic well-being, what our spirit wants and needs, and how we should live in harmony and interdependence with the living and nonliving things of Earth. We have gone through half a century in the world's development with what seems to be a shift away from the spiritual wisdom of philosophers, such as Confucius and Lao Tzu, towards an economics-based rationale for living. In relation to fostering economic growth, Lebow (1955) states that "we convert the buying and use of goods into rituals, that we seek our spiritual satisfactions, our ègo satisfactions, in consumption." Spirituality is perceived as the major competing interest to growth, which needs to be overcome. Jackson (2009) refers to gross domestic product (GDP) as the means by which nations sum up market exchanges including household, community, business and government expenditure on goods and services. He states that this expenditure in the GDP is taken as a proxy for measuring satisfaction and well-being. Tied in with this, Jackson summarizes Sen's point of view as follows: "The baseline for social functioning is always the current level of commodities. The avoidance of shame—a key feature of social flourishing—will drive material demand forward relentlessly."

The trend of placing economics as the underpinning of national growth started to discard ancient wisdom and successfully replaced spirituality with ego-driven consumerism. It seems that the state of the world today has reached a point where a growth-based economy is considered conventional—the norm, and that this is unsustainable. How do we bring sustainability back into our thinking? Is there wisdom in ancient philosophy that can guide us?

Confucius saw that customs were key to establishing order in a nation and he himself sought to learn from past wisdom. He said that "a man born in our days who returns to the ways of antiquity is a fool and brings misfortune upon himself" (Jaspers, 1957). The ways of antiquity were a priority for Confucius; however, his process in finding solutions, according to Jaspers, was to ask: "What is the old? How can we make it our own? How can we make it a reality?"

Self-modeling was a starting point for Confucius. He developed what he saw as the essential qualities for a community and national leader and also the qualities for everyday people to transform themselves to be the best they could be. His teachings did not take anything for granted and included details of how to walk, greet, behave in different situations, how to bury the dead, how to administrate and work, how to be a family. If we apply this thinking today, perhaps we could be asking: what would be the equivalent customs for a sustainable person? How would they travel? What would they eat? How would they engage with diversity? How would they create work cultures in harmony with nature? "A man of humanity does not strive for life at the cost of injuring humanity." (Jaspers, 1957)

Confucius promoted civic sense, saying that a good citizen would not neglect their neighbors. They would honour the worthy and be able to work with diversity. High on his agenda was respect for parents. "If respect is absent, wherein should we differ from the beasts?" (Jaspers, 1957) To follow this family code of conduct might require restructuring of our modern day life imperatives where economic pressures prevail and are the highest on the list of priorities.

What is the Wisdom of Confucius and Lao Tzu for Sustainability?

The greatest strength of Confucianism is the wisdom regarding government. He advised that there were "aspects of government that had to be developed and there were aspects that had to be nurtured" (Jaspers, 1957). This nurturing can be interpreted as very early notions of a developmental, participatory approach to assist with change management and capacity building. Linked to the ability to achieve change, Confucius stated that a good government was led by a person who engendered the confidence of the people and provided opportunity for education. In his lifetime, he did not find a leader (a prince) with the qualities he saw as necessary but he did not give up on his teachings. Confucius did not lower his standards—as some thought he should. He founded a school for future statements, trusting in the long-term. Lao Tzu is said to have disapproved of Confucius' planning process, his study regime and demanded that people remain impartial. However, we today can draw wisdom from the strengths of both of these great Chinese philosophers and see that both elements are essential.

Both sages, Lao Tzu and Confucius, revered nature and the cosmos as sacred. It was with this foundation that Confucius developed his teachings of good citizenship, good leadership and how to run a successful nation. The same focus was used by Lao Tzu to develop his teachings and processes for engagement with nature and the celestial spheres. This underlining valuing of nature and the cosmos as scared is a critical point of difference between Confucius' wisdom on governance and management and our current corporate systems, which seem to disconnect people from the spirituality and sacredness of the physical world. This detached objective approach is part of a package often included in what is seen as the western paradigm where consumerism has replaced spirituality and ethics, as was the intention in the Lebow (1955) plan.

As part of his teachings, Confucius called for impartiality in the leader, allowing for an open mind to absorb new ideas. This, again, can be argued as the birth of community development or participatory planning processes, with the impartial leader guiding the discussion, but not imposing the way forward. The impartiality is related to the objectivity required in corporate planning. However, it is not separated from strong ethical foundations in its teaching or its application. Lao Tzu lived in the world of nature and the cosmos. His response to Confucius according to Jaspers is:

> To make up one's mind to be impartial is in itself a kind of partiality ... You had best study how it is that Heaven and Earth maintain their eternal course, that the sun and moon maintain their light, the stars their serried ranks, the birds and beasts their flocks, the trees and shrubs their station. Thus you too shall learn to guide your steps by Inward Power, to follow the course that the Way of Nature sets; and soon you will reach a goal where you will no longer need to go round laboriously advertising goodness and duty ... All this talk of goodness and duty, these perpetual pinprinks unnerve and irritate the hearer ... The swan does not need a daily bath in order to remain white. (Jaspers, 1957)

Confucius, however, had this inner power and referred to it often as an essential ingredient of his teaching. His focus was the ethical-political state, the qualities and customs of a good citizen of the Earth and a good leader of a nation. Lao Tzu's focus was to create time, space and methods for one to commune with nature and the cosmos.

Tu (2001) refers to New Confucian humanism as a source of inspiration for human flourishing in the twenty-first century. According to Tu (1998), the age in which we live is one where the modern West has the most dynamic and transformative ideology in human history. He sees the achievements we have today—science and technology, industrial capitalism, market economy, democratic polity, mass communication, research universities, civil and military bureaucracies, and professional organizations, as part of the whole enlightenment mentality. The Confucian Golden Rule "Do not do unto others what you would not want others to do unto you" seems to rest forgotten, so is his understanding "In order to establish myself, I have to help others to enlarge themselves". (Tu, 1998) His teachings reinforced the need for society to have ethical foundations and values of a consciousness that goes beyond anthropocentricism to that which embraces the whole of the Earth and beyond.

Confucianism is originally a philosophy, a way of life—not a religion. However, it provides a good ethics underpinning ordering of communities that is compatible with the foundations of many world religions. According to Tu (1998), Western, Eastern and Indigenous spiritualities have informed the Enlightenment mentality while the Confucian tradition avoids anthropocentrism (human-centeredness) in favour of anthropocosmism (seeing humans as part and parcel of the cosmos). A re-examining of the link between modern religious traditions in the West is needed to position the matter/spirit, body/mind, sacred/profane, human/nature, creator/creature realities in the new mentality and to go beyond anthropocentrism. (Tu, 1998)

At the core of Confucianism is the appreciation that human beings are sentient, social, political, historical and metaphysical beings. (Tu, 1998) Confucianism refutes any reductionist models that collapse people into anything less; however, the human being has to learn how to be human through transformation in communion with self, community, nature and the transcendent.

According to Moller (2011), Confucianism and Taoism both view nature, human beings and the cycles of nature as a holistic system in which humans must not only be in harmony with other beings, but also with nature itself. They see people as part of a network of ecological and social relationships undergoing constant change. Being part of the ecology, humans should not use it according to their own interests. This concept leads to a notion of nature-based sustainability and helps to ensure the protection of nature and its resources. When developing its economy, has China's past practice followed these principles?

How Can We Draw on the Wisdom of Confucius and Lao Tzu?

According to Confucius, one should not only love his or her parents, but also spread this love to nature. Furthermore, he also advised that one should control personal selfish desires and should not sacrifice the environment for achieving economic needs. Nowadays, people should be more philosophical in their treatment of natural resources and seek to adhere to a more harmonious relationship between human and nature. Confucius, Lao Tzu and other Chinese philosophers and ideologists treated people as equals to nature.

The Confucian thoughts of kindness and responsibility can thus be seen to be based on the notion that humans should see themselves as equal to other natural lives and resources. This means that people should not try to conquer other living entities but should instead protect them. Therefore, people should not try to overcome nature, but rather they should love it as much as they love their parents and relatives including humans and other creatures and resources.

Lao Tzu suggested in the *Tao Bible* that everything on earth is produced by *Dao*, the natural rules, and he believed that *Dao* produces one; one produces two; and two produces three. Therefore, humans have the responsibility to take good care of the other creatures and resources of nature. Protecting and caring for nature are thus viewed as the best of human moral expressions. According to Lao Tzu in *Tao Bible*, *Dao*, Heaven, Earth and Human are the four biggest things in the universe and he believed that humans depend on the Earth to live, the Earth depends on Heaven, Heaven follows *Dao*, and *Dao* eventually follows the principles of nature. This means that humans are the children of nature who have to respect Heaven and Earth. Their actions or behaviours need to follow the natural rules (*Dao*). Humans are allowed to improve the natural conditions because they are not passive; however, they have to act under humane and righteous motives. (Pan, 2013)

In general, Confucius advocated that people should treat nature nicely and should exercise self-control in relation to their desires, by applying appropriate and environmentally friendly behaviours. According to Confucius, when dealing with the natural environment and its resources, if righteousness and benefit conflict each other, the former should be treated as the greater imperative. When we are not able to achieve both, Confucius advised that people should forgo benefit and follow the right rules (*Dao*) of the earth. People should follow this notion of treating the natural environment and exploiting their needed life materials under the condition of not damaging the ecology. The benefits are obvious for all involved. People should follow and respect the natural principles of the environment and balance the economic and personal choices in order to achieve any material needs in the best way. According to Confucius, people should be able to satisfy themselves with enough resources if they treat nature well and follow wisely the natural rules. (Pan, 2013)

Conclusion

The environmental damage caused by China's pursuit of unsustainable GDP growth is becoming more serious, and the country needs to be prepared to face these difficulties. In particular, there is need for the government to seek a balanced developmental strategy model to achieve this. China's environmental pollution and deterioration may challenge and delay future economic growth. Immediate actions are thus needed to adjust the current growth pattern. This includes achieving the goal of building a harmonious society, outlined by the government, including reducing corruption and enhancing environmental protection laws, regulations and education. (Morrison, 2013) Much of Confucianism and Taoism can be seen as being important in informing how to achieve these.

The ideas of Confucius, Lao Tzu and the other ancient philosophers can be used to direct and empower people of this day and age to deal with the environmental crisis, while still gaining access to needed resources. Confucius believed that the Earth was big enough to secure life with the condition that humans must treat nature with care, following the natural rules. (Pan, 2013) China, as the largest developing country, can set a good example by demonstrating that it is actively working to tackle climate change, restore and maintain the health of the natural environment. There is a lot of useful wisdom regarding sustainability that can be derived from ancient Chinese ideologies such as Confucianism and Taoism.

Indeed, it is the case that Confucianism has already been accepted not only in China but across the world. (Hsü, 2005) People need to remember to look back more often to seek the wisdom from their ancestors when developing economic and environmental policy. They need to pay more attention to the finite nature of many key resources and the planet itself. The sense of sustainability is not a new concept for China. Instead, the root of the sustainability concept was planted more than five thousand years ago. The nation's ancestors set a good example in respecting and taking care of nature, which has sustained human life for many generations. The thoughts of Confucius and other Chinese ancient philosophers informed today's basic sustainability concept of keeping the balance between economic development and environmental protection to achieve harmony.

(ZACHER L W. (ed.). Technology, society and sustainability[M]. Cham: Springer International Publishing AG, 2017.)

Comprehension Check

A. Questions for Discussion

1. Is the concept of sustainability new to China?
2. What is the wisdom of Confucius and Lao Tzu for sustainability?
3. How can we draw on the wisdom of Confucius and Lao Tzu in our contemporary challenges regarding climate change and environmental sustainability?

B. Detail Understanding

Match the persons and their opinions.

Person	Opinion
1. Aitken	A. New Confucian humanism is a source of inspiration for human flourishing in the twenty-first century.
2. Lebow	B. Environmental protection laws should be enhanced to adjust to the current growth pattern.
3. Tu	C. In the time of Confucius, the natural environment was held as sacred.
4. Hsü	D. Confucianism and Taoism both view nature, human beings and the cycles of nature as a holistic system in which humans must not only be in harmony with other beings, but also with nature itself.
5. Morrison	E. People seek their spiritual satisfactions from consumption.
6. Moller	F. Confucianism has already been accepted not only in China but across the world.

Suggestions for Further Reading

1. WARE J R. The sayings of Confucius[M]. New York: The New American Library, 1955.
2. PAN S D. Learning the wisdom of ancestors and understanding the truth of harmony (in Chinese) [EB/OL](2013-03-01)[2018-09-04]. http://www.chinavalue.net/general/blog/2013-3-1/959751.aspx.
3. 杨敏，王克奇，王恒展. 中国文化通览[M]. 北京：高等教育出版社，2006.

Unit 8　The Image of China

Diversity will be the engine that drives the corporation of the 21st Century.

—Stephen H. Rhinesmith

Objectives:

To understand what public diplomacy can do for the image of China;

To understand the image of China through the silk road;

To learn how to promote the image of China.

Warm-up Activity

Please put the following sentences into English and then explain their connotations.

(1) 志合者，不以山海为远。

(2) 朋友多了，路才好走。

(3) 志存高远，脚踏实地。

(4) 朋友越走越近，邻居越走越亲。

(5) 授人以鱼，更要授人以渔。

(6) 逢山开路，遇水架桥。

Part One

Intensive Reading

A New Era in Cultural Diplomacy: Promoting the Image of China's "Belt and Road" Initiative in Asia

In a multi-polar international system that is becoming more and more globalized, countries today are paying greater attention to cultural diplomacy, as part of a central component that represents their national and international interest and image in the international arena. China is one such country that through the reestablishment of the Old Silk Road, of the Silk Road Economic Belt and the 21st Century Maritime Silk Road, commonly called the "Belt and Road Initiative"(BRI), has transcended into a new era of cultural diplomacy. By means of the use of soft power in promoting its image and furthering its relations through the establishment of its strategic drive, it seems China is destined to connect the globe through this momentous initiative, more so than ever as a resourceful means in achieving its national and international interest.

Significantly, the growing popularity and expanding international recognition of Chinese culture and traditions over the years has demonstrated the increasing development and the importance of China's soft power. Fundamentally, through the Belt and Road Initiative, China has now been able to transform and demonstrate the vibrant contribution and impact of this policy, through such aspects of a multi-culturalism, multi-ethnicity, social, political and economic sphere. Additionally, China is able more so than ever with its peaceful image in sync with the new era of spreading cultural diplomacy through education, tourism, media, languages, performing arts, Confucius ideology, etc., by means of being perceptive, and developing the aptitude to utilize culture as the basis of soft power in its strategic drive.

China's rise in the world today not only symbolizes a significant shift based on its growing trade activities in Asia and beyond, but importantly, through its use of cultural diplomacy as a soft power, which has changed its reputation and image in the 21st century not only to be perceived as a global leader of trade to be contended with but also as a soft power strategist, projecting a non-confrontational image and friendly diplomacy.

Admittedly, soft power in China is leadership-driven and more or less is seen to be strongly associated with the Chinese culture. Fundamentally, when examined, it is noted that Chinese soft power relies mainly on sources of the aspects of public diplomacy, which is a form of cultural diplomacy, since in China, many of the aspects that public diplomacy covers such as television (TV), radio, cultural and educational exchanges, scholarly, newspaper publication, etc. are in actuality classified as culture.

Conversely, over the years China has garnered a central role in the utilization of cultural diplomacy as a soft power tool as an alternative approach in effectively stimulating, building and developing a more secure and stable image in the international system as a rising regional and global power. Notably, in today's world, there is clear indication that soft power has become a popular discourse in China's foreign policy and no doubt drives China's objective in Asia. Critically, China's soft power practice such as culture, purposely promotes an avenue to maintain friendly relations with other nations in the Asian region as an opportunity to avoid political and regional disputes, which in of itself promotes common prosperity, cultural exchanges and creates a medium for peace and regional connectivity.

Proposed by Chinese President Xi Jinping, the Belt and Road Initiative (BRI) is predominantly projected to be the longest economic corridor in the world, which will continue to promote the spirit of the ancient route (Ancient Silk Road) covering 4.4 billion people, accounting for 63% of the world population. Therefore, in looking at the focus of the Belt and Road Initiative in Asia, undoubtedly it is fueled through guaranteeing a viable economic hub, and acceptable also is that soft power plays an important role in setting the relationship in Asia, eventually opening doors for economic development, regional cooperation and connectivity, which will reshape and integrate the regional geo-political and economic landscape of the Asian region.

In effect, it is possible to say that China has been successful in using specific soft power techniques to build its image, as a trustworthy regional power with the ability to offer developmental growth in the Asian region now and optimistically will continue to do so in the future. From this conception, almost all countries in the world generally pursue peace in the international arena and the BRI is seen as an important initiative in the enhancement of peace to acquire developmental opportunities for all the countries party to this policy. Thus, in general, it is perceived that peace promotes and bridges a platform for communication, enhances cooperation, which in essence results in a happy and friendly society and over a period in turn promotes economic prosperity that a country and its citizen can enjoy.

Scholar, for instance, states that the BRI possesses rich Chinese cultural connotations and activates the essence of a harmonious Chinese culture in the new historical circumstance. Additionally, it is further elaborated that the bright future of the BRI is closely related to its historical origin and cultural charm. Historically, China's Old Silk Road was an established viable peaceful trade hub route in which goods were sold and bought along the customary path from China and beyond. This past practice resulted in shared harmonious heritage in the exchange of commodities. Moreover, it also resulted in the exchange of various aspects of culture, such as languages, ideologies, and a rich history of religious and harmonious cultural exchanges. Which fundamentally today, with the revival of the Old Silk Road by Chinese President Xi Jinping in 2013, marks a significant milestone which rhetorically gives importance to the shared historical cultural heritage of the past and the new emerging China. In effect, China is building directly on this legacy through mutual cooperation, respect and trust in Asia with the BRI, with the means of implementing projects to transform the infrastructural growth, increase global competitiveness and refocusing the countries party to this policy, as well as through the development of China's soft power. The other is that, the BRI has induced varied emotions of enthrallment, attraction, wonderment and trepidation on China's grand strategic vision of the BRI and its capability to "charm" through its use of its soft power tools.

The discourse over the years, understandably has varied and has now focused largely not only on the economics of the BRI, but now also on its soft power strategy such as culture that has now become an avenue, a gateway for China with the capability to influence. More so than ever, China undeterred with the BRI does have the strength and potential to influence and transform Asia with its soft power strategy peacefully, which eventually will boost its image regionally and globally.

In recent years, an increase number of scholars have pointed to China's past history of overcoming a century of humiliation at the hands of oppressive powers, thus of significance, this is one factor that plays a considerable major role in the way China conduct international affairs in today's society. Thus, it's clear and obvious in the way China expresses and communicates its ideas regionally and globally. Therefore, China's use of cultural diplomacy as a soft power strategy has become a powerful and meaningful innovative tool as a platform in promoting its image, influence, diplomatic ties, economic prosperity, etc.

Paying tremendous importance to the use of soft power strategy by China, in 2014 President Xi Jinping stated that, we should increase China's soft power, give a good narrative and better communicate China's message to the world. Likewise, former Chinese President Hu Jintao echoed similar sentiments by stating, "the great rejuvenation of the Chinese nation will definitely be accomplished by the thriving of Chinese culture". In fact, this more or less showcased the importance China places on culture and its use in promoting its image in the world through the use of soft power techniques.

Principally, Winter (2016) argues that based on the following historical narrative premise of connectivity, it is stated that both culture and economy reduce suspicion and promote common prosperity. For this reason, it should be clearly understood that culture does indeed shape the economic corridors of China, and evidently it is obvious through the newly revived Belt and Road Initiative, which in essence allows for economic growth, that will provide and lead towards the enhancement of regional connectivity and in particular that of cultural connectivity through shared heritage in order to gain mutual trust, further loyalty and influence China's image among countries in Asia.

Given the importance soft power plays, what essentially is soft power? The notion of "soft power" is an ability to coapt people to achieve political ends through attraction rather than coercion or payment. Thus, it is further stated that soft power relies on the ability to shape the agenda in world politics based on ones principles and ideas. Additionally, it is further elaborated that the concept of soft power is to exert power in such a way that others will do your bidding without being coerced. On the other hand, making a clear distinction between hard power and soft power, it is posited that, "hard power" is the ability to get others to act in ways that are opposed to their initial preferences and strategies. Essentially then, this is the ability to force, through the use of threats and inducements. Soft power is indeed as important as hard power and even more so in international politics. In today's contemporary society, when the concept of hard power is examined, in practicality it is very costly for countries that use hard power through the use of military means as coercive diplomacy, military interventions, threats or the use of force, economic sanctions, etc. , as part of its nationwide and foreign policy.

While in relation to soft power, it is "free", unconditionally in the sense that it does not require large resources and has limited consequences in case of failure. Essentially, soft power is a matter of "seduction" and behaviors such as arrogance, which might be counterproductive involving repulsion rather than attraction. Additionally, soft power can be conceived as being "passive" or in the eye of the beholder; and it is also identified as emerging from how outsiders perceive a country's values and systems from rather than being promoted from the inside.

By and large, when we reflect on the past the strong influential focus of China in promoting its image of peaceful inclusiveness is not a new occurrence. Years ago, China's influence has been filtered through the import of Chinese cultural values in the Asian region by means through the internalization of providing extensive training for Asian language teachers, sending more Chinese native speakers to work in schools in the Asian region, the creation of Chinese media organizations such as radio and television, etc. Currently the BRI has now allowed for added integration of the internalization of the Chinese culture not only through its vision of boosting economic integration, but also increasing connectivity, people to people exchange programs, infrastructure, etc. , through the tool of cultural diplomacy as a soft power strategy, largely leading to the development of cultural awareness and interest in Asia.

Since the revival of the BRI, it has been described by many as the most significant and most far reaching initiative that China has ever put forward. Hence, in 2015 at the Boao Forum for Asian Annual Conference, Xi Jinping in his speech stated that the BRI will promote intercivilization exchanges to build bridges of friendship for our people, drive human development and safeguard peace of the world. Principally, when one takes a keen look at China and the BRI in promoting its image in Asia, it is noted that China is investing immensely in numerous resources in Asia in connecting its past history by creating and establishing expos, festivals, universities, language training centers, museums, Confucius Institutes, television shows that represent the Chinese culture and innumerable other display of cultural diplomacy that promotes its image, and the development of cultural awareness by way of its soft power tools.

Nye, Jr. (2009) postulates that the major elements of a country's soft power include its culture (that is when it is pleasing to others), its values (when there are attractive and consistently practiced), and its policies (when they are seen as inclusive and legitimate). This in essence is what China has and is in no doubt intended to accomplish with the BRI. China has now placed significant values on its soft power strategy and has made its culture, its values and its policy attractive, inclusive and legitimate and this in turn has promoted China's image regionally in Asia as a peaceful and trustworthy partner, attractive giver, etc. , to the region, creating and bringing forth more cultural awareness of its cultural traditions and heritage. Acceptable is that China with its soft power strategy, is able to conduct its affairs in a peaceful manner without more or less overseas interference, thus attracting more support regionally.

Indeed, China is already promoting and supporting language training in many countries in Asia and over the years the numbers of language training center, Confucius institutes has risen steadily, resulting additionally in the increase of more Asian studying mandarin in the region. For example, In Malaysia, private language school enrollment in Chinese classes has increased immensely. In the Pakistan-China Institute in Islamabad, in collaboration with the University of Karachi's Latif Ebrahim Jamal National Science Information Centre, launched a basic Chinese language course in all public Universities across Pakistan, to be delivered via video conferencing to develop their Chinese Language skills (Confucius institutes expanding rapidly to meet demand for Chinese language skills, 2014). This nonetheless shows the increase influence of China's soft power, its image culturally through the BRI and its soft power strategy in increasing its influences and therefore the increased cultural awareness of China's culture.

The conceptual meaning of the BRI with its strong implication, despite numerous questions and doubts surrounding arguments of its success to succeed and needing to have a clear plan, evidently has been welcomed. Nevertheless, the initiative and the use of soft power strategy has set the tone for cross regional connectivity, fostering bilateral and multilateral cooperation, and in turn will create a platform in opening more doors for better understanding and awareness of the Chinese tradition and culture, thereby, equally creating a channel for the ease of better communication, between China and its Asian neighbors.

Evidently, the BRI is undoubtedly intended to change the landscape of Asia over the coming years through its economic ties, traditional and cultural appeal, diplomatic relationship, infrastructural partnership, multilateralism, etc. Through the use of cultural diplomacy as a soft power strategy, which stems from the perception of China's foreign policies, its five principles of peaceful co-existence and its alignments to the United Nations Charter, further propels the development of cultural awareness leading to cultural interest, which essentially will lead to a harmonious society in Asia.

China realized that establishing good relation is required with the BRI not only for security stability, regional, economic reasons, etc. Therefore, China in promoting its image and the development of cultural awareness in Asia, has been engaging and participating actively in a number of regional organizations and cooperations such as ASEAN, the Shanghai Cooperation Organization, East Asian Summit, Asian Development Bank (ADB), Asian Infrastructure Investment Bank (AIIB), etc. In this way, China's soft power will increase in the Asian region with the BRI and likewise increase cultural awareness of China's traditional and cultural values and further developing mutual understanding of its developmental strategy, resulting therefore in promoting a harmonious society in Asia.

In recognizing the significance of cultural diplomacy through the BRI, it is necessary to understand that it requires collective effort between governments, non-governmental organizations, regional organizations and soft power tools in order to promote the use of cultural diplomacy in Asia. China in effect, has realized that this is necessary for the BRI to be effective. Thus, ultimately the power to connect culturally, deepening cultural exchanges, sustain economic growth, security cooperation and bonding people regionally, can result in collectivity making the Asian countries and regions more culturally aware of the

Chinese culture and the development of cultural interest in developing a harmonious society.

(STERLING D P. A new era in cultural diplomacy: promoting the image of China's "Belt and Road" Initiative in Asia[J]. Open Journal of Social Sciences, 2018, 06(2): 102-116.)

Vocabulary

vibrant *adj.*	full of energy and enthusiasm
sync *n.*	match or happen together
perceptive *adj.*	be good at noticing or realizing things, especially things that are not obvious.
aptitude *n.*	ability to learn it quickly and to do it well.
utilize *vt.*	make work or employ (something) for a particular purpose
confrontational *adj.*	disapproval of the fact
garner *vt.*	gain or collect
activate *vt.*	causes it to start working
elaborate *vt.*	describe something that is very complex
trepidation *n.*	fear or anxiety
enthrallment *n.*	a feeling of great liking for something wonderful and unusual
undeterred *adj.*	not discouraged or dissuaded
humiliation *n.*	embarrassment and shame
oppressive *adj.*	treat people cruelly and unfairly
sentiment *n.*	an idea or feeling that someone expresses in words.
bidding *n.*	an authoritative direction or instruction to do something
exert *vt.*	put to use it in a strong or determined way
coerced *vt.*	to cause to do through pressure
repulsion *n.*	an extremely strong feeling of disgust
filter *vt.*	pass through
legitimate *adj.*	be acceptable according to the law
collaboration *n.*	act of working jointly
alignment *n.*	an organization of people (or countries) involved in a pact or treaty

Exercises

A. Words in Use

Fill in the blanks with the words given below. Change the form when necessary. Each word can be used only once.

sync	perceptive	exert	garner	legitimate
elaborate	sentiment	humiliation	filter	utilize

1. He has __________ extensive support for his proposals.
2. A spokesman declined to __________ on a statement released late yesterday.
3. The movie is not in __________ with reading, so let me show you a little about the reading.
4. I must agree with the __________ expressed by John Prescott.
5. He was one of the most __________ U. S. political commentators.
6. News of the attack quickly __________ through the college.
7. Sound engineers __________ a range of techniques to enhance the quality of the recordings.
8. She faced the __________ of discussing her husband's affair.
9. He __________ considerable influence on the thinking of the scientific community on these issues.
10. The French government has condemned the coup in Haiti and has demanded the restoration of the __________ government.

B. Questions for Discussion

1. What do you think is the soft power?
2. What's the significant impact of China's revival of the Old Silk Road and the construction of the BRI?
3. What do our soft power strategy contribute to a harmonious society?

C. Translation

1. The growing popularity and expanding international recognition of Chinese culture and traditions over the years has demonstrated the increasing development and the importance of China's soft power.
2. Conversely, over the years China has garnered a central role in the utilization of cultural diplomacy as a soft power tool as an alternative approach in

effectively stimulating, building and developing a more secure and stable image in the international system as a rising regional and global power.

3. Hence, in 2015 at the Boao Forum for Asian Annual Conference, Xi Jinping in his speech stated that the BRI will promote inter-civilization exchanges to build bridges of friendship for our people, drive human development and safeguard peace of the world.
4. Evidently, the BRI is undoubtedly intended to change the landscape of Asia over the coming years through its economic ties, traditional and cultural appeal, diplomatic relationship, infrastructural partnership, multilateralism, etc.

D. Case Study

Case 1

Chinese students at Columbia University, in New York, have had an unusual response after non-Western name tags were ripped from dorm room doors during the Chinese Lunar New Year. In a campaign later joined by other international students, the Chinese students attempted to explain to the English-speaking community the meaning carried by different characters in their names in a video entitled "Say my name".

In the video, students introduce their names, explain the origin of their name, its meaning in Chinese, and why the names are important to them. Students say the names are part of the Chinese culture and contain their parents' wishes and expectations for them, which they take seriously.

Question

Why did the incident incite outrages among the Chinese and the East Asian students' community?

Case 2

Learning culture through proverbs.

Proverb 1: The true friendship seeks to give, not take; to help, not to be helped; to minister, not to be ministered unto.

Proverb 2: A hedge between keeps friendship green.

Question

Work in pairs and exchange views on the meanings, and then find out their Chinese equivalents if there is any.

Part Two

Extensive Reading

The Creativity and Exchange

The Silk Road

Over a history of 5,000 years, Chinese people have produced numerous inventions. At the same time, the Chinese people have always kept an open heart toward friends and cultures from other lands. Wherever the Chinese travelers arrived, they carried out material and cultural exchanges under the principle of peace.

The Silk Road refers to a transport route connecting ancient China with Central Asia, West Asia, Africa, and the European continent. It appeared as early as the second century and was traveled mainly by silk merchants. The term "Silk Road", or "die Seidenstrasse" in German, was first noted down by the German geographer Ferdinand von Richthofen at the end of the 19th century.

The Silk Road began in Chang'an (present-day Xi'an, capital of Shanxi Province), passing through Gansu and Xinjiang to Central Asia, West Asia, and lands by the Mediterranean. There were no signs of communication between ancient Chinese civilization and Mediterranean civilization in earlier history. In about the seventh century BC, the ancient Greeks began to learn about an ancient civilization in the east, but knew little about it. Before the Silk Road, according to archeological findings, there had already existed an intermittent trade route on the grasslands from the Yellow River and the Indus River drainage areas to the Euphrates and the Tigris, and the Nile drainage areas. Yet real communication between China and Central and West Asian countries, Africa and the European continent did not develop until the opening of the Silk Road.

The Silk Road functioned not only as a trade route but also as a bridge that linked the ancient civilizations of China, India, the Mesopotamian plains, Egypt, and Greece. It also helped to promote the exchange of science and technology between east and west. The Silk Road served as the main channel for ancient China to open up to the outside world, as well as for fresh impulses from other cultures to enter the country, which contributed a significant share in the shaping of Chinese culture.

Zhang Qian, Trail Blazer

The pioneer who blazed the trail of the Silk Road was Zhang Qian, a general of the Western Han Dynasty. In Zhang Qian's time, the Chinese had little knowledge about Central and West Asian countries, Africa or Europe, although they were aware of the existence of many different countries and cultures in faraway places to the west.

During the reign of Emperor Wu, there were 36 small kingdoms in the Western Region (present-day Xinjiang and parts of Central Asia). All of them were later conquered by the Huns, who then posed a direct threat to the Western Han and blocked the dynasty's path west. Under these circumstances, Emperor Wu appointed Zhang Qian to lead a team of more than 100 envoys to the Western Regions. The mission was to unite the Indoscythic people against the Huns, who once killed their chieftain. Zhang Qian's team set out in 138 BC. No sooner had they entered the Hexi Corridor (northwest of present-day Gansu Province) than they were captured by the Huns. After being held under house arrest for over ten years, Zhang Qian and only one remaining envoy managed to escape and returned to Chang'an in 126 BC. Their accounts about the Western Regions were a revelation to the Han emperor and his ministers.

In the next two decades, Emperor Wu launched three major campaigns against the Huns, forcing them to retreat from the Western Regions. In 119 BC, the emperor sent Zhang Qian on a second mission to the Western Regions. This time Zhang Qian went further west, while his deputies reached more than a dozen countries in South and West Asia, and the Mediterranean.

Zhang Qian's two missions to the Western Regions opened up the road to the west. Emperor Wu adopted a series of measures to strengthen ties with the Western Regions, including encouraging Han people to trade there. Soon the route was bustling with caravans of camels carrying goods of all types and reverberating with the tinkling of their bells. Through the Silk Road, trade flourished between China and Central, South and West Asian countries, Afica, and Europe. In 166 AD, envoys from Rome arrived via the Silk Road in Chang'an, where they set up an embassy.

The Silk Road also facilitated active trades among India, Southeast Asia,

West Asia, Africa, and Europe. The exchange of new goods and technologies from different continents greatly helped to promote the development of all the civilizations involved.

Opening to the "West"

The Silk Road exerted an inestimable influence on the lives of the Chinese people. While Chinese culture and technology, such as papermaking and printing, were introduced to countries to the west, China also absorbed many elements from the arts, philosophy and religions of many other countries. This helped to promote an open policy toward other cultures from the Han to Tang dynasties.

The Silk Road highlights a period of history when China looked west for a farther vision of the world. To the east, apart from the islands of the Pacific and Japan, the country faced only a huge ocean. To the west, in contrast, there were many countries in the Western Regions and beyond. By the tenth century, Chinese explorers had already realized there were rich countries, attractive goods and artworks, and different peoples beyond the Western Regions. This aroused great interest in the "west" among ancient Chinese people.

Buddhism, for example, was first introduced to Khotan Kingdom (covering present-day Hetian area of Xinjiang) in the Western Regions before or after the epoch of the Gregorian Calender, and then gradually spread to the Central Plains along both the southern and northern routes of the Silk Road. This religion has since exerted a huge influence not only on Chinese beliefs but also on the development of Chinese thinking. Nestorianism and Islam were also introduced to China through the Silk Road.

Cultures and arts from other lands have left valuable legacies along the Silk Road, such as the murals in the Gaochang, Kuche and Dunhuang grottoes. They stand as evidence of a stunning blend of Chinese and western art and culture.

Zheng He's Voyages to the Western Seas

On the 11th day of the 7th lunar month of 1405, a huge fleet of 208 ships appeared on the blue seas of the earth. With more than 27,500 people aboard, it was the greatest fleet with the largest crews the world had ever seen. Carrying cargoes of porcelain, silk, tea, and numerous other treasures, the fleet navigated the South China Sea, passing through the Strait of Malacca, and traversing the Indian Ocean to arrive at countries on the coasts of Asia and Africa. Over the next 28 years, six more fleets of a similar scale, with crews totaling more than 100, 000 people, left China for further voyages to the Western Seas and arrived in more than 30 countries along the way. "Western Seas" was the term used in ancient China to refer to the west regions of the South China Sea. In West Asia, they visited the holy city of Mecca; in Africa, they reached as far as the port of Beira.

The commander of the fleet was Zheng He (1371-1433), an important official in the court of Emperor Yongle of the Ming Dynasty. Born in a Muslim family, Zheng He also believed in Buddhism and Mazu (Chinese goddess of the sea). Intelligent and knowledgeable about navigation, he was entrusted by the emperor to direct all these seven adventurous missions.

Advanced Navigation Civilization

From the 15th century on, humans had accelerated their pace in combing the oceans. Christopher Columbus (1451-1506) came upon the continent of the Americas in 1492 by traveling across the Pacific with his Spanish fleet. The Portuguese fleet of Vasco da Gama (1460-1524) passed around Africa's Cape of Hope and across the Indian Ocean, to arrive at Calicut on the west coast of India in 1498. Ferdinand Magellan (1480-1521) and his Spanish fleet claimed the first round-the-world navigation in 1522.

Compared with these explorers, Zheng He's voyages took place much earlier and on a much larger scale. On each of the seven voyages to the Western Seas, his fleet consisted of more than 100 ships, with 62 large and medium-sized ships forming the main body. Crews and other personnel added up to more than 20,000. Columbus fleet had only three ships and an 88-member crew. Obviously, Zheng He's fleets were unparalleled in terms of size, navigation technology, organization and amenities.

Zheng He's ships were also constructed with advanced technology and craft. A large-sized ship in the fleet was 150 meters long, 60 meters wide and 12 meters deep. It had a cargo capacity of about 1,000 tons, with four levels to house more than 1,000 crew and passengers. The foredeck had an area of 9,000 square meters, equal to the size of half a football field. The ship had nine masts with 12 sails. Its iron rudder needed more than 200 people to lift. The large ships of Zheng He's fleet would still look extraordinary even today.

Spreading Peace

When Emperor Yongle sent Zheng He on the missions to the Western Seas, he expected to show off the prosperity of the Ming Empire as well as to put his ideals into practice, of making friends with and spreading peace to other countries near and far. Zheng He's huge fleet was indeed proof of the strength of China at that time. At the same time, the navigator was also fulfilling the emperor's wishes of developing China's international relations.

Zheng He's family chronicles, which came to light in the 1930s, include record of Emperor Yongle's exhortations before his departure: "Follow the ways of Heaven and the world, do not bully small or weak countries, and spread the blessing of peace." On all his voyages, Zheng He strictly followed the emperor's instructions.

Although Zheng He brought a large armed force along on all seven long journeys, only on three occasions during those 28 years did he deploy troops. The first time was to wipe out pirates in the Palembang area (southeast of present-day Sumatra), to restore order and transport routes. The second and third times when he used force were for self-defense: against an attack by a king of Ceylon (now Sri Lanka), and against a gang of rioters from the Sumatra area. None of these acts constituted a violation of the principle of peace laid down by Emperor Yongle.

Of the many places that Zheng He's fleets reached, they never occupied an inch of anybody's territory, nor took away the slightest bit of anybody's property, nor left a single soldier on anybody's land. Instead, they always presented all sorts of gifts to local kings and their families, chieftains at different levels, and to Buddhist temples. The gifts ranged from cash, silk, porcelain and clothing, to utensils made of iron, copper, silver and gold. Zheng He even brought bricks, tiles and glazed tiles for locals to build temples in some parts of Southeast Asia. Following principles of fair trade, Zheng He's crew bartered porcelain, silk, tea, and metal utensils with local governments and ordinary citizens for jewelry, spices, medicine, and rare animals. They also introduced to the countries they visited items such as: the Chinese calendar, Chinese medical sciences, and technologies in farming, manufacturing, navigation and shipbuilding.

On every one of his missions, Zheng He would bring envoys from other lands back to China. For example, in the ninth lunar month of 1422 (20th year of Emperor Yongle's reign), more than 1,200 envoys from 16 states of Southern Africa came to visit China with Zheng He's fleet. There were also several kings who traveled on Zheng He's ship back to China. Three of them from Sulu (now Sulu Archipelago of the Philippines), Borneo (today's Kalimantan Island) and Gran Molucas (now Mindanao Island of the Philippines) stayed in China until they died due to illness. When the king of Borneo died in 1408, Emperor Yongle called a recess of the court for three days of mourning.

People in some Asian countries still retain fond memories of Zheng He's visits. One can find many commemorative buildings in these countries such as the temple named after Zheng He in the Indonesian port city of Semarang. In the Malacca Straits area there can be found a well said to have been dug by Zheng He. In 2004, in celebration of the 30th anniversary of the establishment of diplomatic ties between Malaysia and China, the Royal Opera House in Kuala Lumpur staged a large bilingual song-and-dance drama in Chinese and Malay. Based on *Sejarah Melayu*, or *The Malay Annals* (编年史), the drama presented the story of Princess Hanbaoli, daughter of Emperor Yongle, who was escorted by Zheng He and a 500-member retinue to her wedding with Sultan Mansur Shah of Malacca. This is one of the many fine stories about the travels of Zheng He.

(YE L, ZHU L Z. Insights into Chinese culture[M]. Beijing: Foreign Language Teaching and Research Press, 2014: 61-81.)

Language focus

archeological *adj.* 考古学的
drainage *n.* 排水系统
revelation *n.* 启示；揭露
reverberate *vi.* 反响
mural *n.* 大型壁画
porcelain *n.* 瓷器
foredeck *n.* 前甲板
bully *vt.* 欺负；威吓
rioter *n.* 暴徒；暴民
commemorative *adj.* 纪念的
intermittent *adj.* 断断续续的
envoy *n.* 使者
deputy *n.* 代表
bustle *n.* 喧闹
stunning *adj.* 震耳欲聋的
amenity *n.* 便利设施
exhortation *n.* 训词；劝告
deploy *vt.* 部署；展开
barter *n.* 物物交换
bilingual *adj.* 双语的

Exercises

A. Text Reading

Decide whether the following statements are true (T) or false (F).

1. ______ There wasn't communication between China and West Asian countries before the opening of the Silk Road.
2. ______ The first mission of Zhang Qian was to know more cultures about the faraway places to the west.
3. ______ The Silk Road helped China learn many technologies from the countries in the west.
4. ______ The expression "Silk Road" was not recorded until about 1,700 years after its appearance.
5. ______ The destinations of Zheng He's voyage are countries located on the coasts of Asia and Africa.
6. ______ Buddhism, Taoism and Islam were introduced to China through the Silk Road.
7. ______ Zheng He was appointed as the commander of the missions because he was an important official in the court of Emperor Yongle.
8. ______ The purposes of Zheng He's mission were mainly to show off the prosperity of the Ming Empire and put into practice Emperor Yongle's ideals.
9. ______ Zheng He's crew traded their porcelain and metal utensils for spices and rare animals.
10. ______ Zheng He deployed troops for three times on his seven missions.

B. Terms Understanding

Find the definitions of the following terms or events in the text. If you cannot find the exact definition, try to use your own words to interpret it.

1. The Silk Road
2. Buddhism
3. Zheng He's voyages to the western seas

C. Classroom Activities

1. What does "real communication" in paragraph 2 mean?
2. What did Zhang Qian's two missions resulted in?

3. Today, the ancient trade route—the Silk Road—is renewed with the Belt and Road Initiative. Could you explain how the Silk Road are consistent with the Belt and Road Initiative?

Part Three

Academic Reading

The Chinese Dream

Chinese Communist Party leader Xi Jinping said during a museum tour in November of 2012, the Chinese dream meant for him the "great renewal of the Chinese nation".

Background: Connotations of Chinese Dream

In November of 2012, soon after the conclusion of the 18th National Congress of the Communist Party of China (CPC), President Xi Jinping put forward, for the first time, the idea of the Chinese Dream on a visit to "The Road towards Renewal" exhibition at the National Museum of China. The great rejuvenation of the Chinese nation "is a dream of the whole nation, as well as of every individual", he said.

In March of 2013, Xi further elaborated on the Chinese Dream in his speech at the closing ceremony of the First Session of the 12th National People's Congress. Since then, he has talked about the concept on a number of occasions.

Xi stressed that the Chinese Dream means the great rejuvenation of the Chinese nation. It embodies achieving prosperity for the country, renewal of the nation and happiness for the citizens. Only when the country is doing well can the nation and people do well.

Xi emphasized that the Chinese Dream in essence means the dream of the people. The Chinese Dream is to let people enjoy better education, more stable employment, higher incomes, a greater degree of social security, better medical and health care, improved housing conditions and a better environment. It is to let our children grow up well, have satisfactory jobs and live better lives.

Xi stressed that all the Chinese people who live in our great country at this great time have the opportunity to enjoy a successful life, the opportunity to realize one's dream, and the opportunity to grow and progress together with the country.

Xi also emphasized that the Chinese Dream is a dream for peace, development, cooperation and mutual benefit for all. It is connected to the beautiful dreams of the people in other countries. The Chinese Dream will not only benefit the Chinese people, but also people of all countries in the world.

Xi proposed taxonomy of five dimensions from which to analyze the concept—national, personal, historical, global and antithetical. The "national Chinese Dream", as Xi described, is a big dream for the Chinese nation: "History tells us that everybody has one's future and destiny closely connected to those of the country and nation."

The "personal Chinese Dream", for instance, focuses on the well-being of individual citizens and thus modifies traditional notions of the primacy of the collective over the individual. In the global prospect, the Chinese Dream will change the global landscape, which was shaped by Western countries over the past two centuries during industrialization. The new global landscape will be established through international rules and experiences of both developed and emerging countries, he said.

Potential of the Chinese Dream

The Chinese Dream integrates national and personal aspirations, with the twin goals of reclaiming national pride and achieving personal well-being. It requires sustained economic growth, expanded equality and an infusion of cultural values to balance materialism.

Dreams are powerful. In advancing the Chinese Dream the government is uniting people around a shared mission and driving change, especially people in lower-tier cities and rural areas, as they experience increased affluence and opportunity.

Externally, the Chinese Dream can improve the image of China as a fast-growing nation striving to improve the welfare of its people and secure its place as a respected leader of the international community. In addition, the Chinese Dream can help elevate the overseas perception of Brand China, the collective reputation of products and services that originate in China.

Like many developments in modern China, awareness of the Chinese Dream happened with great speed. Chinese social media is full of postings about the Chinese Dream, in which people express their demands for free education, better air quality and safe food. The government has raised awareness of its view of the Chinese Dream with a poster campaign and other publicity.

When the Chinese people say they support the Chinese Dream, they mean it. They take national pride seriously. According to the Wire and Plastic Products Group (WPP) research from The Futures Company, 67 percent of Chinese say showing national pride is very or extremely important. Only 60 percent of Americans and 48 percent of Britons agree showing national pride is important.

When we asked Chinese what country they feel is the most ideal today, they answered the United States. When we asked them what country would be ideal in 10 years, they said China. This optimism may be driven by a phenomenon articulated by The Futures Company, which suggests that personal satisfaction is determined less by one's current status and more by the prospects of improvement in the future. In its *Global Monitor 2013*, a consumer intelligence tool, The Futures Company found that 58 percent of Chinese say they are very or extremely satisfied with their lives, compared with 48 percent of Americans and only 33 percent of Britons.

At the same time, Chinese realize that their lives have room for improvement, with an overwhelming 79 percent agreeing that they'd be happier with more possessions. Only 16 percent of Britons and 14 percent of Americans say they need more stuff. Based on the Global Monitor research, The Futures Company concludes that once people worldwide satisfy their basic material needs, adding more possessions doesn't usually increase happiness. Chinese aren't there yet. But they are determined to reach this threshold. For the past 30 years Chinese have been manufacturing and exporting products to meet the materialistic aspirations of consumers in the West. Chinese are now ready to consume what they produce, to realize the materialistic aspect of the Chinese Dream. The only question is whether this acquisition of material goods will unfold as Western-style conspicuous consumption in China or in a more considered way, informed by a Chinese cultural appreciation for keeping life in balance.

Realization of the Chinese Dream is important to Chinese for practical reasons, because it will improve the lives of people, particularly in lower-tier cities and rural areas. And it is important for reasons of national identity, to bring a country with a proud history out of the shadows of the troubling last couple of centuries. This commitment to the dream is consistent across all age groups and highest among younger people, ages 30 to 39. These people, who mostly grew up during the period of China's rapid economic growth, tend to be more individualistic and determined to advance either by finding a good job or starting their own businesses. Two-thirds of the Chinese people surveyed said the Chinese Dream makes them feel more confident about their personal future and 61 percent say the Chinese Dream makes them feel more confident about the future of the country. They also rate the dream high for strengthening social cohesion, making the country more energetic and influencing positive social change.

In contrast, achievement of the national dream is not as urgent in the U. K. or the U. S. , developed nations that continue to evolve, but not at the pace of fast-growing China. Only 39 percent of British people say that achieving the British Dream is important to them. And the result drops off dramatically with age. Only one-third of Britons over age 50 say achieving the dream is important. The absence of a clearly articulated national dream in the U. K. may reflect an overall sense of national confidence that a nation with a rich heritage can endure without a national dream. Or the absence may indicate a missed opportunity to inspire people and reenergize the country for successful engagement with the modern world. Younger Britons are more open to having a British Dream. Over half of people ages 18 to 29 say a national dream is important. America falls in the middle, with about two-thirds saying that achieving the American Dream is important to them individually. That response stays fairly consistent regardless of age, with a modest decline after age 50.

In the U. S. and the U. K. , there is also a link between the extent to which the national dream inspires people to feel confident both about their personal future and the future of the nation. The intensity of these beliefs is much lower, however, compared with China. In the U. S. , 45 percent of people polled said that the American Dream makes them feel more confident about their own future; 42 percent said the American Dream makes them confident about the future of the nation. That compares with 66 percent and 61 percent in China.

The American Dream is cultural wallpaper. It surrounds Americans in film, advertising and other popular media, sets the tone for how they think about the nation, but it remains in the background until particular circumstances prompt a political leader or someone else to point it out. Less defined, the British Dream lacks the presence and pattern of wallpaper. It's more like a room filled with random memorabilia that reminds Britons of their history and heritage.

Unlike the American Dream or the British Dream, the Chinese Dream is part of daily conversation.

The Chinese Dream in Western Eyes

In China, the Chinese Dream stirs hopes and sets expectations; internationally, it provokes questions and elicits concerns. President Xi Jinping's overarching vision of the Chinese Dream has become a grand driver of China's continuing reform and development. The Chinese Dream differs from the American Dream in that it expresses China's collective aspirations— "the great rejuvenation of the Chinese nation"(in Xi's words) —and it differs from the Chinese Dream in Chinese history by embracing the personal dreams of individual Chinese people for attaining happy, healthy, abundant and productive lives.

That the entire world derives material benefits from the Chinese Dream is apparent in a global economy. Higher standards of living mean greater consumption of goods and services in China, which works to create jobs and prosperity in a multiplier effect worldwide. China's commitment to science enables all peoples to share in China's success, often by making new technologies widely available at low costs.

Misperceptions, however, can distort motivations. Western anxiety is rooted in the fear that for China to fulfill the Chinese Dream, China will become more assertive, more aggressive and more expansionist in foreign affairs, especially when dealing with smaller neighbors. Even though China's leaders avow "No matter how strong China becomes, China will never seek hegemony", there's still the worry that sometime in the future, newer reasons will emerge to belie the older promises. One never knows, foreigners fret, when the "gentle giant" will have a change of heart, when the "awakened lion" will not be so "peaceful, pleasant and civilized".

In his speech "China's Challenge to American Hegemony", former U. S. ambassador Charles W. Freeman Jr. (the chief interpreter during President Nixon's legendary trip to China in 1972) advises us "to see China as it is, not as we wish or fear it to be" nor as China itself may today sincerely proclaim. He argues: "China is inadvertently echoing the American isolationists of the 19th and early 20th centuries. The United States did not then seek to dominate or control the international state system, nor did it pursue military solutions to problems far from its shores. In time and in reaction to events, however, America came to do both."

Freeman concludes: "The more likely prospect is that China will take its place alongside the U. S. and others at the head of a multilateral system of global governance. In such an oligarchic world order, China will have great prestige but no monopoly on power comparable to that which the U. S. has recently enjoyed."

Li Junru, former vice-president of the Central Party School, said that it is a misunderstanding to worry about China's expansion when the country is seeking rejuvenation. Rather, he said, "we put forward the concept of rejuvenation based on our historical experience that lagging behind leaves one vulnerable to attacks."

What about that danger of "self-fulfilling prophecy"? It cuts both ways. If foreign powers, led by the U. S., do in fact strategize to "contain China" (artlessly applying George Kennan's classic Cold War narrative of "containing" the Soviet Union), then China will react adversely and confrontation will be made more likely, not less. Similarly, if China robotically interprets all U. S. policies as "containment", and reacts adversely, it could inadvertently make actual containment more likely. It's "Game Theory 101". These political equations can only be solved in parallel, not in series, with "transparency" being the key operator. China and the U. S. must strive for openness and candor, particularly in matters of defense.

Foreigners are wary of relying on China's goodwill, no matter how genuine. This frustrates China, but China must not cast blame or conjure up conspiracies. Better is to show how China's national interest would be undermined by trying to assert hegemony. China's main mission is to elevate the standard of living of its citizens and international troubles undercut China's capacity to achieve this goal.

Looking back, future historians will likely assess the Chinese Dream as a visionary milestone that energized President Xi's transformation of China across a broad spectrum of complex economic, social and governance issues. The entire world should benefit—though missteps along the way will be easy to make. Vigilance and diligence are not optional.

Making "Chinese Dream" a Reality

The plenum of the Central Committee of the Communist Party of China (CPC) promised reforms necessary to pave the way for the realization of Chinese dream.

"China's society is extremely complex compared to the past, so a comprehensive approach to reform is required." said U. S. expert Robert Lawrence Kuhn, Chairman of Kuhn Foundation. Addressing a forum called "International Dialogue on the Chinese Dream" held in Shanghai, Kuhn said the Chinese Dream cannot be achieved without reform.

Chinese President Xi Jinping came up with the "Chinese Dream" and it has since become a buzzword both at home and abroad. Xi said everyone has his or her own ideals and pursuits, in addition to this shared dream, "realizing the nation's great rejuvenation is the greatest dream of the nation", Xi said.

For Kenneth Lieberthal, senior researcher at the Brookings Institution, the meaning of Chinese Dream is wide ranging, with six key components required to make the dream real: a development model based on efficiency and institutional capacity; ecological urbanization; fair distribution of the benefits of economic development; political reform; reduction of governmental interference in the market; and social stability.

The decision on major issues concerning comprehensively deepening reform was adopted in response to people's concerns and requests. It requires reform to be complete by 2020, the same deadline as that of building a moderately prosperous society.

Kuhn has recognized the historical significance of the third plenary session of the 18th CPC in November as similar to the third session of the 11th led by Deng Xiaoping to institute economic reform. The agenda includes difficult areas, such as state-owned enterprises and land reform, he said, which demonstrates that China is trying to move forward. The result is a blueprint for development, though not a guarantee of success, Kuhn added.

Other experts at the forum discussed financial reform, demographics and ecology, calling the Chinese Dream a prompt to consensus among the middle class, which is crucial for further reform.

Gustaaf Geeraerts, director of the Brussels Institute of Contemporary China studies, said that the Chinese Dream needed new ideas in the economy, politics, culture, society and the environment.

"These will require big changes in organizational structure, administrative functions and personnel." said Martin Jacques, a visiting senior fellow from IDEAS Centre for the Study of International Affairs, Diplomacy and Grand Strategy of the London School of Economics and Political Science. Martin does not expect western style reform. "The Chinese state and the government has never been the same as western countries, but I expect the reform in information publicity, representation and responsibility for the people."

Rejuvenating China, the Chinese Dream will benefit the world with experiences for other regions and countries to follow and help establish win-win relationships among world players, Martin added.

(①Background: Connotations of Chinese Dream[N]. 2014-03-05[2018-09-04]. http://www.chinadaily.com.cn/china/2014npcandcppcc/2014-03/05/content_17324203. ②Potential of the Chinese Dream[N]. 2014-03-26[2018-09-04]. http://usa.chinadaily.com.cn/epaper/2014-03/26/content_17380146.htm. ③The Chinese Dream in Western eyes[N]. 2014-04-17[2018-09-04]. http://www.chinadaily.com.cn/china/2014-04/17/content_17465392.htm. ④Making the 'Chinese dream' a reality[N]. 2013-12-08[2018-09-04]. http://www.chinadaily.com.cn/china/2013-12/08/content_17160305.htm.)

Comprehension Check

A. Questions for Discussion

1. How was the concept "Chinese Dream" initiated and developed?
2. To which dimensions is the concept to be explained?
3. Discuss and compare Chinese Dream with American Dream.

B. Detail Understanding

Match the persons and their viewpoints.

Person	Viewpoint
1. Gustaaf Geeraerts	A. The reform on organizational structure and personnel is necessary to realize the Chinese Dream.
2. Martin Jacques	B. It is unnecessary to worry about China's rejuvenation for some Westerners.
3. Xi Jinping	C. The prompt to consensus among the middle class is important for further reform.
4. Robert Lawrence Kuhn	D. Chinese Dream means the great rejuvenation of the Chinese nation.
5. Li Junru	E. Chinese Dream includes six key components.
6. Kenneth Lieberthal	F. The Chinese Dream cannot be achieved without reform.

Suggestions for Further Reading

1. CHEN D D. The rise of China's new soft power[N/OL]. The Diplomat, (2015-06-09)[2018-09-04]. http://thediplomat.com/2015/06/the-rise-of-chinas-new-soft-power/
2. Just what is Xi Jinping's "Chinese Dream" and "Chinese Renaissance"[N]. South China Morning Post, 2013-02-06.
3. 罗新星. 跨文化传播视野下的文化软实力[J]. 湖南社会科学, 2011, (2): 167-170.

Keys

Unit 1

Warm-up Activity

In this case, people's different reactions reveal not only their individual personality, but also the orientation of their nation's mainstream culture: the English's seriousness, the French's arrogance, the Spanish's generosity, the Japanese's critical approach, the Arab's sarcasm and the American's humor.

Part One

A. Words in Use

1. neutral 2. sentiment 3. sophisticating 4. imperative 5. pervasive
6. mutual 7. implicit 8. concrete 9. recognition 10. ambiguity

B. 略

C. Translation

1. 问题的要点是，语言和文化是分不开的，即使交流双方讲相同的语言，但如果文化不同，也会出现沟通障碍。
2. 文化意识指对文化多元性的意识和对文化差异的宽容态度。
3. 在文化意识的最后一个阶段，我们要以重视、欣赏的眼光对待自己的文化，无论它是本土的，还是借鉴外族的。对待其他文化，我们也能持相同的态度。
4. 文化意识之旅最终还是由个人去完成，他们很可能像萨克斯诗歌中的六位盲人一样，永远不知道全部的真相或最好的答案，但这些障碍不应该阻止他们去探寻。

Part Two

A. Text Reading

1. F 2. T 3. T 4. T 5. T 6. T 7. F 8. F 9. T 10. T

B. Terms Understanding

1. A situation or position in which a person feels secure, comfortable, or in control.
2. Culture can be defined as human creation. It is the human part of the environment. Cultures are not fixed. It may be fundamental, while it is not innate.
3. The encoding of a message is the production of the message. It is a system of coded meanings, and in order to create that, the sender needs to understand how the world is comprehensible to the members of the audience.
   In the process of encoding, the sender (i. e. encoder) uses verbal (e. g. words, signs, images, video) and non-verbal (e. g. body language, hand gestures, face expressions) symbols for which he or she believes the receiver (that is, the decoder) will understand. The symbols can be words and numbers, images, face expressions, signals and/or actions. It is very important how a message will be encoded; it partially depends on the purpose of the message.
4. The decoding of a message is how an audience member is able to understand, and interpret the message. It is a process of interpretating and translating the coded information into a comprehensible form. The audience is trying to reconstruct the idea by giving meanings to symbols and by interpreting the message as a whole. Effective communication is accomplished only when the message is received and understood in the intended way. However, it is still possible for the message recipient to understand a message in a completely different way from what was the encoder was trying to convey. This is when "distortions" or "misunderstanding" arise from "lack of equivalence" between the two sides in communicative exchange.
5. Perception is defined as "the internal process by which we select, organise and interpret information" from the outside world. In other words, our perceptions of the world are what we tend to notice, reflect upon and respond to in our environment that is meaningful and significant to us.

6. Beliefs are the judgments we make about what is true or probable. They are usually linked to objects or events that possess certain characteristics that we believe to be true with or without proof.
7. Values are defined as "an enduring set of beliefs that serve to guide or direct our behaviour". They represent the norms of a culture and specify, for instance, what is good or bad, right or wrong, rude or polite, appropriate or inappropriate. In other words, they provide us with a set of rules for behaving, making choices and reducing uncertainty.

C. 略

Part Three

A. 略

B. Detail Understanding

A. *Linguistics Across Cultures*; first attempted to link language and culture in teaching
B. Developed the principles of intercultural communication
C. Identified human universals in visual perception and cognitive processing
D. *Narrative, Literacy and Face in Interethnic Communication*
E. Propagated the concepts of individualistic vs. collectivist cultures
F. Illustrated the different ways various cultures have of expressing themselves
G. Provided implications for the teaching of English reading and writing for non-English speakers

Unit 2

Warm-up Activity

Situation 1

"*What's this*?" sounds too abrupt and impolite. It is better to make some appreciative comment first. Such as "This is delicious. What is it?" (if you have just tasted it) or "That looks interesting. What is it?" (if you have not tasted it yet).

It's not wrong to say "*Is this sweet or salty*?", but the difference—like the Chinese 甜 and 咸—is better described as sweet and savoury. Savoury is a general word used to describe main course dishes like meat and vegetables as well as others, like cheese and crackers (salty biscuits). A cocktail party may offer savouries (small portions of slightly salty foods) as well as drinks and sweets. Note that the most common word for the sweet food at the end of a Western meal is dessert, but it may also be called sweet or pudding.

In "*What are the materials*?" the word "materials" should be replaced by "ingredients", which are the things mixed together to make a particular type of food or drink.

Situation 2

Sometimes it can cause offence to say bluntly that you don't like something. It is better to indicate you have already had enough. Such as "*No, thanks, I am doing very well for the moment.*"

Part One

A. Words in Use

1. digestive 2. opinionated 3. obsession 4. asserted 5. indulge
6. strain 7. lethargy 8. boost 9. reinforce 10. irritated

B. Questions for Discussion

1. ①Before you travel to another country, learn as much as you can about the geography, history, politics, and education system of that country. ②If an orientation program is available for you, attend it. You will learn lots of details about the university, the place in which you will live, and the transportation system. ③Think about what makes you happy and bring some of these objects with you, such as music, pictures and so on.
2. 略
3. ①Recognize that overseas adaptation is a process composed of many large and small adjustments, and that almost everyone experiences some negative emotions when they move to another country. ②Do not forget that there would be physical and physiological changes during the first week or two. ③It is important to remind yourself that each culture has an internal logic to it. Stop yourself from making negative comments about the new culture.

C. Translation

1. 尽管不是所有的人都经历同样的阶段，但是对大部分初次体验不同文化的人来说，他们都会经历悲喜，都会遇到积极和消极的境遇。

2. 体验者面对"文化休克"所产生的症状包括在生理上会使人身体不适、没胃口、头疼、咳嗽、萎靡不振等；在心理方面，也会导致人的敏感和易怒。
3. 如果你对自己的英语水平不自信，你就想一下并不是所有的英国人都会说一门外语。这样想会提高你的语言自信。
4. 不要只和你的同胞或者其他外国人交流，而要多与英国本土人士交流，这会让你适应得更快。而提出问题是促进交流的有效方式。

D. Case Study

Case 1

Westerners usually sit wherever the host points to or where they themselves like to sit, regardless of the kind of seats there might be. While choosing to sit in a less comfortable place is a sign of modesty in China.

Case 2

1. The Chinese student felt disappointed at British hospitality because she used the Chinese way of showing hospitality to judge the British one.
2. Stew is a dish with meat, vegetables, etc., cooked together in liquid.
3. British people show their hospitality in a different way.

Part Two

A. Text Reading

1. T 2. F 3. T 4. T 5. T 6. F 7. T 8. F 9. T 10. T

B. Terms Understanding

1. Culture shock is an experience a person may have when one moves to a cultural environment which is different from one's own; it is also the personal disorientation a person may feel when experiencing an unfamiliar way of life due to immigration or a visit to a new country, a move between social environments, or simply transition to another type of life. One of the most common causes of culture shock involves individuals in a foreign environment. Culture shock can be described as consisting of at least one of four distinct phases: honeymoon, negotiation, adjustment, and adaptation.
2. During this period, the differences between the old and new culture are seen in a romantic light. For example, in moving to a new country, an individual might love the new food, the pace of life, and the locals' habits. During the first few weeks, most people are fascinated by the new culture.

They associate with nationals who speak their language, and who are polite to the foreigners. Like most honeymoon periods, this stage eventually ends.

3. After some time (usually around three months, depending on the individual), differences between the old and new culture become apparent and may create anxiety. Excitement may eventually give way to unpleasant feelings of frustration and anger as one continues to experience unfavorable events that may be perceived as strange and offensive to one's cultural attitude. Language barriers, stark differences in public hygiene, traffic safety, food accessibility and quality may heighten the sense of disconnection from the surroundings.
4. After some time (usually 6 to 12 months), one grows accustomed to the new culture and develops routines. One knows what to expect in most situations and the host country no longer feels all that new. One becomes concerned with basic living again, and things become more "normal". One starts to develop problem-solving skills for dealing with the culture and begins to accept the culture's ways with a positive attitude. The culture begins to make sense, and negative reactions and responses to the culture are reduced.
5. In the mastery stage individuals are able to participate fully and comfortably in the host culture. Mastery does not mean total conversion; people often keep many traits from their earlier culture, such as accents and languages. It is often referred to as the bicultural stage.
6. Ego may refer to several related concepts:
   (1) Ego (Freudian), one of the three constructs in Sigmund Freud's structural model of the psyche.
   (2) Self-concept, a collection of beliefs about oneself that embodies the answer to "Who am I?"
   (3) I (pronoun), the first-person singular nominative case personal pronoun in modern English

C. 略

Part Three

A. 略

B. Detail Understanding

1. B 2. D 3. E 4. A 5. C

Unit 3

Warm-up Activity

1. Silence 2. Silence 3. Destiny 4. Destiny 5. Courage 6. Courage

Part One

A. Words in Use

1. accuse 2. predominant 3. controversial 4. confrontation 5. supreme 6. provocation 7. conciliatory 8. consensus 9. eloquence 10. corporate

B. Questions for Discussion

1. language is part of the culture and also a carrier of the culture. Culture shapes its people's behavior. When you observe people's behavior, you can better understand the culture if you understand the words or expressions they are using.

   The following are common proverbs in English. Each proverb communicates a cultural value that is so important to Americans.

Proverbs	Chinese Equivalents	Values
Remember the roots of your family tree, but you are known by your fruit, not by your root.	不可忘本，但是扬名不是靠出身，而是靠成就。	Equality
Discontent is the first step in progress.	不知足是前进的第一步。	Change
Men live like fish; the great ones devour the small.	弱肉强食。	Competition
God helps those who help themselves.	天助自助者。	Independence
Work while you work, play while you play.	工作时工作， 玩耍时玩耍。	Concentration
Great gain makes work easy.	所获甚丰，辛劳也觉轻松。	Materialism
Time lost cannot be won again.	时间一去不复返。	Cherishing time

续表

Proverbs	Chinese Equivalents	Values
Poverty is not a sufficient cause for disgrace, but poverty without resolution to help oneself, is a disgrace.	贫穷并不可耻，穷而不争气才可耻。	Self-reliance
Well done is better than well said.	说得好不如做得好。	Action

C. Translation

1. 甚至在处理孩子的问题上，美国人都会尽力给孩子提供自己的卧室，尊重孩子的隐私，让孩子自己解决问题，尽力给孩子灌输独立自主的意识。
2. 正如康登提醒我们的那样，如果笛卡尔是日本人的话，他会说："我们思，故我们在。"
3. 日本人在众人面前不喜欢发表个人的不同见解，正如日本人的谚语："钉子竖起来，锤子打下去。"
4. 如果必须表示不同意，日本人常会礼貌、委婉的表达。经常会使用"据说……"或者"有人说……"这类委婉语。
5. 因此，日本和美国语言表达上的所有这些差异从根本上反映出两国不同的价值观。日本人是集体主义价值观，而美国人则是个人主义价值观。

D. Case Study

Case 1

The best choice is D. The British people maintain their etiquette and social manners even when they are very excited. Even more important, the Filipino couple did not introduce their Filipino friend to him and in addition, the Filipinos were talking in their own native language. No doubt the British felt left out, which is unacceptable and rarely occurs on social occasions in Britain. In a foreign country, when an immigrant meets their native people or things they well, they usually have a strong emotional reaction. At these moments they tend to take no notice of their surroundings, including those around them. Such behavior is likely to be considered rude, which requires attention.

Case 2

The foreign visitor was almost forced to say something like "But these flowers are beautiful" or "I wish I could do so well".

Part Two

A. Text Reading

1. T 2. F 3. F 4. T 5. F 6. T 7. T 8. T 9. F 10. T

B. Terms Understanding

1. Both Taoism and Buddhism have a deep respect for nature. Humans are born from nature and depend on her for survival and development. "harmony of man with nature" in Confucianism and Taoism is a perfectly harmonious values, which will benefit the people through enhancing their moral taste, sense of homeland, guiding their production and consumption with perfectly harmonious values.
2. "Peace Enjoys Priority" is the philosophies and ideals of the Chinese people since ancient times in their pursuit of the harmony between man and nature and the harmony among people, building up a harmonious society and achieving harmonious development are the dream and aspirations of Chinese. It is the belief that peace and progress, harmonious development, living in amity, cooperation and mutual benefit, and enjoying a happy life are the common ideals of the people throughout the world.
3. The philosophical origins of Chinese medicine have grown out of the tenets of Daoism (also known as Taoism). Daoism bases much of its thinking on observing the natural world and manner in which it operates.

   The direct meanings of *Yin* and *Yang* in Chinese are bright and dark sides of an object. Chinese philosophy uses *Yin* and *Yang* to represent a wider range of opposite properties in the universe: cold and hot, slow and fast, still and moving, masculine and feminine, lower and upper, etc. In general, anything that is moving, ascending, bright, progressing, hyperactive, including functional disease of the body, pertains to *Yang*. The characteristics of stillness, descending, darkness, degeneration, hypoactivity, including organic disease, pertain to *Yin*.

   The function of *Yin* and *Yang* is guided by the law of unity of the opposites. In other words, *Yin* and *Yang* are in conflict but at the same time mutually dependent. The nature of *Yin* and *Yang* is relative, with neither being able to exist in isolation. Without "cold" there would be no "hot"; without "moving" there would be no "still"; without "dark", there would be no "bright". The most illustrative example of *Yin-Yang* interdependence is the interrelationship between substance and function. Only with ample substance can the human body function in a healthy way; and only when the functional processes are in good condition, can the essential substances be appropriately refreshed.

4. The Taoistic theory of the Five Elements can be seen as a further, more refined step to understand and categorize or analyse the *Yin-Yang* philosophy. The Theory of the Five Elements describes the interaction and relation between *Yin* and *Yang*, between phenomena.
   Wood—rising, development (of an action), impulse, expansion, decampment
   Fire—embodiment, definition, action, dynamic phase, design
   Earth—alteration, transformation, transmutation, change, conversation
   Metal—sinking, contraction, declining
   Water—contemplation, calmness, (re) consideration, observation, reflection
   All Five Elements are equally important and should form a balance, while being in constant move and cyclical change (phases).
5. Health Preserving Theory is an important part of the theory of *Inner Canon of Huangdi*, and correspondence between human and nature is the fundamental basis of thought.
   Health preserving is a concept in Chinese traditional medicine to enhance physical fitness, prevent diseases, postpone aging and prolong the life by spiritual toning, therapeutic diets and medicated diet, healthy exercises and other methods. Such concept takes the natural point of view in ancient China as the theoretical basis, such as Five Elements Theory, *Yin-Yang* Theory, Pneumatism and Connecting with Macrocosm.
   Based on those theories, Chinese people established the rich and effective methods of health preserving, such as spiritual toning, guiding and breathing, health care in four seasons, food and medicine diets to keep health, thus forming a miracle of the traditional Chinese medicine—Health Preserving Theory

C. 略

Part Three

A. 略

B. Detail Understanding

1. D 2. B 3. A 4. C 5. F 6. E

Unit 4

Warm-up Activity

略

Part One

A. Words in Use

1. auspicious 2. blaspheme 3. neutral 4. ferocious 5. affirmative 6. embezzle 7. eulogized 8. conceited 9. notorious 10. derogatory

C. Translation

1. 水牛的涵义来源与美国的“西进运动”有关。那时候美国西部人民猎取大量的水牛,企图通过水牛的毛皮生意牟利。但是后来们发现与预想的不同,猎取水牛难度很大。因此,人们会说“We are buffaloed.”,借此表达自己的无助和失望。后来慢慢延伸出了“威胁”与“欺骗”的涵义。
2. 许多人会把自己比作海燕。在中国人心中,海燕不畏艰难险阻,冒着暴风雨顽强地翱翔。它是勇敢、顽强、不屈不挠精神的象征。
3. 在英国文学史上有大量的文学作品歌颂西风。比如英国著名诗人雪莱的著名诗篇《西风颂》。因为英国的西风徐徐吹来,温暖宜人。而对于中国人来说。西风却是凛冽刺骨的寒风。“东风”才是中国人最喜欢的和煦之风,其含义恰恰与英国的西风相似。
4. 某些词语在不同文化语境下的涵义是不一样的。比如,在中国文化里,“松、竹、梅”因其挺拔多姿、不畏严寒的特征,被人们赋予了了长寿、高风亮节、不怕困难的涵义,从而地位凌驾于其他花木之上。但是它们在西方却没有这样的涵义。

D. Case Study

Case 1

在这个案例里,Johnson 先生由于不懂中西文化差异弄了个不愉快。在英美人看来,朋友双方送些书、钟之类的东西既实用又贴心。但他们不知道,在中国，送钟给别人会让人有“送终”的不愉快的联想，别人当然不接受这个礼物了。

语言是文化的载体，同时又是文化的一个重要组成部分。在语言的各要素中，词汇是基本要素，因而文化差异在词汇上必然有所体现。不同的民族由于在地理、民俗、宗教及价值观念等方面存在着差异，表达同一理性概念的词，在各自独特的文化传统作用下必然会产生附加在词汇本身概念之上的不同的联想意义。这种联想意义与词义本身没有必然联系，而是在说者和听者的文化知识基础上，在特定的语境中，对于一个词所产生的某种特定感受。不了解这种联想意义的差别就不能完全接受一个词所承载的全部语言信息量。尤其是在跨文化交际中，对于词汇联想意义的理解有助于人们更恰当地了解和掌握所学语言的文化，从而达到真正交际的目的。

Case 2

Smith 先生是一个很正直的人，但是他很怯懦。当他发现被自己非常亲密的朋友欺骗了以后，他怒气冲天，却什么也没说。上个星期五是个不幸的日子，他出了场车祸。最近他看起来气色不大好，常常感到忧伤。我看到他的时候他正陷入沉思中，我希望不久他就会康复。

Part Two

A. Text Reading

1. T 2. F 3. F 4. T 5. T 6. T 7. F 8. T 9. T 10. T

B. Terms Understanding

1. The relationship between the speaker and his addressee determines the choice of linguistic forms. There are two major forms of address in American English: the use of the first name (FN) and the use of a title with the last name (TLN). The use of these forms of address is governed by the relationship between the speakers. It is not predictable from properties of the speaker alone or the addressee alone.

   There are two reciprocal patterns: the reciprocal exchange of FN and the reciprocal exchange of TLN. FN includes full first names, familiar abbreviations, and diminutive forms. In American English, male first names seldom occur in full form. However, female first names are often left unaltered. Titles in this study include Mr., Mrs., Miss, Dr., Senator, Major, and the like. The distinction between the two patterns is one of degree of acquaintance, but the degree required for mutual FN is less for younger people than for older people, and less where the members of the dyads are of the same sex than where they are of different sex.

It seems likely that the two reciprocal patterns are on a dimension that ranges from acquaintance to intimacy. In English of the past, the mutual FN is farther displaced from the mutual TLN. However, in modern American English the distance between the two points is small with the mutual FN usually representing only a very small increment of intimacy over the mutual TLN; as small as 5 minutes of conversation. The principal factors predisposing to intimacy seem to be shared values (like kinship, nationality, sex, etc.) and frequent contact.

2. In the nonreciprocal pattern, one member of the dyad says FN and the other TLN. There are two kinds of relation that can generate this pattern. The first is a difference of age: an elder by 15 years or more receives TLN and gives FN to his junior. The second is a difference of occupational status. Age and occupational status are correlated and most instances of nonreciprocal address involve differences on the two dimensions. However, there is proof that a difference on either dimension alone is able to generate the nonreciprocal pattern. The proof is the existence of nonreciprocal dyads matched on one dimension but not on the other. The question is what happens to address in dyads where the elder has the humbler occupation. In the plays there are many examples in which the criteria oppose one another. In all these examples occupation prevail over age.
3. People observe the symmetrical nature of social interactions in a variety of contexts. Symmetrical interactions send the moral message "we are all the same."
4. Asymmetrical interactions may send the message "I am special; better than you."

Part Three

B. Detail Understanding

1. Chinese: Seem to be rich with complicated honorifics

   English: Much simpler, the consideration of interpersonal distance overrides the consideration of formality
2. Chinese: Start a business correspondence with some kind of phatic talk to

show respect

English: "Get down to business" straight away

3. Chinese: Letter writers denigrate themselves, elevate the letter receivers.

   English: This is not found in English.

4. Chinese: Letter writers set up a kind of inferior to superior relation.

   English: This is not found in English.

5. Chinese: comprises three parts: willing to provide more information, looking forward to a reply, and thanking

   English: The same as Chinese

6. Chinese: rich and varied

   English: almost monotonous

7. Chinese: sign names

   English: sign names followed by titles or positions

Unit 5

Warm-up Activity

略

Part One

A. Words in Use

1. pushy 2. commodities 3. summon 4. tardiness 5. beckon
6. trickle 7. abide 8. assemble 9. duplicating 10. compartmentalized

C. Translation

1. 同样的，如果我作为一个外来人，食指向上弯曲来招呼密克罗尼西亚人，这一手势会被认为在招呼动物，是很不礼貌的。（在美国，这一动作表示召唤某人。但是在许多东南亚国家，以及文中作者提到的密克罗尼西亚，这一手势只用于召唤动物。因此，对人用这一手势，是非常不礼貌的。在印度尼西亚和澳大利亚，这一手势也指召唤性工作者。在欧洲许多国家，用食指指着别人是不礼貌的。）
2. 美国人（的生活）与时间紧密相关，他们把时间仔细分割成一段一段的，以免造成浪费。而密克罗尼西亚是"存在文化"，人们做事随心情而定。（作者提到美国和密克罗尼西亚对待时间的态度不同。美国是 doing culture 国家，许多美国人对一生时间的短促相当敏感，他们认为如果时间浪费了，那是无法弥补的，他们要让每分钟都有价值；而密克罗尼西亚是 being culture 国家，人们做事随心情而定，没有“浪费时间”说。compartmentalize 意为“分割”，即把时间分割成不同时间段，将所做的事情放入不同时间段中完成。）

3. 在波纳佩，隐私问题对我来说是一个很大的挑战。作为典型的欧美人，我非常注重隐私。但在密克罗尼西亚，人们对隐私的概念是不同的，亲密无间是他们的常态。（个人主义国家和集体主义国家对于隐私的界定大不相同。美国是典型的个人主义国家，非常重视个人隐私，不打探他人私事，未经允许不进入他人房间、不动用他人物品。密克罗尼西亚是集体主义国家，当地人对于个人隐私的概念没有美国人敏感，由于隐私问题产生的文化冲突非常常见。）

D. Case Study

Case 1

This is a typical case of misunderstanding caused by different perceptions about body distance. There is a lot of evidence to show that body distance varies with different people, different circumstances, and different cultures. In Denmark. at a formal event. the intimate space is usually between 20 to 30 centimeters; while in Australia, such an occasion requires a body distance of 40 to 50 centimeters. Therefore, when a Dane talks with an Australian, the problem arises: the Dane is accustomed to a close distance while the Australian is comfortable with a great distance. In this case, Mark, by trying to establish his normal intimate space, infringed on the Australian lady's space. Because of this, she felt somewhat threatened and lost her sense of comfort. At that moment, the nearby man offered her the opportunity to excuse herself from Mark. If Mark had some knowledge about the expected personal space for Australians, the encounter might have been total different.

Case 2

略

Part Two

A. Text Reading

1. F 2. T 3. T 4. T 5. F 6. T 7. T 8. F 9. T 10. F

B. Terms Understanding

1. Face theory is also called “politeness theory”. Politeness theory accounts

for the redressing of affronts to a person's "face" by face threatening acts.

(1) The concept of face was derived from Chinese into English in the 19th century.

(2) Erving Goffman would then go on to introduce the concept into academia through his theories of "face" and "facework".

(3) Although politeness has been studied in a variety of cultures for many years, Penelope Brown & Stephen Levinson's politeness theory has become very influential.

(4) In 1987, Brown & Levinson proposed that politeness was a universal concept, which has created controversy within academia.

(5) Politeness is the expression of the speakers' intention to mitigate face threats carried by certain face threatening acts toward the listener.

(6) Another definition is "a battery of social skills whose goal is to ensure everyone feels affirmed in a social interaction". Therefore, being polite can be an attempt for the speaker to save their own face or the face of who he or she is talking to.

2. Negative face was defined as "the want of every 'competent adult member' that his actions be unimpeded by others", or "the basic claim to territories, personal preserves, rights to non-distraction—i. e. the freedom of action and freedom from imposition".
3. positive face involves a desire for connection with others, negative face needs include autonomy and independence.
4. Collectivism is characterized by a rigid social framework that distinguish between in-groups and out-groups. People expect their in-group to look after them, and in exchange for that they fell they owe absolute loyalty to the group. Collectivism means greater emphasis on ① the views needs, and goals of the in-groups rather than oneself. ②social norms and duty defined by the in-group rather than behavior to get pleasure.

Part Three

A. 略

B. Detail Understanding

1. Japan 2. America 3. Middle East, Asia, South America 4. Arab
5. Arab 6. Russia 7. South India 8. Jordan 9. America

Unit 6

Warm-up Activity

全世界对时间的观念是不一样的，有的甚至是截然不同。如德国人、荷兰人对待时间的态度就与同属欧盟的意大利人不同，前者属于对时间抱有直线式观念，即一次只从事一项主要的活动，他们认为时间是宝贵的，应该好好利用，不能浪费，他们总是高效、精确地组织商务活动；而后者则认为时间是可以变通的，不太愿意对时间进行严格计量和控制，他们对时间的流逝往往熟视无睹，他们更关注现在，因为他们喜欢现在就能生活得很充实。因此在上面这个案例中，来自鹿特丹的商人 Walther Habers 在意大利米兰的遭遇就清楚地表明了不同文化间商务活动中可能会遇到的理念、习惯等的差异。

一般来说，在单一的文化背景下，谈判过程是可以预见并准确把握的。然而跨文化谈判比单一文化背景下的谈判更具有挑战性，因为跨文化谈判是一种属于不同文化的不同思维形式、不同沟通方式、不同行为方式的谈判行为。所以从事跨文化商务活动就要重视和了解谈判双方的文化差异，尊重和理解对方，以期商务活动顺利进行，并提高谈判效率。

Part One

A. Words in Use

1. conjured 2. Righteous 3. tactic 4. femininity 5. impair
6. rendered 7. eradicating 8. slangy 9. erroneous 10. vulgar

B. 略

C. Translation

1. 产品广告和商标的设计代表着产品的形象。广告和商标的跨文化设计包括语言效应和文化效应。
2. 汉语的广告和商标设计通常以“自我”为中心，注重对自己产品和服务功能的宣传；而英语的广告和商标设计是以“顾客”为中心，通常他们更关心产品所传递的文化内涵以及顾客的使用体会。
3. 汉语的广告和商标设计注重生理需求和传统，而英语的广告和商标设计则注重消费者的精神生活和创新。
4. 商标是商品的生产者或者服务的提供者使用在其商品或服务上的，用于区别商品或服务的来源，包括文字、短语、标识、图形、口号等具有显著特征的标志。

D. 略

Part Two

A. Text Reading

1. T 2. F 3. F 4. F 5. F 6. T 7. T 8. T 9. F 10. T

B. Terms Understanding

1. Context in communication refers to the surrounding physical environment and the framework of related facts and events within which a communication takes place. These contextual factors affect the perception of a person which in turn influences the way a message is decoded understood by the recipient.
2. The seller adjusts the project and sells it to the buyer when it's ready for immediate use.
3. Subcontracts are arrangements in which a company pays another company to perform part of the production process in manufacturing a product. For example, Mcdermott International negotiates subcontract labor agreements with suppliers in the Philippines, Thailand, and Lebanon to perform craft duties in Middle East construction projects.

C. 略

Part Three

B. Detail Understanding

1. B 2. C 3. D 4. E 5. A

Unit 7

Part One

A. Words in Use

1. submerge 2. sacred 3. escalated 4. compliance 5. indigenous
6. strife 7. admonish 8. surplus 9. maim 10. fragility

B. 略

C. Translation

1. 在商周时期,人们把“上天”当作一个人格化的神灵,在此基础上孔子提出了自己的见解，认为“上天”就是自然。孔子说，“天何言哉？四时行焉，百物生焉，天何言哉？”这句话的意思是说：天道哪里用得着说呢？它就像四季的更替，万物的生长一样。天道哪里用得着说呢？即世界的规律就在那里，真理就在那里，无需多言。可见孔子认为“上天”就是自然万物。

2. 孔子认为教育的根本目标就是培养人正直的思想和良好的品德。
3. “无为”是老子哲学的核心。认为事物的发生与发展都有其客观性与规律性。人们对待自然，要依照自然发展规律，而不加以任何人为的措施。
4. 老子认为宇宙万物来自虚无，也走向虚无。因此他提倡人们要摒弃外界物欲的诱惑，保持内心的安定清静，确保固有的天性。

D. 略

Part Two

A. Text Reading

1. F 2. F 3. F 4. T 5. F 6. T 7. F 8. F 9. T 10. T

B. Terms Understanding

1. The Hundred Days' Reform was a failed 104-day national, cultural, political, and educational reform movement from 11 June to 22 September 1898 in late Qing Dynasty China. It was undertaken by the young Guangxu Emperor and his reform-minded supporters. Following the issuing of the reformative edicts, the coup detat ("The Coup of 1898", *Wuxu* Coup) was perpetrated by powerful conservative opponents led by Empress Dowager Cixi.
2. Feng Menglong wrote *Three Volumes of Words* (*Clear Words to Illustrate the World*, *Ordinary Words to Warn the World*, and *Lasting words to Awaken the world*), while Ling Mengchu authored *Two Volumes of Slapping*. They are regarded as model illustrations of Chinese feudal society.
3. The eight-legged essay was formulated around a rigid, artificial structure. It tested, among other things, the examinees' knowledge of the Four Books and Five Classics and ability to insert classical allusions and idioms at the places deemed appropriate.

   The eight-legged essay format was invented by the Song Dynasty reformer Wang Anshi. However, it is not certain exactly when the form became the standard for the civil service examinations. A model form for essay writing issued by Emperor Taizu of Ming in 1370 is much less rigid and precise than eight-legged essays eventually became. It specifies only the topics to be tested in the examinations and the minimum length of the candidates' essays. According to Gu Yanwu, the form of the essay became more standardized during the 15th century.

4. The Chinese imperial examinations were a civil service examination system in Imperial China to select candidates for the state bureaucracy. Although there were imperial exams as early as in the Han Dynasty, the system became widely utilized as the major path to office only in the mid-Tang Dynasty, and remained so until its abolition in 1905. Since the exams were based on knowledge of the classics and literary style, not technical expertise, successful candidates were generalists who shared a common language and culture, one shared even by those who failed. This common culture helped to unify the empire and the ideal of achievement by merit gave legitimacy to imperial rule, while leaving clear problems resulting from a systemic lack of technical and practical expertise.

C. 略

Part Three

A. 略

B. Detail Understanding

1. C 2. E 3. A 4. F 5. B 6. D

Unit 8

Warm-up Activity

(1) People of the same commitment don't feel distant even if departed; people in distinct convictions don't feel closed even if enclosed.

(2) More friends, more opportunities.

(3) Aspire for high and grand while planting our feet firmly on the ground.

(4) Friends and neighbors become closer when they visit each other more often.

(5) Give a man a fish and you feed him for a day. Teach him how to fish and you feed him for a lifetime.

(6) When confronted by mountains, one finds a way through. When blocked by a river, one finds a way to bridge to the other side.

Part One

A. Words in Use

1. garnered 2. elaborate 3. sync 4. sentiments 5. perceptive
6. filtered 7. utilize 8. humiliation 9. exerted 10. legitimate

B. Questions for Discussion

1. Soft power is more critical than ever in China's foreign policy. The building of friendship, understanding peoples enhances China's security, and its principle of peaceful co-existence. Soft power supports and deepens diplomatic ties, the sharing of knowledge and expertise, and the cooperation on shared common areas of interest.
2. Since the revival of the Old Silk Road and the construction of the BRI, its significance has gradually increased in magnitude as a component of China's strategic policy, symbolizing the "vision of connectivity", with its huge investment, infrastructural development, etc., aligning the countries along the BRI route and allowing for cross cultural exchanges and sharing of knowledge between people in the Asian region. Analytically, the significant impact of China's the BRI has resulted in different forms of cultural heritage awareness rising in the Asian region and with its increase use of cultural diplomacy through the use of soft power tools, this ultimately will improve and change the lives of many people in the Asian region.
3. China's soft power strategy offers a systematic and important way for it to respond to many challenges it faces relating to the security of its Asian neighbors, providing investment projects and programs, opportunity for employment, education, improving technical skills, the opportunity of learning new ideologies, Mandarin language, educational exchange programs, research cooperation, expertise skills, etc., which will strengthen its economic link and likewise its cultural link in Asia and the support of the Asian countries aspirations, leading to cultural interest and essentially developing a harmonious society.

C. Translation

1. 近年来,中国的文化和传统日益普及并逐渐得到了国际认可,这反映了中国软实力的不断发展及其重要性。

2. 相反，多年来，中国作为一个不断崛起的地区和全球力量，一直寻求在国际体系中树立安全、稳定的形象。而文化外交这一软实力工具在这方面发挥了核心作用。
3. 因此，在 2015 年博鳌亚洲论坛年会上，习近平主席在讲话中表示，"一带一路"倡议将促进文明交流，为人民搭建友谊桥梁，推动人类发展，维护世界和平。
4. 显然，在未来几年里，"一带一路"无疑将通过其经济联系、传统文化吸引力、外交关系、基础设施伙伴关系、多边主义等来改变亚洲的面貌。

D. 略

Part Two

A. Text Reading

1. F 2. F 3. F 4. T 5. F 6. F 7. F 8. T 9. T 10. T

B. Terms Understanding

1. The Silk Road was an ancient network of trade routes that connected the East and the West. It was central to cultural interaction between them for centuries. The Silk Road refers to both the terrestrial and the maritime routes connecting Asia with the Middle East and Southern Europe.

The Silk Road derives its name from the lucrative trade in silk carried out along its length, beginning in the Han Dynasty (202 BC-220 AD). The Han Dynasty expanded the Central Asian section of the trade routes around 114 BC through the missions and explorations of the Chinese imperial envoy Zhang Qian. The Chinese took great interest in the safety of their trade products and extended the Great Wall of China to protect the trade route.

Trade on the Silk Road played a significant role in the development of the civilizations of China, Japan, the Indian subcontinent, Iran/Persia, Europe, the Horn of Africa and Arabia, opening long-distance political and economic relations between the civilizations. Though silk was the major trade item exported from China, many other goods were traded, as well as religions, syncretic philosophies, and technologies. Diseases, most notably plague, also spread along the Silk Road. In addition to economic trade, the Silk Road was a route for cultural trade among the civilizations along its network.

Traders in antiquity included the Bactrians, Sogdians, Syrians, Jews, Arabs, Iranians, Turkmens, Chinese, Indians, Somalis, Greeks, Romans, Georgians, and Armenians.

In June 2014, United Nations Educational, Scientific, and Cultural Organization (UNESCO) designated the Chang'an-Tianshan corridor of the Silk Road as a World Heritage Site. The Indian portion is on the tentative site list.

2. Buddhism is a religion and dharma that encompasses a variety of traditions, beliefs and spiritual practices largely based on original teachings attributed to the Buddha and resulting interpreted philosophies. Buddhism originated in Ancient India sometime between the 6th and 4th centuries BC, from where it spread through much of Asia, whereafter it declined in India during the Middle Ages. Two major extant branches of Buddhism are generally recognized by scholars: Theravada (Pali: "The School of the Elders") and Mahayana (Sanskrit: "The Great Vehicle"). Buddhism is the world's fourth-largest religion, with over 520 million followers or over 7% of the global population, known as Buddhists.
3. Zheng He's voyages to the western seas is a significant event in Chinese history. That voyage took place much earlier and on a much larger scale than foreign explorers. It promoted the navigation civilization of our country and facilitated the cultural exchanges between China and the world. So far, Zheng He's voyages to the western seas still has a profound meaning to adhere to the independent foreign policy of peace.

C. 略

Part Three

A. 略

B. Detail Understanding

1. C.　2. A.　3. D.　4. F.　5. B.　6. E.